The European Union: Annual Review of the EU 2000/2001

Edited by

Geoffrey Edwards
and
Georg Wiessala

General Editors: Iain Begg and John Peterson

Copyright © Blackwell Publishers Ltd

ISBN 0-631-22751-2

First published 2001

Blackwell Publishers Ltd
108 Cowley Road, Oxford OX4 1JF, UK

Blackwell Publishers Inc.
350 Main Street,
Malden, MA 02148, USA

British Library Cataloguing in Publication Data
A catalogue record for this book is available from the British Library

Library of Congress
Cataloging in Publication Data applied for

This journal is printed on acid free paper
Printed in the UK by J.W. Arrowsmith Ltd, Bristol

CONTENTS

Journal of Common Market Studies

Volume 39, Annual Review
September 2001

Editorial: Visions and Realities

GEOFFREY EDWARDS
University of Cambridge
and
GEORG WIESSALA
University of Central Lancashire

Introduction

Rarely has the gap between vision and reality become more apparent than during 2000. On the 50th anniversary of Robert Schuman's declaration that led to the Coal and Steel Community, the German Foreign Minister, Joschka Fischer, initiated a new debate about the future of Europe. By the end of the year, Schuman's words that 'Europe will not come about at a single stroke, nor as a seamless construction. It will come about through concrete realizations which create first of all a de facto solidarity' seemed even more prophetic. Given the criticisms made of the fourth major effort at reforming the treaties in 20 years, there were some leaders, in the early morning of 11 December, who remained to be convinced that a real commitment to solidarity existed among all 15 governments – or even solidarity within a rather key government. But Fischer launched – with Nice only perhaps a temporary distraction – what has proved to be an important transnational debate in Europe. Indeed, it became increasingly incumbent upon all leaders to add their voice to the debate: among others, President Chirac spoke (to the Bundestag) in June, Tony Blair spoke (to the Poles) in October, in addition to Messrs Amato, Lipponen and a flurry of foreign ministers (prominent among them being Robin Cook insofar as he spoke several times on the subject). Their visions differed on a number of counts, such as on the role, inclusiveness and structure of 'pioneer groups', as

President Chriac referred to them, as well as fairly fundamentally on the role of the state. There was an interesting identity of views as far as Robin Cook saw it between Britain and France (which went beyond the fact that he was speaking to the French National Assembly), in that, as he put it and quoting President Chirac, 'we are building a united Europe of states, not a United States of Europe'.[1]

The debate among political leaders was important not only in itself, but because it also stimulated discussion at other levels. A number of useful collections of speeches, reactions, papers, etc. have gradually found their way into the press or online. To take just two as examples, there is the collection edited by C. Jörges, Y. Mény and J.H.H. Weiler, *What Kind of Constitution for What Kind of Polity? Responses to Joschka Fischer,*[2] and the collection edited by Mark Leonard, *The Future Shape of Europe.*[3] Doubtless more are making their way on to the market. The latter, however, included a challenge:

> I think British intellectuals and policy-makers could make some contribution to working out what such a future for Europe might involve. At first sight this looks an unlikely proposition. The British famously have been the 'reluctant Europeans'. The UK has not as yet adopted to the Euro and the majority of the population is at best indifferent towards Europe ... .[4]

Granted, the author went on to suggest that the UK had been a source of 'lively thinking in politics in recent years', but in view of the call for civil society, including universities, to become involved in the 'post-Nice process', it behoves us all perhaps – and not just in the UK – to participate and to be encouraged and enabled to participate in the process.

I. Symbols, Challenges and Charters: Enhancing the EU Constitution

The year 2000, as symbolic as its predecessor seemed shambolic, also framed a number of significant anniversaries in addition to that of the Schuman Declaration. These included the 50th Anniversary of the signing of the European Convention of Human Rights (ECHR). For other reasons, too, there was a noticeably greater emphasis during 2000 on issues of civil liberties, civil society, human rights and citizenship. The response of the EU's Heads of State and Government to the inclusion of the Austrian Freedom Party – with or without its leader, Jörg Haider[5] – in government in some ways set the tone,

[1] Robin Cook, speech to the Foreign Affairs Committee of the French National Assembly, Paris, Wednesday 8 November 2000.
[2] Electronic version (pdf) of the full text available, 1.1 MB (266 pp.) at «http://www.jeanmonnetprogram.org/papers/00/000701.html».
[3] Foreign Policy Centre/ BSMG Worldwide.
[4] Anthony Giddens, 'A Third Way for the European Union?' In Leonard (ed.), p. 70.
[5] Whether Jörg Haider was in or out seemed irrelevant if, as the *Economist* reported (19 February 2000),

with the official opening of the European Monitoring Centre on Racism and Xenophobia in Vienna adding a certain irony to the proceedings. The Austrian case and the discussions about proportionality, effect and justification of the EU's sanctions, and how to resolve the issue once the initial 'threat' of isolation had been ignored, certainly propelled the issue into the foreground. But the prominence of the Austrian case raised expectations even while forcing a recognition that the EU Member States had to be somewhat better prepared, coherent and consistent if they were to deal with other instances of threatened breaches of human rights and freedoms among their own number. But not for some time has recognition of the EU as a value-based organization been so publicly and widely embraced.

In many respects this should not have come as a surprise in that both the Maastricht and Amsterdam Treaties had developed important EU human rights and anti-discrimination competencies. The 2000 Anti-Racism Directive, the European Conferences on Human Rights Protection in Dublin, and on Racism in Strasbourg, and even the (not wholly satisfactory) way in which the Charter on Fundamental Freedoms had been drawn up, provided a sharper focus for interest in problems of European governance, enhanced civic participation and entitlement. It will therefore be interesting to see how the Commission takes up such themes in its work on governance during 2001–02. But it is not just a greater awareness of these problems within the EU; they have been taken up and significantly developed in the EU's international policies. On the one hand, the EU Council of Ministers' Human Rights Reports and the Commission's regular Monthly Review on Human Rights and Democratization have begun to attract much wider attention. On the other hand, in terms of implementation, human rights and governance issues have been brought much more to the fore in the overhaul of EU development policy, the renewed ACP framework of Cotonou, the third Asia–Europe Meeting (ASEM 3) in Seoul, the first ever high-level summit meetings with India and Africa in 2000 and, somewhat closer to home, in the pre-negotiation of Turkey's candidacy to the EU. Further evidence of this more consistent concern can be seen in other EU initiatives during 2000, such as the new strategies on human rights and democratic principles in external relations, electoral assistance and observation, or the funding provided by the European initiative on human rights and democracy.

The European Union's Charter of Fundamental Rights, 'solemnly proclaimed' at the Nice Council, continues to be a significant part of the post-Nice agenda, not least because its mere proclamation sparked acrimonious debates about its symbolism and its legal nature, method, scope and force. The idea of

---

the FP's Vice Chancellor, Susanne Reiss Passer had said that she would co-ordinate policy with him 'before, during and after decisions'.

a Charter, which was promoted in 1999 by the Germans during another anniversary (that celebrating the 50th anniversary of the German Constitution: the *Grundgesetz*), was moved up the political agenda in 2000, by the Commission, its President and the Portuguese and French Presidencies. Although many initiatives in 2000 have put rights and citizenship more under the spotlight, it is the proposed Charter above all, which has shown that, in matters of human rights, there are some still weighty qualifications to Member States' records. Firstly, Member States, themselves, continue to commit infringements of human rights and civil liberties, not least against asylum-seekers, immigrants, minorities or other groups. Despite European Years of Racism and the Commission's communications on asylum and immigration policy in 2000, Member States and the Union alike continue to fail to tackle many of the issues of racism and xenophobia in Europe, some of which, worryingly, continue to enter and pervade mainstream politics. Secondly, Member States are still deeply divided over the extent of human rights protection to be demanded, which means that they have not yet been able to agree on a coherent human rights system for the EU. The 1950 ECHR – still one of the landmarks of human rights achievement of the Council of Europe – was only incorporated into the legal system of the UK in the period under review; that, itself, perhaps, speaks volumes. The lack of publicity or awareness of the event seems again to confirm the results of a 2000 Commission report, which found that some UK newspapers at least, are 'deliberately misleading' their readers some of the time, committing the sin of a 'cavalier disregard for facts'. These and other issues in other Member States may serve as reminders of the profoundness of future challenges for a Union, which strives to match human rights responsibility with internal reform, balanced distribution of power and credibility.

II. Housekeeping

We have been extremely fortunate in gathering up Alexander Stubb and Mark Gray to write the keynote article. Asking 'insiders' to go public is always risky, especially on a subject that aroused just a little controversy – within the French government as much as between France and its partners – insofar as there is always a danger of discretion overcoming them. Alexander and Mark are to be congratulated for weaving a singularly subtle but nonetheless revealing path. We were lucky, too, to be able to nab Jo Hunt, somewhere between Leeds and Cardiff, to undertake the Law section. We are also grateful to all the other contributors who seem to be able to manage to provide brilliant copy with amazing regularity and almost on time. We had one failure in that our Portuguese contributor got lost so that the editors had to try to match Christian Lesquene's excellent piece. For her patience and forbearing, this year we owe even more to Mary Robinson at Photoscript for her sub-editing.

Journal of Common Market Studies

Volume 39, Annual Review
September 2001

Keynote Article: The Treaty of Nice – Negotiating a Poisoned Chalice?*

MARK GRAY
White & Case LLP
and
ALEXANDER STUBB
Group of Policy Advisers, European Commission

Introduction

The European Union is in a constant process of change. For nearly two decades the Union has been either preparing, negotiating or ratifying a new treaty. The process itself has become institutionalized with agreement on the Single European Act of 1987, the Maastricht Treaty of 1993 and the Treaty of Amsterdam in 1999. The last may have incorporated a range of new policies into the Treaty and transferred areas of justice and home affairs to the Community area, but it proved unable to reach agreement on its original objective – the institutional changes required for enlargement. The latest revision, the Treaty of Nice, attempts to address this deficiency.

The IGC 2000 negotiations witnessed a total of 370 official negotiating hours in 30 representatives' meetings, ten ministerial meetings and three European Councils. After a long, and at times, tedious negotiation, the main decisions of Nice can be summarized rather simply. The EU's leaders agreed to maintain one Commissioner per Member State until the Union reaches 27. A new distribution of votes has been agreed for the Council based on three

* During IGC 2000, Alexander Stubb was a member of the Finnish negotiating team and Mark Gray a member of the European Commission's negotiating team. The authors would like to thank Gilles Bertrand, Efthymios Costopoulos, Thijs Debeij, Desmond Dinan, Andrew Duff, David Galloway, Simon Hix, Andrew Moravcsik, John Neary, John Palmer, Antti Satuli, Alexander Schallenberg, Francisco Seixas da Costa, Sir Stephen Wall, Helen Wallace and our two co-editors for their valuable comments. The responsibility for the final text remains with the authors, who are writing in a personal capacity.

criteria: a majority of votes, a majority of Member States and an additional criterion that, if Member States make a specific request, a check will be carried out to verify that the vote covers at least 62 per cent of the Union's population. The number of issues now covered by qualified majority voting (QMV) has been further increased, although particularly sensitive issues remain subject to unanimity. Significant changes have been made to the treaty provisions and statute of the Court of Justice and Court of First Instance and the articles on enhanced co-operation have been amended in an attempt to increase the scope for its possible use after enlargement.

Treaty changes are considered to be history-making decisions. Yet there is surprisingly little analysis on the actual dynamics of IGCs.[1] One of the main reasons for the lacuna is that IGCs are conducted behind closed doors, excluding outside observers. This article is an analysis of the IGC 2000 negotiating process and the Nice Treaty as perceived by two people involved in both the Amsterdam and Nice negotiations.[2] Section I of the article looks at the political context of the negotiating process. Section II looks at the results of Nice, and Section III assesses the implications for the future and suggests a number of changes to the current IGC method.

I. Negotiating the Treaty of Nice

Managing the Negotiation Process

IGC negotiations are multilateral, i.e. they take place among a large number of players making moves and counter moves between visible and invisible players (Stubb, 1998). IGC negotiations should be seen as an incremental learning process, which is dynamic and ongoing as opposed to static, and in which both institutions and the individuals within them matter. Inevitably among the multitude of players, some are more influential than others. However, in any IGC the two key actors are the Presidency and the Council Secretariat. In theory, the Presidency provides the political guidance, and the Council Secretariat assists. In practice, the relationship is much more fluid. On some issues the Presidency takes the lead and, on others, the Council Secretariat sets the agenda. This can, of course, lead to a conflict of influence when the balance between the institutions is being debated. Much depends on personal relationships and expertise, but experience shows that the most efficient Presidencies are those which work as a team together with the Council Secretariat.

---

[1] For analysis of IGCs, see Weiler and Modrall (1985); Cloos (1993); Corbett (1992); Edwards and Pijpers (1997); Oreja (1998); McDonagh (1998).
[2] The article seeks to give an objective assessment of the negotiations, but it does not seek to advocate a particular theoretical approach to treaty revision.

It is impossible to quantify Member State influence in IGCs. Some observers claim that the large Member States run the show (see, e.g., Moravcsik, 1998). Anyone involved in the day-to-day work of IGCs will know that this is not the case. That said, larger Member States certainly have more political clout, more extensive interests and larger administrations to deal with the negotiations. Smaller Member States tend to be more flexible in their approach but, however efficient they may be, when the chips are down, the pressure to compromise is felt much more by the small rather than the large Member States.

In accordance with Art. 48 TEU, the European Commission has the right to issue an opinion before the start of the IGC. Based on historical precedent, it participates in all the meetings and has the right to put forward proposals. The European Parliament only has the right to issue an opinion before the IGC. It does not have the right of assent on the treaty as it does in the enlargement process. But the European Council has accepted that the Parliament should have a role and it has been allowed to appoint two 'observers' to the negotiations. Although on paper the EP's role is marginal, it has steadily increased over recent IGCs.

An IGC is always a cross-sectoral exercise which has an impact on the whole administrative structure of member governments. It is vital for each to have an IGC team able to co-ordinate the position at home. Note-takers play an important part both in terms of advising the main negotiator and influencing the opinion of the national administration. A majority of the note-takers resort to laptop computers in the meeting room, thus sending information to their capitals almost simultaneously at the end of the meeting. The preparatory machine in the capital can thus participate in a virtual IGC. The relationship between the capital and the Permanent Representation in Brussels is also critical to the proper functioning of the system. In many instances, the IGC negotiators have positions which are closer to each other's than those between the various ministries at home. This is notoriously true when the negotiations address issues within the remit of Ecofin. During the negotiations, it is not difficult to detect when a given negotiator has not been able to co-ordinate the position at home. The code phrase is usually: 'we are still studying the question back home'. This tends to lose an element of credibility when the subject in question has been on the table since the 1996–97 IGC. And it has sometimes been used by a delegation to suggest a positive position when in reality it has been impossible for an agreed position to be reached in the capital.

As in any set of EU negotiations, individuals matter. And, as in any working conditions, negotiators form close ties with their counterparts. More often than not these relationships are based on personal preference, rather than a Member State's integration policy. One of the most important aspects of an IGC negotiation are the personal contacts across the institutional boundaries. In addition to the formal negotiations, there are a number of informal networks both in Brussels and between the capitals. In many cases the assistants of the Representatives build informal email networks with their counterparts.

In recent IGCs, the negotiations have been conducted on three levels (Galloway, 2001). At the top are the quarterly meetings of the Heads of State and Government, which culminated in the end game of the European Council in Nice. This is the level where the final bargain is struck. The middle negotiating level consists of the monthly meetings of the foreign ministers. These meetings usually take place in connection with the General Affairs Council (GAC). The third level is that of the personal representatives of the governments. The representatives meet roughly once a week. Most of the detail is ironed out in these meetings.

Preparing IGC 2000

It is difficult to establish when the IGC 2000 actually began since one could argue that the decisions of IGC 2000 had been an eternal leftover (Best *et al.*, 2000). More practically, as the Treaty of Amsterdam was being finalized before signature on 2 October 1997, the focus of attention moved to ratification of the Treaty and the preparation of the *Agenda 2000* negotiations on agriculture, structural funds and financial perspectives. The momentum for a renewed debate on institutional reform followed the decision in May 1998 as to which Member States would participate in the single currency. In December 1998, the European Council of Vienna formally requested that the Cologne European Council take a decision on how and when to tackle the institutional issues not resolved in Amsterdam.

The first official IGC discussions took place in Coreper and the GAC in May 1999. These meetings set the tone for the rest of the IGC preparations. The agenda became an obsession. For many, the scope of the agenda was related to the duration of the IGC which in turn was related to the timetable for enlargement. The equation was:

narrow agenda = short IGC = early enlargement

and conversely:

wide agenda = lengthy IGC = postponement of enlargement

This equation was based on a contradiction – a narrow agenda would leave a number of issues unresolved which would probably require a further IGC before enlargement. In June 1999, the European Council of Cologne decided that the IGC should be restricted to the so-called institutional 'leftovers' – the size and composition of the Commission, the reweighting of votes in the

Council, and QMV, which had been the subject of a declaration attached to the Treaty of Amsterdam. In addition, it was decided that the Finnish Presidency would draft a report on the IGC for the Helsinki European Council in December 1999, the Finns being given the responsibility largely because the Heads of State and Government could not decide on what other body might be used.

The new European Commission under President Prodi was determined to extend the scope of the IGC, deciding that a group of wise men was needed, even though Heads of State had rejected this approach at the Cardiff European Council (EUI, 2000). On the personal initiative of Prodi, a group was duly created with Richard von Weiszäcker and Lord Simon working under the chairmanship of Jean-Luc Dehaene. They presented a report to the Commission on 18 October 1999 (Dehaene, 1999), which confirmed the Commission's thinking on a number of issues. This provided the Commission with the advantage of being able to gauge reaction to the report without being committed to all the proposals it contained.

Meanwhile, the Finnish Presidency had two possibilities in drafting its report. The first was to outline a number of options for resolving the issues that were to be dealt with in the IGC, and the second was to prepare a document which indicated the direction in which the debate was going. The Finns opted for the latter strategy. The Finnish IGC report (1363/99 LIMITE) suggested that the IGC should deal with the three issues outlined in Cologne. This meant that European security and defence policy, and fundamental rights were to be considered as separate exercises parallel to the IGC. The Presidency also considered that a majority of Member States were opposed to bringing flexibility and the simplification of the treaties on to the IGC agenda, though it was agreed at the Helsinki European Council that the Portuguese Presidency could propose additional issues. The debate about the size of the agenda actually focused on a single issue, flexibility. The agenda remained open due to the persistence of the Benelux countries, Italy and the Commission. It is also worth noting that, at this stage, France and Germany were not pushing to include flexibility in the negotiations.

The Portuguese Presidency – Attempts to Stabilize the Agenda

In the weeks preceding the start of the IGC, the Member States and the institutions prepared their positions. The EP contemplated delaying the start of the IGC because its members were unhappy with the narrow Helsinki mandate and the 'observer' status of the Parliament. Retrospectively the EP made a mistake in not submitting a substantial opinion before the start of the IGC (European Parliament, 2000). However, during this defining phase, it was simply unable to take up detailed positions. More serious was its failure to focus on its key objectives even when it had adopted a resolution. It was left to the European Commission to be first in the field with its opinion of 26 January 2000 (Commission, 2000).[3]

The Portuguese Presidency had a difficult task in trying to stabilize the agenda debate (Seixas da Costa, 2001). While the issues were to be kept alive, the aim was to defuse the conflict over the agenda and to work out which additional issues could be put on the agenda. In general, a good Presidency needs three things – organization, objectivity and leadership – and the Portuguese Presidency had all three. Francisco Seixas da Costa and his team managed the IGC extremely well. The meetings were well organized, the Conference documents were objective, and Seixas da Costa showed strong leadership in the negotiations.

The Portuguese Presidency aimed to define the IGC agenda, map out the positions of the Member States, and define concretely some of the possible treaty changes. It achieved these aims in the Feira report (CONFER 4760/00). The build-up to Feira suggested that the real negotiations were about to begin. The Portuguese Presidency was bold, especially with voting, where it proposed that 39 areas should be moved to QMV. The Presidency was also firm on pushing flexibility on to the agenda. This was an interesting change in the Portuguese position since at Amsterdam and even during the Finnish Presidency, it had still been rather reluctant about flexibility (Stubb, 2001a).

The negotiations did not advance in a political vacuum – frustration in the candidate states about the slow progress of the accession negotiations created pressure among the negotiators to achieve results. During the summer and early autumn of 2000, the supporters of a narrow agenda for the IGC won the battle but lost the war. They succeeded in narrowing the scope of the IGC 2000 reforms, but they could not stop Joschka Fischer and others from looking further ahead and reflecting on the long-term nature and organization of the Union.

Bringing enhanced co-operation on to the IGC agenda was a way of discouraging the idea of flexibility outside the Treaty, while also being a way of linking the IGC 2000 to the long-term debate. It gave the IGC 2000 a 'big idea', something that appeared to be more than just a rehash of the institutional 'leftovers'. This also meant that the debate about a further IGC was already emerging. Fundamental rights and the simplification of the treaties were not going to be on the agenda of this conference, but it became increasingly clear that decisions would have to be taken about future procedures.

---

[3] Retrospectively it could be argued that the Finnish Presidency should have produced a similar report. By drafting a report where all the Member States could 'find themselves', the Helsinki European Council might have had an easier time in trying to decide the size of the agenda.

The French Presidency – Starting with a Clean Sheet

The French Presidency did not continue the negotiations on the basis of the Feira report. This was regarded by some participants as a backward step, especially at the first meeting. The French Presidency did not demonstrate that it was going to be an impartial Presidency, but rather one that would advocate a shift in the balance of power in Community decision-making decisively towards the larger Member States. It started by posing conceptual questions rather than moving to the drafting of treaty articles. This introduced a tension between the large and small Member States that was to become an ever-present and corrosive dynamic in the negotiations right up to their conclusion in Nice. It once again illustrates the difficulty of achieving continuity between presidencies, especially in such sensitive negotiations.

The French Presidency focused initially on flexibility and QMV, which were on the agenda of five of the first eight meetings. It can be argued that the French Presidency managed this debate extremely well. The lead in both areas was clearly in the Permanent Representation, in the competent hands of Ambassador Pierre Vimont and his team, whose most difficult negotiations were not with the 14 other Member States. One of the problems of the French Presidency was that Paris was determined to keep control on other points, especially the reweighting of votes. This, combined with *cohabitation* in government, did not make it easy for Vimont to steer the negotiations in Brussels. If a strategy existed, it seemed to be to leave the admittedly difficult contentious issues to the final evening, so that Heads of State and Government would be forced to relent under intense political and media pressure.

Clearing the Air in Biarritz

Going into the informal European Council of Biarritz (13–14 October 2000), it was not clear how the Presidency was going to manage the debate. No background documents, apart from the traditional letter of invitation, had been distributed in advance. In fact, it was not even certain that the IGC would be dealt with in detail as many expected the discussions to focus on the debate on the future of Europe. Biarritz was not a breakthrough in the negotiations, nor was it supposed to be. Its aim was generally regarded as one of giving a political impulse to the negotiations and to establish a 'managed crisis'. The problem was that, at the infamous first dinner, the crisis did not seem to be managed. The Presidency had said in the media that it would be prepared to postpone the treaty if a satisfactory result was not reached on the number of Commissioners and the reweighting of votes. It was a clear indication of the priority of the Presidency – the balance between the Member States.

Biarritz was an important step on the road to Nice – it cleared the air. It was the first time since Amsterdam that the Heads of State and Government had an opportunity to tackle institutional questions. Three main conclusions can be drawn from the meeting. Firstly, flexibility was painted as the big success. Inspired by the oral conclusions of the Presidency, virtually all Member States indicated in their respective press conferences that political agreement had been reached on flexibility. At the time, no one seemed to have noticed that there been no draft article on flexibility on the negotiating table. The first one was discussed only on 30 October 2000. That discussion showed that there was a lot still to negotiate. Secondly, the strategy of the Presidency was to put pressure on the small states, especially on the question of the Commission. The Presidency noted that the 'large' Member States would be able to accept an equal rotation of Commissioners. The ball was now back in the court of the small states which, apart from a few exceptions, wanted to stick to the Commissioner-per-state principle. One of the key problems at that point was that the small Member States failed to build a coalition. Thirdly, it was becoming increasingly clear that most of the issues would be on the table, unresolved, in Nice.

There was a certain negotiating vacuum after Biarritz. The representatives had to go back and tackle the details. The debate on QMV especially, became unmanageable as one draft article after another was put on the table on, for example, taxation and social policy. In a sense, the conference became obsessed with numbers (i.e. how many questions could be moved to QMV) as opposed to substance (the actual content of the article in question).

While the formal negotiations became less important as Nice approached, the various delegations were involved in a frenzy of informal activity behind the scenes. Two key informal representative meetings in Paris and Val-Duchesse made an attempt to settle some of the key issues. The efforts were in vain, partly because of the nature of the negotiations (everything was open until the end), and partly because the small states especially were unable to agree on a common line on, for example, the reweighting of votes. Key elements of the Nice preparations took place on three additional fronts – the *tour des capitales* of Moscovici, the French Minister for Europe and, later, of President Chirac, and the 'confessionals' in Brussels. All three were an attempt by the Presidency to establish the bases for compromise.

Nice – the End Game

European Council meetings are the one occasion when Heads of State and Government are essentially on their own. Once inside the meeting room it is virtually impossible for advisers to reach them – even those entitled to be there were on occasion told to leave the room. European Councils are also a political circus with cameras, lights and not much action for anyone else. Some delegations are so large that 90 per cent of the advisers are not needed. Long periods of waiting are punctured by bouts of intense work by the advisers – many with their laptop computer projections – while the journalists outside desperately search for a different angle to their 3,000 colleagues.

Nice was something of a shock for all of the parties involved. IGC negotiations usually advance in three stages: preparation, negotiation and end game (Stubb, 1998). Although not quite true, this time it seemed as if 18 months of preparation had been thrown out of the window and negotiations started from scratch. An unusually large number of issues were still unresolved. These included the reweighting of votes, the number of Commissioners, key QMV questions (trade, Justice and Home Affairs, taxation and social policy), and the allocation of seats in the European Parliament. Flexibility had almost been settled, apart from some questions relating to the second pillar on the CFSP and defence.

The Nice European Council was the longest in EU history. It started at 9.45 am on Thursday, 7 December and ended at 4.40 am on Monday, 11 December. In actual fact, the real negotiations did not get underway until Saturday morning. On Thursday, the focus was on other issues and on Friday night the Presidency organized a number of bilateral IGC 'confessionals' with each delegation. On the basis of these, the Presidency distributed a new set of documents, which had been substantially changed from the proposals that had been dealt with in preparatory meetings before Nice. On reweighting, for instance, the 'triple majority' and a higher threshold were put on the table for the first time. On Saturday, the negotiations ended rather early because it was clear that agreement was not in sight that evening. There was a sense that the French Presidency was in no rush to finish the negotiations. They trusted that delegates would climb the compromise pyramid one by one and reach a final package in the end. The two obvious defenders of the general interest – the Commission and Presidency – were not able to facilitate the compromise.

The stage was set for a grand finale (Seixas da Costa, 2001; Ludlow, 2001). The most difficult issue on the table remained the reweighting of votes. During the last day and night the negotiations were interrupted eight times for consultations with delegations. Every time the Presidency made an attempt to find a compromise. One by one the Member States began to come on board. Belgium was the last to resist having received a number of significant improvements. The final compromise (see below) was finally approved at 4.40 on Monday morning. Albeit plagued by inconsistencies and blamed for cynical negotiating tactics, the French Presidency had succeeded in its main aim – a political agreement on the Treaty of Nice.[4] Most of the assessments of Nice have noted that the way in which the Treaty was negotiated was unusually tough. This may, indeed, have been the case but, at the same time, one must keep in mind that the issues on the table were extremely difficult. In many ways there was a battle both in the negotiating room and the press room. The ongoing battle in the press can be seen as one of the peculiarities of the negotiations. This was partly due to the fact that the European Council lasted four days. Some delegations distributed negotiating documents, which were often circulating in the press room almost immediately after they had been distributed in the meeting room. Other delegations organized briefing sessions with the press core of other Member States in order to advance their own interests. Oddly, the French Presidency did not appear to give particular importance to the media battle, with the result that they seemed to be the only delegation not communicating effectively.

II. Assessing the Results of Nice

Any analysis of the results depends on one's perception of the objective. The Member States and the institutions clearly had very different ambitions. Many observers have seen the negotiations as a dispute between large and small Member States, though the reality was much more nuanced. At no point during the negotiations were the larger Member States able to achieve an absolute consensus among themselves. The same is true of the smaller Member States. Different perspectives on the desirable levels of integration also cut across these coalitions based on size. A better assessment of the results of the Treaty of Nice can only be achieved by considering the objectives and the results on each of the six main issues (Duff, 2000; European Parliament, 2001; ECSA Review, 2001; Satuli and Stubb, 2001; Wessels, 2001; Yataganas, 2001).

Issues of Power

The composition of the Commission was recognized as an issue for the IGC 2000 even before the Treaty of Amsterdam negotiations had been completed. The compromise reached at Noordwijk in May 1997 meant that the issue would be re-examined in the next treaty negotiations. The same proposals had been on the table for many years, and were as valid at Nice as before. The difference in Nice was that negotiators had not dealt with the issue during the Portuguese

---

[4] For the first time in the history of the Union, the so-called Antici notes were leaked to the press. A first version of the debate in the final hours appeared in *El Pais* and a second version in the *Economist*. This sets a dangerous precedent for European Council meetings, which are supposed to be highly confidential discussions among Heads of State and Government.

Presidency but had rather concentrated on the organization of the Commission. Secondly, the larger Member States took a strategic decision at Biarritz to put pressure on the smaller Member States by offering to accept the model of equal rotation, which implied acceptance of the possibility that they might not have even one Commissioner.

The final deal was a classical EU compromise with one Commissioner per Member State until the Union reaches 27 members, followed by the introduction of a rotation system based on equality, although without precise details at this stage. In essence, it was a deal in which all Member States could claim some success. As an added bonus for the more integrationist-minded delegations, the Presidency suggested in the dying hours of the negotiations that the Commission President be elected by qualified majority voting.

The reweighting of votes was the most important issue for the larger Member States (Moberg, 2001; Felsenthal and Machover, 2001; Wallace, 2001). Strangely, it was the issue on which the least amount of time was spent up to the immediate preparations before and during Nice. Again, this was a leftover from the compromise at Ioannina that had not been resolved at Amsterdam. Numerous proposals and models, both formal and informal, were issued during the negotiations, but the Presidencies had been understandably reluctant to advance a specific proposal. Negotiations continued to alternate between the double-majority approach with increased emphasis on population, a simple reweighting approach, and numerous variants between these systems. At Nice, the main problems were that France and Spain could not accept a double simple majority, France did not want to break its parity with Germany, Spain wanted to be seen as a large state, some Member States focused on the blocking minority, and the Netherlands wanted more votes than Belgium.

The sum of these problems led to an overall triple-majority compromise, which could not have been predicted by anyone in advance. Interestingly, the final result does not differ dramatically from the first proposal tabled by the French Presidency in Nice. The small states were bought off, one after another, with a couple of extra votes. The threshold for QMV was brought down from the original proposal due to the insistence and persistence of the Belgian Prime Minister, Guy Verhofstadt. The final deal seems to benefit few and infuriate many. The most understandable criticism is that decision-making has been made more complex and more illogical. By adopting a position for a Union of 15, a joint negotiating position for a Union of 27 and a separate declaration, Heads of State and Government managed to agree on a system that contradicts itself in a number of places. The irony is that, if France had not insisted on parity with Germany, they might well have come away with a reweighting system which was more advantageous to the larger Member States than the one eventually agreed.

The issue of the number of members of the European Parliament was always likely to be caught up in the final compromise on the reweighting of votes. Amsterdam had set a ceiling of 700 MEPs after enlargement, but had failed to outline a system for dividing the number between the different Member States. It was clear that even a limited enlargement would break the 700 ceiling, so alterations were necessary. When approaching the subject it became clear that any attempt to find a logic, even within the present system, would be fruitless. During the IGC 2000, two basic options were presented: a move towards a more proportional system (digressive proportionality) or a straight cut across the board for all Member States. Like the Commission, the European Parliament had been unable to put forward a single approach to its own composition. The final outcome is one of the most illogical and arbitrary decisions stemming from Nice. The Presidency handed out extra seats like loose change and even then failed to give an equal number to Hungary and the Czech Republic, though they are roughly equal in population to Belgium, Greece and Portugal. One key question for the future will be the impact of the mathematical dominance of the German MEPs.

Issues of Efficiency

The debate on the extension of qualified majority voting was a clear example of a mismatch of objectives of the different Member States. A number of them, the Commission and the European Parliament sought to extend QMV as far as possible. Others were either determined to limit the scope or to avoid progress in some of the most sensitive issues. Although both the Finnish Presidency and the Commission attempted to introduce a number of criteria into the negotiations, the discussions were destined to be undertaken on a case-by-case basis. As each negotiation took place, and the scope of unanimity became more limited, it was only logical that the negotiations became more difficult. This was certainly the case at Nice.

What is extraordinary is that the vast majority of cases were not debated in any detail. The Portuguese and French Presidencies concentrated on six main issues: taxation (Art. 95 EC), social security (Art. 42 and 137 EC), asylum, immigration and related issues (Arts. 62–68 EC), common commercial policy (Art. 133 EC), structural and cohesion funds (Arts. 159 and 161 EC) and environment (Art. 175(2) EC) to such a degree that many of the other points were passed without detailed discussion. It can also be argued that so many drafts were produced on taxation and social security that it was counterproductive. The final deal was a success in numerical terms, but not encouraging substantively. This was no real surprise, although the manner of the final discussions is difficult to fathom. A number of the larger Member States (including Germany and Italy) which, hours before, had been so adamant about extending QMV suddenly fell silent when they had negotiated their compromise on reweighting of votes.

The argument over whether to include enhanced co-operation on the agenda underlined the ideological differences between the different Member States (Philippart and Sie Dhian Ho, 2000; Stubb, 2001a, b). Some saw it as a concept that could be developed further at a later date, while others demanded that a case had to be made for where enhanced co-operation could be used before treaty changes could be made. The main political agreement was reached at Biarritz with the exception of European security and defence policy, which was eventually dropped in Nice due to the other changes made to the treaty on defence.[5] Although frequent discussions took place on enhanced co-operation, many of the details of the articles were not properly debated, leaving a number of contradictions, omissions and unanswered questions.

The IGC reached agreement on three main themes: removing the emergency brake mechanism (veto), reducing the number of states required to initiate enhanced co-operation, and slightly relaxing the tight conditions. The conclusion must be that there has been some progress on making the provisions easier to operate, but that the case has still to be made for where enhanced co-operation can be used in the future. Perhaps the real success is that the justification for working outside the treaty has become more difficult. It is difficult to agree with those who claim that the current flexibility rules allow for the creation of a core of states. Our assessment is that far from creating a single core, the new flexibility rules may become a useful tool for establishing a number of different constellations of Member States. For all of those who dreamed of a predetermined and unitary core which would determine the pace of integration in Europe, Nice must have been a serious disappointment. The Nice provisions may not put an end to the debate about core Europe, but it is likely to calm things down for a few years. Flexibility can now be used inside the treaty, on the basis of common rules.

The reform of the Union's legal system was not debated by the Heads of State and Government. Nonetheless, the implications of the proposed changes may have a more significant impact on the development of the European Union than any of the other changes agreed in Nice. While the Court of Justice will continue to be composed of one judge from each Member State, a 'grand chamber' has been established to deal with cases today handled by plenary session. The Court of First Instance will have at least one judge from each Member State. The system of rotation for appointments has still to be decided.

---

[5] An enabling clause on the implementation of joint actions and common positions was agreed, but the possibility for flexibility in its classical sense was not agreed.

The most important change to the Union's legal system is the redistribution of responsibilities between the Court of Justice and Court of First Instance. The Court of First Instance becomes the common law judge for all direct actions with the exception of those attributed to a specialized judicial chamber and those the statute reserves for the Court itself. The Court of Justice retains responsibility for other proceedings (particularly action for failure to fulfil obligations). The idea is to maintain the Court of Justice as the jurisdictional supreme body of the European Union on the essential Community issues. The different provisions in the Treaty, statute and rules of procedure have also been rationalized which will make it easier to adjust the operation of the Court in the future.

Following a compromise reached between a number of Member States, Europe's leaders agreed a declaration in Nice which provides for an Intergovernmental Conference in 2004. This is to examine at least four issues: the legal status of the Charter of Fundamental Rights, the simplification of the treaties, the role of national parliaments, and the distribution of powers and responsibilities between the Union, national and regional levels. Crucially, the declaration also allows for additional issues to be added to this agenda. Each of the issues highlighted in the declaration attached to the Treaty are points that have been raised in previous IGCs and have failed to gain the necessary support. The negotiations in 2004 on this basis will not be any easier than in Nice.

Overall, the Treaty of Nice meets few of the different objectives of the participants. It is tempting to argue that, if the Amsterdam and Nice treaties are viewed as one process, then an impressive step forward has been made. Nevertheless, this still hides the reality that some of the key institutional questions for the future remain unresolved. Throughout the process, the justification for the changes was enlargement, though the real reason centred more on efficiency and power than on enlargement itself. That does not mean that Nice should be disregarded; some of the changes made in areas that did not gain public attention, such as the Court of Justice, are extremely important. But, in history, Nice is more likely to be remembered for its political disputes than the quality of the changes made to the Treaty.

III. Implications for the Future

The Political Landscape

The implications of Nice are more difficult to judge. An overriding concern must be that the acrimony at Nice may colour a number of the key alliances that have been formed over many years. It is difficult to see the Franco–German alliance being rectified before the elections in both countries in 2002. The relationship between the Benelux countries is also hard to gauge following the mistrust created by both Amsterdam and Nice. The truth may be that when it comes to other areas co-operation will continue, but there will be an underlying resentment within these alliances for many years to come. One clear implication of the Treaty of Nice, however, will be the negative message sent to the candidate states, which were not treated as being the equals of existing members. Even worse were the mixed signals given to Turkey, which was given soothing words on enlargement and then not deemed to be worthy of being considered for the allocation of seats and votes in the institutions.

Each of the Member States will need to reflect on the process of the negotiations and the role they played. One of the most interesting aspects of treaty reform is that the process has become institutionalized. Yet the turnover of staff in the Member State Prime Minister's offices and foreign ministries is huge. One of the key advantages for the Council Secretariat and the European Commission is that they have an institutional memory very rarely matched by member governments. For the larger Member States, the key assessment must be whether they have stretched the institutional balance to an extent that may have created friction for the future. For the smaller Member States, the real concern must be that they were outmanœuvred by their larger brethren, largely as a result of their inability to adopt a common negotiating position after Biarritz. This led to the salami tactics in Nice, which resulted in many failing to achieve a number of their key objectives.

The European Commission and the European Parliament must also reflect on their roles. A clear political choice was taken by these two institutions to outline similar positions. They must question whether their coalition in the IGC actually strengthened or weakened their position, with the latter distinctly possible. The European Commission is perceived to have been ignored during the negotiations. In reality, like each delegation, it made some wise proposals and others, which with hindsight were misguided. One of its key problems was that, over the last ten years, it had been unable to adopt a clear position in four debates on its own composition. The Commission also felt that the reweighting of votes was an artificial problem. While its opinion was generally respected, a range of proposals presented during the Portuguese Presidency were seen as a step too far by many delegations. For its part, the European Parliament was hampered from the start. By threatening to delay the start of the process and then being unable to adopt a detailed resolution until April 2000, the Parliament struggled to stamp its authority on the agenda or the rationale behind each of the issues.

A New Method for Preparing and Negotiating Treaties?

IGCs are a necessary evil – but an evil that can be changed. The call for a change in procedure is an understandable one and change has long been overdue. Michalski and Bertrand (2000) rightly point out that the IGC method has diminishing returns. Although the IGC method is a legal requirement, at least until 2004, this should not be used as an excuse to avoid reform. The rejection of the Nice Treaty by the Irish public on 7 June 2001 further reinforces the case for fresh thinking on treaty change.

The method for preparing for the 2004 IGC has still to be agreed. Consensus only seems to have been reached on one point, that the process should be more open, and dialogue should take place with all interested parties. When considering changes to the preparation of the 2004 IGC, many observers have looked to the process that led to the Charter of Fundamental Rights and have suggested that the convention method should be used. Others have stressed that constitutional change should be the sole prerogative of Member States. A widening of the preparatory phase would be a positive development. A revised Convention model should give rise to little fear as long as it is recognized that Member States must take the final decisions in an Intergovernmental Conference format. A number of other practical improvements can be made to the system. Some have been outlined by McDonagh (1998), Dorr (2000) and Gray (2000). The vast majority of these proposals would not require treaty change. Some of the most important are outlined below.

Firstly, greater political direction is needed throughout the process. As in Amsterdam, the ministerial level was virtually non-existent during the IGC 2000. Ministers only debated the issue for an hour every month in the GAC. The suggestion made during the French Presidency of adding a further level was rightly rejected. The ministerial level of the process must be strengthened to give political orientation to the negotiations, possibly by only appointing ambassadors to the technical group and ensuring that the GAC has a detailed discussion each month rather than a one-hour session with the European Parliament. Secondly, the model of the enlargement and *Agenda 2000* negotiations might be used. The Presidency might present a series of negotiating 'boxes', which are then completed with a series of successive approximations, so avoiding the situation of all the issues remaining open until the final summit. Finally, a more radical suggestion to avoid the difficulties encountered in both Amsterdam and Nice would be for Heads of State and Government to review the compromise resulting from the summit in the cold light of day. This might risk reopening the negotiations, but it would at least avoid the mistakes and discrepancies on issues like reweighting of votes, which then require weeks of subsequent negotiations. Nice was similar to Amsterdam in that the negotiations did not end in the European Council, and Coreper had to negotiate the inconsistencies in the actual text that had been agreed.

IV. Conclusions

Ultimately, each IGC is unique to the time, place, agenda and personalities involved. Nothing in an IGC negotiation is quite as it seems. Personal relationships cut across institutional boundaries, proposals are submitted on behalf of other delegations and the same meeting will produce 18[6] different sets of minutes, which rarely correspond. Although hundreds of hours of negotiations went into the process, the vast majority of the text of the new treaty was dependent on the viewpoint of only a limited number of actors – often cutting across Member State or institutional boundaries, so that the impact of personalities needs to be considered in much greater detail than in the past. A number of examples illustrate this point. The enhanced co-operation and European political parties issues would not have been an agenda item without the respective presence of Francisco Seixas da Costa and Dimitris Tsatsos. Article 133 would not have been resolved without Antti Satuli and Pascal Lamy. The influence of personalities is significant even to the extent of the seating arrangement in the final European Council meeting. The decision to locate all European Councils in Brussels would not have taken place without the Deputy Secretary-General of the Council, Pierre de Boissieu. Countless other examples exist.

Much of the IGC was blighted by an artificial debate on the agenda. In reality, all issues will be considered if the proposal is initially supported by a number of delegations. One of the main problems affecting this IGC, and potentially that scheduled for 2004, is the reliance on an agenda covering only institutional issues. This inevitably leads to the discussions focusing on issues of power, which reduces opportunities for each delegation to be able to find their fingerprints on the Treaty.

Inevitably, much of the literature on the Treaty of Nice will focus on whether the negotiations have led to the intergovernmental approach becoming more prevalent. The perception may be that the Commission and European Parliament were peripheral actors in the process. Once again, the reality is more nuanced. This type of negotiation is by nature extremely intergovernmental; it is therefore surprising that even in Nice, supranational bodies were able to shape and influence events on certain issues. The fact that Member States brokered the deal on the weighting of votes should not blur the

---

[6] Each of the 15 Member States, the European Commission, the Council Secretariat and the European Parliament (when invited) produce reports of the meetings. None of these is available to the public.

involvement of others in the vast majority of issues. It was surprising, though, that there were only very few Member States who were willing to defend the Community method, and these were not the countries traditionally seen as holding this standard. The IGC also demonstrates once again that Heads of State and Government are most likely to continue down a step-by-step approach to European integration rather than creating a totally new system.

Although it is tempting to suggest that a better result should have been achieved, it is not clear that a different approach would have led to a different set of treaty texts. The EU will not stop, simply as a result of the rancorous atmosphere in Nice. What remains clear is that treaty change is only one part of the picture. The concrete measures already being undertaken to reform the institutions are as important, if not more important than anything agreed in the Treaty. Although the Kinnock proposals have received widespread attention, also hugely important are the proposals outlined in the second report of the Trumpf-Piris recommendations on reform of the Council's working methods. What may have begun to change are the coalitions that have underpinned the Union for the last 50 years and the logic and balance that are essential to the Union's future.

References

Best, E., Gray, M. and Stubb, A. (2000) *Rethinking the European Union – IGC 2000 and Beyond* (Maastricht: EIPA).

Cloos, J. (ed.) (1993) *Le traité de Maastricht, genèse, analyse, commentaries* (Bruxelles: Bruylant).

Commision of the European Communities (2000) 'Adapting the institutions to make a success of enlargement'. *COM*(2000) 34 – C5-0072/2000, 26 January.

CONFER, all Conference documents are available on the Council's website: «http://db.consilium.eu.int/cig».

Corbett, R. (1992) 'The Intergovernmental Conference on Political Union'. *Journal of Common Market Studies,* Vol. 30, No. 3, pp. 271–98.

Dehaene, J-L. (1999) *Report of the Group of Wise Men* (Brussels: CEC).

Dorr, N. (2000) 'The IGC Agenda: An Irish Perspective'. In Best *et al.* (eds), pp. 29–42.

Duff, A. (2000) 'The Treaty of Nice: From Left-overs to Hangovers'. Briefing on the outcome of the IGC and the European Council of Nice, 7–11 December.

ECSA Review (2001) *Forum: Analyzing the Treaty of Nice,* Vol. 14, No. 2, Spring.

Edwards, G. and Pijpers, A. (1997) (eds) *The Politics of European Treaty Reform* (London: Cassell).

European Parliament (2000) 'European Parliament's Proposals for the Intergovernmental Conference. 14094/1999, 13 April.

European Parliament (2001) 'Draft Treaty of Nice (initial analysis)'. PE 294.737.

European University Institute (2000) *A Basic Treaty for the European Union: A Study of the Reorganisation of the Treaties* (Florence: EUI).

Felsenthal, D. and Machover, M. (2001) 'The Treaty of Nice and Qualified Majority Voting'. Unpublished paper, revised version February.

Finland (1999) 'The Finnish IGC Report'. 1363/LIMITE.

Galloway, D. (2001) *The Treaty of Nice and Beyond: Realities and Illusions of Power in the EU* (Sheffield: Sheffield Academic Press).

Gray, M. (2000) 'Negotiating EU Treaties: The Case for a New Approach'. In Best *et al.* (eds), pp. 263–80.

Ludlow, P. (2001) 'The European Council at Nice: Neither Triumph nor Disaster'. Background Paper, CEPS International Advisory Council, 1–2 February.

McDonagh, B. (1998) *Original Sin in a Brave New World* (Dublin: Institute for European Affairs).

Michalski, A. and Bertrand, G. (2000) 'The Future of EU Institutions: Insights from the Scenarios Europe 2010 Project'. In Best *et al.* (eds), pp. 281–98.

Moberg, A. (2001) 'The Voting Rules in the Nice Treaty'. Unpublished paper, Stockholm.

Moravcsik, A. (1998) *The Choice of Europe* (London: UCL Press).

Oreja, M. (1998) *El Tratado de Amsterdam: Analisis y comentarios* (Madrid: McGraw-Hill).

Philippart, E. and Sie Dhian Ho, M. (2000) 'The Pros and Cons of Closer Cooperation within the EU. Argumentation and Recommendations'. The Hague, WRR Working documents, No. 104.

Satuli, A. and Stubb, A. (2001) 'Nizzan hallitustenvälinen sopimus? Hyvään tulokseen huonolla tavalla'. Ulkopolitiikka, Helsinki, 1/01.

Seixas da Costa, F. (2001) 'Portugal and the Treaty of Nice: Notes on the Portuguese Negotiating Strategy'. Negócios Estrangeiros, March, Lisbon, English translation.

Stubb, A. (1998) 'Flexible Integration and the Amsterdam Treaty: Negotiating Differentiation in the 1996–97 IGC'. PhD thesis, London School of Economics and Political Science.

Stubb, A. (2001a) 'From Amsterdam to Nice and Beyond: Negotiating Flexible Integration in the European Union' (Basingstoke: Palgrave), forthcoming.

Stubb, A. (2001b) 'The European Union After Nice: Goodbye Core, Hello Flexibility' (Oxford: Oxford Analytica).

Wallace, H. (2001) 'Nice Votes if you can Get Them'. *Integration,* No. 2.

Weiler, J.H.H. and Modrall, J. (1985) 'Institutional Reform: Consensus or Majority?'. *European Law Review,* 10/05.

Wessels, W. (2001) 'Nice Results: The Millennium IGC in the EU's Evolution'. *Journal of Common Market Studies,* Vol. 39, No. 2, pp. 197–219.

Yataganas, X.A. (2001) 'The Treaty of Nice: The Sharing of Power and the Institutional Balance in the European Union – A Continental Perspective'. Harvard Jean Monnet Working Paper 01/01.

Journal of Common Market Studies

Volume 39, Annual Review
September 2001

Governance and Institutions 2000: Edging Towards Enlargement

DESMOND DINAN

George Mason University

Introduction

On the surface, institutional affairs in the year 2000 were dominated by the Intergovernmental Conference (IGC), which is examined elsewhere in the *Review*. The IGC was supposed to prepare the EU institutionally for enlargement, but it touched only the tip of the iceberg. The mass of the iceberg – the daily grind of EU institutional operations and governance – was largely unaffected by the IGC and its possible outcome. Yet EU institutional actors were well aware in 2000 that the EU's ability to absorb new members would depend as much on internal institutional reform as on treaty-based reform, if not more so. Changes in the rules of procedure of the Commission, Council, and European Parliament (EP), for example, or in the conduct of the co-decision procedure, would arguably have a greater impact on the EU's ability to withstand the shock of enlargement than would a reduction in the number of Commissioners or greater use of qualified majority voting in the Council.

Although the potentially disruptive impact of enlargement on governance and institutions overshadowed the EU in 2000, the institutions themselves undertook few if any concrete measures to improve their efficiency in anticipation of an influx of new Member States. This was especially true of the General Affairs Council (foreign ministers), a body urgently in need of reform.

Despite having called for reform of the Commission and the Council, the EP has so far avoided the kind of internal administrative overhaul that impending enlargement surely requires. Only the Commission undertook a major reform effort, but that was driven by exposure of past practices rather than expectation of future shocks. The Commission's landmark White Paper on reform, released in March 2000, hardly mentioned enlargement.

Following the turmoil of 1999, when the EP was instrumental in obliging the Commission to resign, the two institutions worked out a new *modus vivendi* in 2000. Relations among the three members of the EU's institutional triangle (the Commission, Council, and the EP) were relatively harmonious at a working level, despite a few public spats on issues such as the seemingly interminable attempt to conclude a statute for members of the EP (MEPs) and efforts to improve public access to documents. The nature of EU governance received unexpected attention when Commission President, Romano Prodi, promised in early 2000 that the Commission would publish a White Paper on the subject in 2001. Musings about EU governance complemented the launch of the 'post-Nice' debate on the future of the EU, a debate that actually began seven months before the Nice summit in December 2000.

Finally, the year 2000 had a surprise in store for observers of EU governance and institutions: the Austrian imbroglio. Regardless of the merits of the issue, the other Member States' response to the possible, and then the actual, formation of an Austrian government that included the far-right Freedom Party was a fascinating case study of the EU's emerging political persona and the entanglement within the EU of domestic and 'European' affairs and of bilateral and multilateral relations.

I. The Commission

Having taken a hammering in 1999, the Commission licked its wounds in 2000 and attempted to regain its former institutional prominence. The reform strategy unveiled by Commissioner Neil Kinnock, first in a consultative document in January, then in a White Paper in March, and implemented gradually thereafter, was central to this endeavour. Kinnock used a memorable metaphor to describe the reform process: it was like a swan gliding across a lake, placid on the surface while paddling furiously under the water. Inevitably, however, reform could not take place without making waves. Reorganization involved disruption; staff unions resisted change; Commission officials fretted about their futures; and the EP and Member States expressed some concerns.

The College of Commissioners

Within the College, the most striking aspect of the new Commission's first full year in office was the contrast between the effectiveness of most Commissioners and the ineffectualness of President Prodi. In the first part of the year, especially, Prodi often seemed befuddled and poorly briefed. Nor did the way in which he championed enlargement and pushed the Commission's position in the IGC bolster his reputation or standing. Prodi's political weakness was most apparent at meetings of the European Council, where the Commission president has a unique opportunity to influence EU policy at the highest political level.

Prodi's poor performance since becoming President in September 1999 gave rise to a highly critical article in April 2000 in *Der Spiegel*, the influential German magazine, which claimed that other Commissioners were pressuring him to resign. This may have had a salutary effect on Prodi, who soon tried to reassert his authority by reshuffled some top civil service positions. The main victim was Carlo Trojan, Secretary General of the Commission, who was packed off to Geneva to head the Commission's delegation to the World Trade Organization. Trojan was closely associated with the old Santer regime; it was surprising that he had survived Prodi's initial reshuffle in October 1999. In a move that revealed how Member States continued to view senior Commission appointments as a matter of national interest, the Dutch government protested against the unexpected removal of the highest-ranking Dutch citizen in the Brussels bureaucracy. Yet the fact that Prodi did not even inform the Dutch government before the reshuffle showed that Member States were gradually losing their grip on personnel policy in the Commission. Similarly, later in May, with much less publicity, the Commission gave golden handshakes to two senior officials, a director-general and a former *chef de cabinet*, who would previously have been protected by their Member States (both big countries).

It was not until October 2000, however, that Prodi began seriously to try to regain lost ground. The occasion was a speech to the EP on 3 October in which he strongly defended the Commission's role in the EU system and warned against what he saw as the danger of creeping intergovernmentalism. The speech was significant less for what Prodi said than for how he said it: he was concise, authoritative and persuasive. Nevertheless Prodi's performance at the Nice summit reflected his continuing inability to punch his weight in the European Council.

Other Commissioners performed admirably during the year, especially those with responsibility for areas of undoubted Community competence. This was most striking in the cases of Mario Monti and the idiosyncratic Frits Bolkestein, Commissioners for competition and the single market, respectively. Their successful advocacy of greater competition and market integration testified to the Commission's centrality in key areas of Community life, despite speculation about the Commission's increasing marginalization in the EU system. By contrast, Chris Patten, the external relations commissioner, was manifestly frustrated by the division between his responsibilities and those of Javier Solana, the High Representative for the Common Foreign and Security Policy (CFSP), a Council appointee. Solana's higher profile and greater involvement in security and defence issues obviously irritated Patten, and demonstrated the Commission's relatively limited role outside the first pillar of the EU.

Internal Reform

Kinnock had a busy year overseeing internal reform, with the help of budget Commissioner, Michaele Schreyer. Kinnock brought energy and enthusiasm to a difficult and thankless task. The first fruit of his labour was a consultative document of 19 January, in which he organized the reform effort around three themes: financial management and control; strategic planning; and personnel policy. The draft White Paper drew on a variety of sources, including the two reports of the Committee of Independent Experts which had helped to bring down the previous Commission. It proposed, *inter alia*, establishing a new internal audit service and decentralizing financial control; introducing a system of Activity Based Management to help match responsibilities and resources (human, administrative, and financial); and improving recruitment, promotion and disciplinary procedures. The consultative document also iden-tified approximately 80 actions deemed necessary to implement the reform strategy during the next two years.

On the basis of this draft, Kinnock consulted Member States, the EP (which produced four reports on Commission reform in the course of the year, and held a public hearing in October), Commission officials, and staff unions. He also raised two issues that were separate from but closely related to the reform strategy: a revision of the 'method' for calculating and adjusting pay and an overhaul of the creaking pension scheme. The current method, in use since 1991, was due to expire in July 2001. Because of staff sensitivity on pay and pensions, especially at a time of wholesale reform, Kinnock proposed that they not be tackled for another two years. Accordingly, a revision of staff regula-tions (under the auspices of the reform strategy), an agreement on a new method, and an overhaul of the pension scheme could be negotiated as part of the same global package (the Council finally agreed to Kinnock's request on 19 December).

In their responses to the consultative paper, Member States were most concerned about the health of the pension scheme and the cost, feasibility and effectiveness of the reform strategy. Although they could not say so openly, some feared a further loss of influence over promotion at the highest levels in the Commission. That concern was somewhat allayed by a tacit agreement with the Commission whereby each Member State would be guaranteed at least one of the most senior positions, with the rest being awarded on the basis of merit rather than nationality.

The Kinnock reforms drew heavily on British and Scandinavian models of public administration. These ran counter to the French model on which the Commission was largely based, a model used also to a considerable degree in Germany, Italy, Belgium, Luxembourg, Spain, Portugal and Greece. Nevertheless, opposition to the reform strategy was not mobilized along national lines, although the French government and many French nationals in the Commission were noticeably discomfited by the reform strategy's implicit rejection of the Commission's original organizational principles and ethos. This may have accentuated a general unease in France about the direction of the EU and the apparent decline of French influence in it, an unease that was even more apparent in the IGC.

In its comments on the reform strategy, before and after the final version of the White Paper appeared, the EP welcomed the reform effort while criticizing specific aspects of it. In particular, the EP expressed misgivings about the effectiveness of decentralized audits by Commission directorates-general, as opposed to detailed parliamentary scrutiny. In effect, the EP was concerned about a possible diminution of its budgetary control over the Commission. Given the role that the Budgetary Control Committee had played in the Commission's downfall in 1999, this was by no means an inconsequential consideration for Kinnock to take on board. Despite some specific and entrenched objections from Member States, the EP, Commission officials, and staff unions to elements of the proposed reform strategy, the consultation process generally strengthened agreement among all parties on the need for reform and resulted in a broad endorsement of the White Paper. The final version, presented to the EP on 1 March, differed in detail but not much in substance from the January draft. The first part again outlined the reform strategy, under three main headings: 'Priority Setting, Allocation and Efficient Use of Resources'; 'Human Resources Development'; and 'Audit, Financial Management and Control'. The second part (a separate document) contained the detailed action plan.

The Commission began a phased implementation of the White Paper almost immediately, although it was not until 31 October that it adopted a 'road map' for the most important reforms, to be approved over the next 12 months, in areas such as staff policy and financial management. Other, related reforms took place throughout the year. These included a major redeployment of staff to operational DGs, such as Justice and Home Affairs, and Enlargement; a thorough reorganization of some DGs, notably Health and Consumer Protection, and Environment; and a comprehensive review of Commission resources and priorities by a 'peer group' of Commissioners, under Prodi's direction. The scale and pace of Commission reform in 2000 was certainly impressive, and the extent of union and other opposition to it suggested that the proposed changes were indeed consequential. But would they be adequate to bring about a 'fundamental change of culture, behaviour, and attitudes', as Kinnock, in one of his innumerable newspaper interviews, hoped that they would? The immediate impact of the reform strategy within the Commission seemed to be negative, with many officials feeling demoralized, disoriented and defensive, and overburdened by new requirements for financial and other controls. These were perhaps inevitable reactions to the events of the previous year, with the Commission struggling in the aftermath of the resignation crisis to reinvent itself organizationally and politically, under Prodi's weak leadership. Regardless of the President's shortcomings, Commission officials hardly doubted the necessity of reform or the benefits of its achievement. Nevertheless, there hung about the various Commission buildings scattered throughout Brussels a sense of regret that the good old days were over, and that the Commission would never be quite the same again.

The Governance Debate

Despite his perceived weakness as Commission President, Prodi launched a potentially important initiative in February 2000: a debate on EU governance. Concerned about public disillusionment with the EU, and about the twin challenges of enlargement and globalization, Prodi included in the Commission's strategic priorities for 2000–05, which he unveiled to the EP on 15 February, a commitment to new forms of governance. Moreover, Prodi promised a White Paper on the subject within the first few months of 2001.

At the time, Prodi's preoccupation with governance was not well received. His presentation to the EP and numerous subsequent pronouncements on the subject were often so vague and full of buzz words ('civil society', 'networked Europe', and the like) that they reinforced the media's unfavourable image of him. Yet Prodi's initiative anticipated the 'post-Nice' debate on the EU's future that Germany's Foreign Minister launched in Berlin in May. Indeed, Prodi had told the EP three months earlier that 'a large-scale debate has to be organized, in the post-IGC epoch, to rethink not only all our institutions but also all our policies'. Prodi's emphasis on citizens' concerns, decentralization, the role of the regions and radical institutional reform were later echoed, without due credit to the Commission President, by almost every contributor to the post-Nice debate.

The Commission approved a work programme for the putative White Paper in October. By that time the Commission's initiative had effectively been subsumed into the post-Nice debate, although Prodi strove to keep it separate. Later in the year, when the Member States decided in Nice to hold an IGC on EU governance in 2004, the White Paper inevitably came to be seen as an early Commission contribution to it. In addition to tackling such issues as accountability, transparency and effectiveness, the Commission's White Paper, and presumably the 2004 IGC, would propose ways to promote public interest in the EU; apportion decision-making authority between and among the regional, national and Brussels levels of governance; and improve the relevance and quality of Community legislation.

II. The European Parliament

Following the excitement during the previous year of the Commission's resignation and the direct elections, 2000 was a busy but relatively uneventful year for the EP. The Socialist Group circulated a paper on parliamentary reform in October, but nothing came of it. Suggestions for improving the EP's performance and public appeal included better organization of plenary sessions; livelier parliamentary debates; delegation of powers in certain cases to committees; rationalization of voting procedures; and a reduction in the number of amendments to draft legislation.

Ideological and procedural problems associated with the political group system were more marked in 2000 than in recent years. This was especially true of the European People's Party–European Democrats (EPP–ED) group, the largest in the EP. With 35 affiliated parties from all 15 Member States, the EPP–ED presented a managerial challenge of epic proportions. A problem unique to the EPP–ED was that the Euroscepticism of its British Conservative members jarred with the group's traditional Christian Democratic enthusiasm for deeper integration.

The most significant political group issue concerned the Technical Group of Independents (TGI), a collection of 19 MEPs, some independent, others members of national parties or lists, held together by a desire to avail themselves of the privileges of group membership. In September 1999 the EP dissolved the group because it lacked 'political affinity', a prerequisite for a political group according to the EP's rules of procedure. Given that the group included such diverse elements as the far-right French National Front and the moderate Italian Bonino List (headed by a former Commissioner), there was no disputing the absence of political affinity. The TGI nevertheless challenged the legality of the EP's rules of procedure and, having won its case in the Court of First Instance in November 1999, promptly reconstituted itself. What

followed in 2000 was a lengthy and inconclusive debate about the rules
concerning party group formation and the rights of independent MEPs. By the
end of the year the EP was moving towards a position that would give
independent MEPs the same rights and access to resources as affiliated MEPs,
a move that could affect the cohesion of the larger and more heterogeneous
groups.

III. The Council and European Council

Council reform proceeded in a lackadaisical way in 2000. Member States
finally acted on one of the provisions of Trumpf-Piris report on Council
reform, issued the previous year and endorsed by the European Council in
December 1999, when they reduced the number of Council configurations to
16 in April 2000. This was one more than the European Council had called for,
but it represented a step in the right direction.

The main problem plaguing the Council in 2000 continued to be the
workload of the General Affairs Council (GAC). A proliferation of bilateral
and multilateral international agreements, usually involving annual ministeri-
al-level meetings tacked on to the GAC's agenda, overburdened the GAC. That
left less time for other business, notably legislative decision-making, general
policy co-ordination, and preparation of the European Council. Minor procedural changes under the French Presidency in the first half of 2000, such as
shifting external relations agenda items to the morning session, had no
appreciable impact on the GAC's efficiency.

At the end of his first year as High Representative for the CFSP, Solana,
who was also Secretary-General of the Council Secretariat, observed that one
GAC meeting a month was inadequate, that GAC agendas were set too far in
advance, and that 'a more flexible process' was needed to meet the growing
demands on foreign ministers' time. Such sentiments were echoed in a seminar
on Council reform organized by the former Commission President, Jacques
Delors, in Paris in September 2000. Delors called for the GAC to be split into
two, with the foreign ministers working exclusively on external relations
issues and deputy prime ministers or European affairs ministers meeting twice
a month to deal with other GAC business. At about the same time as the Paris
seminar, the foreign ministers discussed Council reform at their informal
'Gymnich-type' meeting in Evian. However, no further changes in the Council's composition or organization took place before the end of the year.

As in years past, the GAC's relative disarray stood in marked contrast to the
organizational efficiency of Ecofin (finance ministers), its main rival in the
Council structure. Ecofin's stature rose in 2000 as EMU grew in importance
and impact. More specifically, the Eurogroup, the subset of Ecofin consisting

of the finance ministers of the EMU Member States, became more central to economic policy-making in the EU. With the finance ministers effectively answerable only to the European Council, the GAC lost co-ordination of a wide swathe of EU public policy.

The European Council continued its triumphant march to institutional pre-eminence in 2000 not only because of the increasing number of issues coming within its purview, but also because of the decision at the Lisbon summit in March to hold an annual follow-up summit on the subject of enterprise and information technology. The Nice summit resulted in another potentially important boost for the European Council: a decision to hold all regularly scheduled summits in Brussels instead of in the country holding the Council Presidency. The way in which this decision was taken is revealing: it was proposed by the Committee of Permanent Representatives (Coreper), the power behind the Council throne, and rubber-stamped by the European Council, some of whose members later expressed ignorance of it. Coreper hopes that holding most summits in Brussels will improve the quality of the European Council's work – as well as further enhancing its own influence.

IV. Inter-Institutional Relations

Relations between the Commission and the EP, which were fraught in 1999, remained tense at the beginning of 2000. There was lingering resentment in the EP because the Prodi Commission was not being reconfirmed in January, as it began its full five-year term, but had been confirmed instead the previous September for both its interim and full terms in office. The EP retaliated against a perceived Commission slight by postponing the long-planned announcement of Prodi's five-year programme at the January plenary session until the next plenary, in February.

Such pettiness, which may have been due more to divisions within the EP than to the state of Commission–EP relations, boded ill for interaction between the two institutions in 2000. Yet relations between the Commission and the EP during the next 12 months belied that poor beginning. Apart from renewed tension in April, when the EP's Budget Control Committee delayed granting discharge to the 1998 budget, the Commission and the EP worked well together, with noticeably more visits to the EP by Commissioners and senior Commission officials than in previous years. The Budget Control Committee's action, reminiscent of the events that brought the previous Commission down, did not reflect continuing concern in the EP about the Commission's conduct, but divisions within the committee between a group of conservatives intent on embarrassing the Commission and others who saw no reason why discharge should not be granted. The issue was sorted out, to the discomfiture of the EP, in plenary sessions in April and July when a majority of MEPs overturned the committee's recommendation and granted the necessary discharge.

As part of the fallout from the Commission's collapse in 1999, the Commission and the EP had to negotiate an inter-institutional agreement on their working relationship to replace the 1995 Code of Conduct. The EP based its proposal for the agreement on a September 1999 parliamentary resolution, which covered a range of issues from the conduct of individual Commissioners to the institutions' role in the legislative process. Although the Commission had some misgivings about the EP's inevitable assertiveness in the light of developments in 1999, negotiations between the two institutions were relatively smooth and swift, resulting in the conclusion of an agreement in early July.

It was the Council, rather than the Commission, which objected to what it saw as excessive deference by the Commission to the EP in the inter-institutional agreement. During negotiation of the agreement, the Council repeatedly warned about possible limits on the Commission's freedom of action, the consequences for collegiality, and the danger of treaty infringement. The Council's main concern, however, was about a provision of the agreement on the transmission of documents. Specifically, the Council feared that the Commission would transmit Council documents to the EP without the Council's permission. Immediately after the conclusion of the agreement, Coreper issued a statement reiterating the Council's continuing concern.

The question of access to documents in the inter-institutional agreement touched a raw nerve because the Council and EP were locked in a fierce dispute in 2000 on access to sensitive information concerning defence and security policy. Under the terms of Art. 255 TEC, the EU had to devise rules for public access to documents, using the co-decision procedure, within two years of the Amsterdam Treaty entering into force. The Commission tabled a draft regulation in January 2000, in plenty of time for legislation to be adopted by May 2001. Rapid developments in the area of security and defence policy added a new dimension to the debate about the proposed legislation, and to the transparency debate generally, as the year progressed. The Council, or at least a majority of its members, did not want the EP, let alone the public, to have access to certain security and defence-related documents. Matters came to a head in August when the Council decided, during the summer vacation when little EU business is ever conducted, to prevent public access to documents 'classified as secret, top-secret and confidential in the fields of foreign policy, military and non-military crisis-management'. The timing and substance of the Council's action infuriated the EP, which brought a case against the Council to the Court of Justice, and poisoned the atmosphere of the parallel negotiations for a regulation on public access to documents.

© Blackwell Publishers Ltd 2001

In his capacity as both CFSP representative and Secretary-General of the Council Secretariat, Solana tried to assuage the EP first by reassuring it that the Council's decision, which he had instigated, would in effect cover only NATO documents, and then by offering access to those documents to a select group of MEPs. The EP rejected Solana's offer of privileged access; had it accepted, the EP would have had to share with the Council responsibility for withholding information from EU citizens. Nor did Solana's offer deter the EP from taking legal action against the Council. Support for the EP from a handful of traditionally 'open' Member States – Sweden, Finland, Denmark and the Netherlands – illustrated the divisive nature of the transparency issue within the Council itself (the Netherlands also lodged a separate Court appeal against the Council decision). The EP and sympathetic Member States objected not to the principle of military secrets, but to the practice of prohibiting access to documents based on a general categorization rather than case-by-case justification.

Differences among Member States made it difficult for the Council to adopt a common position on the draft regulation, or even to agree on whether the proposed legislation should take the form of a regulation, which could affect freedom of information laws in the more open Member States. The EP set itself on a collision course with both the Commission and the Council when, on 16 November, it adopted by an overwhelming majority a highly critical report on the draft regulation by its Citizens' Rights Committee. There the matter stood at the end of the year, thus presenting to the incoming Swedish Presidency a complex and politically charged dossier. Regardless of whether and how the issue was resolved before the May 2001 deadline, transparency would undoubtedly remain one of the most contentious aspects of EU governance for many years ahead.

The MEPs' statute was a longer-running, although less far-reaching, bone of contention between the Council and the EP than was access to documents. Efforts to conclude a statute to standardize MEPs' pay and conditions, called for in the Amsterdam Treaty (Art. 190.5 TEC), were unavailing in 2000. A 'Technical Group' of Council and EP representatives met weekly in the latter part of the French Presidency to put the finishing touches to the draft statute's 20 articles, while a senior 'contact group' negotiated the more controversial items: expenses, remuneration and taxation. Taxation was the most difficult of these, with Britain, Germany, Sweden and Finland insisting on the application of national regimes to MEPs' salaries. The EP was also divided, some members (notably the President of the Parliament) being more conciliatory than others. In the end the gulf between the more recalcitrant Member States and the more conciliatory MEPs proved unbridgeable. In January 2001 this poisoned chalice also passed to the Swedish Presidency.

For the EP, the statute was a matter of principle and institutional pride. Highly sensitive to perceived interference in its own affairs, the EP resented the Council's refusal to reach an agreement on the EP's terms. Principle also motivated the hard-line Member States: the principle that MEPs should be subject to the same taxation regime as national parliamentarians. Should the public ever become interested in the affair, opinion would most likely support the hard-line governments. The much lower Community rate of taxation is generally viewed as a perk, and perks in the EU are not popular with the public. Moreover, the EP's intransigence contrasts unfavourably with its crusade against the Commission in 1999 and with its continuing refusal to conclude a statute for MEPs' assistants.

Despite bitter disputes between them over a number of procedural issues, the Commission, Council and EP worked well together in the crucial area of legislative decision-making. In particular, they made a success of the cumbersome co-decision procedure, the scope of which increased markedly following implementation of the Amsterdam Treaty. The relatively smooth functioning of co-decision in 2000 was due in part to the opportunity presented by the Amsterdam Treaty to reach an agreement during the first reading (on average, 25 per cent of legislative acts are now adopted at that stage). Because more issues were settled in the first and second readings, relatively fewer had to be dealt with in the time-consuming and contentious conciliation stage.

The successful operation of co-decision required greater adaptation by the Council than the EP; after all, co-decision represented a loss of power for the Council and a gain for the Parliament. The Council acknowledged as much at an informal inter-institutional seminar on co-decision in November, where various proposals for operational improvements were discussed. Some of these found their way into a report that the Presidency and the Council Secretariat presented to the European Council in December. The report also expressed the wildly ambitious wish that citizens become more aware of how co-decision works.

V. The Austrian Imbroglio

'The Union is founded on the principles of liberty, democracy, respect for human rights and fundamental freedoms, and the rule of law, principles which are common to the Member States'. So says the first paragraph of Art. 6 TEU, as revised by the Treaty of Amsterdam. This short treaty change of 1997 was an important milestone in the history of European integration. Whereas the EU, and the Communities that preceded it, were political constructions, they had not been explicitly imbued with core political values. For the first time, the EU clearly stated what those values were. Member States also revised Art. 7 TEU in order to introduce measures to protect the values enshrined in Art. 6. The authors of the Amsterdam Treaty had prospective Member States from central and eastern Europe in mind when they drafted Art. 7. Their attention turned to the existing EU in January 2000, when the Christian Democratic Party (ÖVP) of Wolfgang Schüssel opened negotiations with the far-right Freedom Party (FPÖ) of Jörg Haider to form a government in Austria. Haider was a dema-gogue who exploited latent racism and xenophobia, especially in the context of EU enlargement. His notoriety spread far beyond Austria: for many Europeans he personified the risk of resurgent right-wing extremism. While appreciating that Haider was not Hitler and that Austria at the dawn of the twenty-first century was manifestly different from Austria in the 1930s, most European politicians were appalled at the prospect of having a party such as the FPÖ in government in the EU.

Member States could have expressed their concerns either individually or collectively. They could have monitored the situation in Austria with a view to taking action under Art. 7 should 'a serious and persistent breach' of the EU's principles become apparent. Austria's partners (the 'Fourteen') went beyond that, however, by issuing a joint declaration on 31 January, when the ÖVP and FPÖ were negotiating a coalition agreement, threatening action against Austria if such a government were formed. Specifically, the Fourteen would suspend official bilateral meetings with Austria, restrict contacts with Austrian ambassadors in EU capitals, and not support Austrian candidates for jobs in international organizations. These threats were unavailing: the ÖVP and FPÖ formed a government on 4 February, under Schüssel's leadership. As a result, the Fourteen acted against the new government.

Although the Fourteen were defending EU values, their so-called 'sanc-tions' lacked a legal basis in the treaties. For that reason the Fourteen denied that they were acting in an EU capacity. Yet the co-ordination of their action by the country in the Council presidency suggested otherwise. More important, claims by the Council presidency that, despite the imposition of sanctions, the EU would continue with business as usual, were obviously illusory. On the one hand, the Fourteen asserted the right to involve themselves in Austria's internal affairs because European values were at stake; on the other hand, they argued that bilateral relations among Member States could be divorced from the conduct of EU business. In fact, the blurring of distinctions between domestic and international, bilateral and multilateral, national and supranational had long ago become commonplace in the EU. The main outcome of the affair was to reinforce that point.

The Austrian situation therefore had a direct bearing on EU governance and institutions. The importance of informal institutions, ranging from bilateral contacts to meetings of party leaders on the eve of European Councils, became even more apparent. Particular institutional issues, such as the role of the Council presidency, the heterogeneity of political groups in the EP, and the Commission's ability to transmit ideas and opinion between 'Brussels' and national capitals, were highlighted. The coincidence of the Austrian affair and the IGC focused attention on specific institutional and political problems, notably the continuation of national representation in the College of the Commission and the apparent rift between small and large Member States. The coincidence of the Austrian affair, the Danish referendum on EMU, and a debate in Germany about a possible referendum on enlargement showed how fearful EU leaders were of plebiscitory democracy in the EU. What soon turned into an imbroglio demonstrated both the emerging political nature of the EU and the political shortcomings of the EU's leadership.

The idea that the other Member States could act bilaterally against Austria without affecting EU business seemed silly even when the sanctions were announced. Yet the Portuguese Presidency stuck doggedly to that line. Summing up his country's Presidency, António Guterres, Portugal's Prime Minister, explained to the EP on 3 July that 'the opinion of one sovereign Member State regarding another and the problem of bilateral relations is one thing; the functioning of the EU is quite another'. Predictably, he claimed that Portugal had never mixed up the two.

Yet the Austrian affair cast a shadow over Portugal's Presidency and obviously intruded into the institutional life of the EU. Some French and Belgian ministers refused to speak to their Austrian counterparts at Council meetings. Guterres pointedly skipped Vienna during his tour of EU capitals in the run-up to the Lisbon summit in March, and the French government excluded the Austrian ambassador in Paris from preparations for the forthcoming French Presidency.

Austria's assertion to the contrary, that bilateral and EU business could not be separated, was borne out by events. Having ostentatiously bypassed Vienna before the Lisbon summit, Guterres, nonetheless, had a preparatory bilateral with Schüssel in Brussels. The Heads of State and Government discussed the Austrian situation over dinner at the Lisbon summit, and even more extensively at the Feira summit in June. As Schüssel remarked in the midst of the crisis,

> the EU can only work if all 15 Member States are included in the dialogue, without discrimination ... one cannot make a distinction between bilateral and Community affairs ... the Amsterdam Treaty obliges us to remain united, among all Fifteen ... . It is not possible to differentiate between bilateral and (multilateral) dialogue, because bilateral dialogue is needed to prepare EU business.

The *de facto* breakdown of sanctions, despite a rhetorical commitment to unity among the Fourteen, demonstrated the impracticability of such measures as well as growing doubts about the wisdom of taking them in the first place. Within a few weeks of the declaration, most Member States had quietly abandoned punitive action against Austria. Yet the Fourteen's continued rhetorical commitment to a common front against Austria demonstrated the importance of consensus – specifically, the appearance of consensus – in EU decision-making on sensitive political issues. No Member State was willing to break ranks publicly.

The Commission was as concerned as the Fourteen about the consequences of the FPÖ entering government in Austria, but it had to act differently. As Prodi repeatedly pointed out to critics of the Commission's seemingly softer line, as a supranational institution the Commission does not have bilateral relations with Member States. Nor is it in the interest or ethos of the Commission to try to isolate a Member State. Although some observers saw the Fourteen's lack of consultation with the Commission before issuing the joint declaration as a snub, the Commission must have been grateful for not having been party to the original decision. The unfolding imbroglio allowed the Commission to stress its political role as guardian of the treaties, as well as its independence of the Member States. Austria appreciated the Commission's more nuanced approach to the problem, and sought Commission involvement in bringing the sanctions to an end. While the Commission could not officially mediate between Austria and the Fourteen, it was no accident that one of the 'Wise Men' who produced the report that helped resolve the crisis was a former senior Commissioner.

Initially, Franz Fischler, the Commissioner from Austria, was in an invidious position, not least because he was a leading member of ÖVP. Soon, however, Fischler emerged as a key interlocutor between Brussels and Vienna. It was Fischler who urged the new government to publish a programme that unequivocally endorsed integration and rejected racism. On 4 February, Fischler declared that 'one part of my responsibility is … to convey the present international concern to my countrymen … . But another part … is to help defend Austria's [position] abroad'. Thus Fischler put his finger on one of the central but unwritten responsibilities of any member of the Commission: to act as a conduit of information between the Commission and the Commissioner's national capital. That reminder was particularly timely at the onset of an IGC in which the possibility of breaking the link between the number of Member States and the number of Commissioners was on the agenda. Without national representation in the Commission, how could a Member State's voice be adequately heard in Brussels?

Just as the debate about the size of the Commission came to be seen in terms of big *v.* small Member States, the Austrian situation acquired similar overtones. Would the Fourteen have acted as quickly and harshly against a big

Member State in a similar situation? Although action against Austria had been orchestrated by a group that included two small Member States (Belgium and Portugal), other small Member States, notably Denmark, Finland and Ireland, as well as Austria itself, interpreted the affair as further evidence of the vulnerability of small Member States. All the more reason, they reckoned, to insist on continued representation for small Member States in the Commission.

The Danish government had an additional reason to fret about the Austrian imbroglio. Sanctions against Austria were particularly unpopular in sovereignty-conscious Denmark, an unpopularity eagerly exploited by advocates of a 'No' vote in the run-up to the referendum on EMU on 28 September. Denmark's governing Social Democrats breathed a sigh of relief when the Fourteen abandoned sanctions less then three weeks before the referendum, although by then the political damage in Denmark may have been done.

The Fourteen's fear of a referendum in Austria on the sanctions issue, rather than sensitivity to Denmark's plight, undoubtedly brought the imbroglio to an end. On 5 May Schüssel announced that unless the Fourteen came up with concrete proposals before end of June to lift the sanctions, Austria would hold a plebiscite on the issue in the autumn. The result of the referendum, everyone knew, would have been an embarrassment for the EU. It would have been doubly embarrassing coming on the heels of what turned out to be a negative result in the Danish referendum. Also in early September, Commissioner Gunther Verheugen reportedly called for a referendum in Germany on enlargement, an idea that EU leaders quickly dismissed.

By early September, fear of a real referendum in Denmark, a possible referendum in Austria, and a notional referendum in Germany had gripped the EU's leadership. Intellectually, EU leaders knew that the EU system of governance needed to be more open and accountable; politically, they also knew that rampant Euroscepticism, or at least widespread Eurofatigue, was not conducive to holding referendums on EU-related issues. That paradox, at the core of EU politics, helped ensure that the Wise Men presented their report promptly and that the Fourteen acted on it quickly. Rarely has there been such a swift and humiliating climb-down from a political high horse.

Like national politicians, most members of the EP, a body notorious for political correctness, denounced the ÖVP for forming a government with the FPÖ. The situation presented a particular problem for the EPP–ED, of which the ÖVP was a member. The EPP's socialist rivals, as well as some national delegations in the EPP, called for the ÖVP's suspension from the EPP–ED. The ÖVP averted a vote on the issue in early April by voluntarily suspending its membership in the EPP, while nevertheless continuing to participate in the parliamentary group. It rejoined the party as a whole following the submission of a report by a small group of EPP–ED members that vindicated the ÖVP's record in the Austrian government.

The Fourteen adopted a similar strategy to end the Austrian affair. The sanctions were open-ended; by implication they would be lifted only when the FPÖ left government. The need to find a solution before then left the Fourteen clutching at straws. The Wise Men reported that minority, immigrant and refugee rights were as well protected in Austria as elsewhere in the EU. However, they also reported that action by the Fourteen had helped to increase awareness in Austria of such rights and of common EU values. Thus, according to the Fourteen, the Wise Men's report justified both the lifting of sanctions and the imposition of them in the first place.

The way that the Fourteen, and especially the more adamant among them, had handled the Austrian situation demonstrated a striking lack of political sensitivity and judgement. Belgium and France, concerned about the far right in their own countries as well as the defence of EU principles, had orchestrated action against Austria and arguably hijacked the Portuguese Presidency for that purpose. Yet each of the Fourteen is culpable for acting precipitately, for not engaging in a dialogue with the Austrian government, and for not including a procedure for ending sanctions. 'This is a great day for the birth of a political Europe', enthused the president of the Socialist group when the EP adopted a resolution on 2 February condemning the possibility of an ÖVP–FPÖ coalition. Seven months later, euphoria had given way to awkwardness. The abiding memory of the affair is not one of high-mindedness, but of self-righteousness and political ineptitude.

Journal of Common Market Studies

Volume 39, Annual Review
September 2001

Conscientious Resolve:
The Portuguese Presidency of 2000

GEOFFREY EDWARDS
University of Cambridge
and
GEORG WIESSALA
University of Central Lancashire

Introduction: More than a 'Through-Train'

Portugal became the first Member State to assume the Council Presidency in the new millennium. It inherited a considerable and diverse agenda from preceding European Councils but managed not only to move a number of highly significant dossiers – including taxes on savings – but also to give its own imprint to the six months. Among the objectives already set out, not least during the Finnish Presidency, were those relating to security and defence policy, opening the accession negotiations with the 'Helsinki Six' while continuing those with the other candidates and, of course, formally opening the Intergovernmental Conference, which was done on 14 February 2000.

All were issues that point to the transient nature of the EU's Presidency: to take the IGC, Portugal might well have opened it – having been able to set the final agenda and isolate points of difference – but the prospect was of completion under the French Presidency in Nice in December. However, even if the rewards (and the criticisms) of treaty-making might fall to France, Portugal, nonetheless, from the Prime Minister down, approached and managed its term in office with drive, thoroughness, ambition and energy. Jaime Gama, the Portuguese Minister of Foreign Affairs, indicated the tone and atmosphere of the Portuguese six months in office when he presented the Presidency programme to the European Parliament:

If we cannot make efficient and convincing use of the means we have at our disposal, in other words of the Europe we have already succeeded in building, then clearly we shall never be able to rely on the willingness of our fellow-citizens to accept the construction of 'more Europe'.

I. Lisbon's Dot-com Summit

One area on which the Portuguese sought to stamp their own imprint was that of employment. The Prime Minister, António Guterres, had often made a point of presenting the Portuguese as the initiators of new European employment strategies, avoiding the traditional dichotomy between European harmonization versus national autonomy and state employment versus unlimited regulation – all positions taken up with varying degrees of intensity by its EU partners. The Lisbon extraordinary European Council dedicated to 'Employment, Economic Reform and Social Cohesion – Towards a Europe of Innovation and Knowledge' on 23–24 March, both reflected and extended these ambitions. While past discussions can be traced back to the European Employment Strategy (EES), originating in the Delors White Paper in 1993 and taken further in Luxembourg in 1997, the Lisbon Council further enlarged the agenda to encompass issues such as new technologies, the information society, 'eCommerce', and the 'knowledge economy'. Indicative of the Prime Minister's own commitment was the fact that the preparatory work was done less by the Portuguese Permanent Representation and the Commission than by his own 'sherpa', Professor Rodriguez. Hailed as the 'dot.com' summit, the Council was also regarded by some as a milestone in defining a new method of 'open co-ordination' in EU policy-making in this area (Ferrera et al., 2000), with objectives such as the creation of 20 million jobs in a decade. Heads of State and Government reaffirmed these objectives at their later meeting at Feira in June.

II. Presidency Busyness

While trailed as rather more of a low-key Council after Lisbon, the Feira Council did manage to reach agreement on a further wide raft of issues, including Greece's accession to the euro-zone. There also seemed to be agreement, at least in principle, on the issue of a withholding tax and/or banking secrecy. The work was largely done by finance ministers – among them the British Chancellor, who had been long and loudly opposed to a withholding tax, the German minister, Hans Eichel, and the Presidency, which finally pressed the Luxembourgers and Austrians into agreement – and endorsed by Heads of State and Government, though there remained doubts as to quite how binding the agreement was. Other decisions reached at Feira related to the Security and Defence Policy. The Portuguese, in the chair of both the EU and the WEU in 2000, were able to maintain the rapid momentum that had been built up since the Franco-British declaration at St Malo in December 1998. Important strides were made by the interim military structures established by Helsinki and agreement was reached, à Fifteen, on the particularly thorny issue of relations between the EU and NATO. The Feira Council agreed to establish 'inclusive' structures that allowed for routine regular dialogue, which would be intensified in any pre-operational phase with an ad hoc committee of contributors in an operational phase. It also identified four areas for developing the relationship with NATO: security issues, capability goals, the modalities for EU access to NATO assets, and the definition of permanent consultation arrangements. But, the Council Conclusions also pointed to the need to recognize the different nature of the EU and NATO and insisted that any consultations 'must take place in full respect for the autonomy of EU decision-making'. The Turkish government may not have been impressed but it marked an important stage on the road to the establishment of the ESDP in Nice.

Feira was also important because it saw final agreement on the agenda of the IGC. The Portuguese, as some others, were concerned that an agenda restricted only to the Amsterdam 'leftovers' (see the keynote article) would not offer enough scope for successful bargaining or, as Francisco Seixas da Costa, the Portuguese European Minister, put it: 'the situation this time round is more difficult than at Amsterdam because a limited agenda leaves little room for trade-offs' (Jones, 1999–2000). They therefore pushed for the inclusion of other issues, particularly that of 'enhanced' or 'closer' co-operation. While that was agreed, the Member States remained divided over the inclusion of the Charter on Fundamental Rights, which remained to be settled separately. The Portuguese Presidency helpfully, if somewhat vainly given subsequent actions by the French Presidency, drew up a progress report on the negotiations of well over 100 pages.

In external matters, the Presidency was noteworthy for the way it reflected the historical and geographical position of Portugal. There was, for example, work on the Common Strategy towards the Mediterranean, a policy area in much need of revitalization. At the same time, there was also a need to push on the Mediterranean, given the pressures from the immediately preceding Presidency to deal with the Northern dimension, and with the Swedes as prospective President in 2001 also eager for the momentum to be maintained. But the Portuguese, as befitted their past, also oversaw, in conjunction with the Organization for African Unity, the first EU–Africa summit in Cairo on 3–4 April. During the Portuguese Presidency, the EU also managed to drive forward the overhaul of development policy and its relationship with the African Caribbean and Pacific states (ACPs) that resulted in the agreement signed in Cotonou in June.

III. Shadow of Success

One shadow over the Presidency was the complicated situation that arose with the decision by Heads of State and Government to ostracize the Austrians on the establishment of a coalition with the Freedom Party led by Jörg Haider. While the Portuguese may have agreed with the principle, they still had to deal with the various Councils in which, of course, the Austrians participated. Their dilemma over invitations to attend informal Councils was particularly acute. The establishment of the 'wise men' to monitor Austrian compliance with its undertakings on human rights and other issues may have led ultimately to a face-saving solution, but continued to create problems for an otherwise extremely active and successful Presidency.

References

Ferrera, M., Hemerijck, A. and Rhodes, M. (2000) *The Future of Social Europe. Recasting Work and Welfare in the New Economy – Report for the Portuguese Presidency of the European Union*, May.
Jones, T. (1999–2000) 'Portugal Launches Crusade to Turn EU into a Genuine "Knowledge Economy"'. *European Voice*, 16 December–5 January.

Journal of Common Market Studies   Volume 39, Annual Review
                                                         September 2001

The French Presidency:
The Half Success of Nice

CHRISTIAN LEQUESNE

Centre d'Etudes et de Recherches Internationales

Introduction

For many French observers, the Presidency of the EU in the second semester of 2000 was not a success. The main reason for this was the loose compromise reached at the European Council of Nice (7–9 December 2000) on institutional reform. The logic of 'petty' bargains, which prevailed among the Fifteen in the Intergovernmental Conference (IGC) did little to allow the French Presidency to find answers satisfactory to everyone on the four institutional 'leftovers' in the perspective of the next enlargement. Nonetheless, poor outcomes on the institutional dossiers should not conceal the sensible progress achieved in other policy sectors during the six months.

I. Progress in Policy Sectors

The French Presidency produced interesting results particularly in the defence field (Howorth, 2000). The European Council of Nice pursued the debate started in Cologne and Helsinki by approving a commitment to mobilize military forces for crisis management and the prevention of conflicts. A new EU military instrument to bring national military forces together will be operational by 2003. This will require a strategic partnership between the EU and NATO. The improvement of the partnership for France was not necessarily the priority it was for a majority of the other Member States. It was also decided in Nice that the EU will have specific permanent bodies to manage the new Security and Defence Policy: a political and security committee (COPS), a military committee and a common headquarters.

Secondly, the French Presidency gave a positive impulse to the EU's social policy at a time when neoliberalism appeared to be increasingly out of touch. This led to the adoption of a European social agenda covering strategies over five years relating to employment, measures against social exclusion and all forms of discrimination and gender policy. It was during the French Presidency that the Charter for Fundamental Rights, brought together through a Convention rather than the Intergovernmental Conference, was agreed, and which remained outside the Nice Treaty. And, after 30 years of deadlock, agreement was finally reached under the French Presidency on the status of a 'European public company'.

Third, regulatory policies were set in place during the French Presidency in several fields that have been particularly sensitive to public opinion, including food safety and maritime safety. Confronted by the crisis of BSE, EU governments agreed to most of the proposals made by the French Presidency on the ban of animal feeds and the introduction of new tests for cows. They also decided in principle to set up a new European Food Agency.

Public opinion in France and elsewhere in the Union did not really take on board the progress actually achieved – which has a great deal more impact on their daily lives than the institutional reforms that were also agreed (Dehousse, 2000). In focusing the public's attention on the IGC and the EU's institutions, the French Presidency lost an opportunity to make the Union more visible and more legitimate in the eyes of its people.

II. Poor Results on the Institutional Dossier

The institutional reforms finalized in Nice were neither a success for the French Presidency nor for the EU as a whole (Zecchini, 2000). In the absence of any greater ambition among the Fifteen, together with the propensity of each Member State to protect its own, particular interests, the French Presidency could not go further in stimulating a more ambitious project. Among the four Amsterdam leftovers (dealt with elsewhere in this volume by Gray and Stubb), the extension of qualified majority voting (QMV) in the EU Council of Ministers is arguably the most important. The French Presidency did not take a maximalist position on this, insisting on the preservation of unanimity in several sectors, including trade in cultural goods. This provided an excellent excuse for other Member States which were opposed to the extension of qualified majority in other fields, as in fiscal matters for the UK.

By refusing to take a more ambitious position on QMV, the French Presidency missed an opportunity to assert its leadership *vis-à-vis* EU countries like Germany, Italy or the Benelux, which were more prepared to deepen the European institutions within the framework of enlargement. It also gave encouragement to the minimalist countries like Denmark, the United Kingdom and Sweden, which were more or less satisfied with an institutional *status quo*. In terms of its relationship with Berlin, Paris's policy was a failure. Instead of seeking possible preliminary agreements on a systematic basis with Chancellor Schröder's government, the French Presidency all too often gave the impression of being afraid of German leadership on Europe. The firm insistence on maintaining parity with Germany on the weighting of votes in the Council of Ministers was symptomatic of a French malaise *vis-à-vis* Germany. This malaise derives from French political and bureaucratic elites rather than from French society as a whole, which has expressed few specifically anti-German feelings.

Cohabitation is also a factor which explains the lack of leadership on the part of the French Presidency. Stuck in the perspective of the presidential election of 2002, President Jacques Chirac and Prime Minister Lionel Jospin are in competition. This did little to help the definition of an ambitious French position on European integration. To take one example: some days before the French Presidency started, the Minister for Europe, Pierre Moscovici, declared publicly that President Chirac's speech to the German Bundestag on 27 June 2000, which referred to a European constitution, did not commit the French government as a whole.

III. Conclusion

More generally, the French Presidency of the second half of 2000 raised the question of the leadership that a Presidency can still bring to an enlarged EU. The lack of an ambitious agenda on the part of the French Presidency itself did not help the Fifteen to move quickly on institutional matters. But the very idea of leading the EU for six months becomes more and more difficult when the number of actors and the number of interests increase.

References

Dehousse, R. (2000) 'Rediscovering Functionalism'. In Joerges, C., Mény, Y. and Weiler, J.H.H. (eds) *What Kind of Constitution for What Kind of Polity?* (Florence: Robert Schuman Center), pp. 195–202.

Howorth, J. (2000) *L'intégration européenne et la défense: l'ultime défi* (Paris: Institut d'Etudes de Sécurité de l'UEO).

Zecchini, L. (2000) 'La présidence française de l'Union européenne a été gâchée à Nice'. *Le Monde*, 29 December.

Journal of Common Market Studies

Volume 39, Annual Review
September 2001

Internal Policy Developments

HUSSEIN KASSIM

University of London

Introduction

Making the European Union the world's most competitive and dynamic knowledge-based economy – the strategic goal agreed by Heads of State and Government at the special European Council held in Lisbon in March – informed action on a number of fronts during the year. Beyond the Lisbon agenda, reforms agreed as part of *Agenda 2000* were implemented with respect to finance, regional policy, and agriculture, and major initiatives were launched in food safety and environmental policy.

I. Economic and Related Policies

Internal Market Developments

In May, the Commission submitted its first annual review of the five-year strategy for the single market, approved by the Helsinki European Council in December 1999. The strategy specified four main objectives – (1) improving citizens' quality of life; (2) enhancing the efficiency of the EU's product and capital markets; (3) improving the business environment; and (4) exploiting the achievements of the internal market in the global economy – and set deadlines for the implementation of key policies. The review laid down a revised set of priorities and targeted areas relating to these objectives:

- better enforcement of internal market rights and deepening dialogue with citizens and business (1);
- rapid agreement on a regulation to create a Community patent (2);
- further liberalization of gas, electricity, postal services, and transport (2);
- fully integrated financial markets before 2005 (2);
- a reduction in the levels of state aid (3);
- improving the integration of services (3);
- new initiatives to reduce red tape (3);
- liberalizing public procurement (3);
- eliminating tax distortions (3);
- streamlining the internal market in preparation for enlargement (4).

At the same time, the Internal Market Commissioner, Fritz Bolkenstein, expressed regret that only 26 of the 53 targeted actions would be completed before the target date of 30 June.

The implementation of internal market directives presented more positive news. In November, the Commission reported a substantial improvement. Twelve of the EU-15 recorded an implementation deficit of less than 4 per cent compared with nine in May 1999 and only two in November 1997. The laggards were Greece (6.5 per cent), France (4.5 per cent) and Portugal (4.4 per cent) all with implementation deficits three times greater than the best performing countries, Denmark (1.1 per cent), Sweden (1.2 per cent), Finland (1.3 per cent), and Spain (1.6 per cent) – though only the first three of these fell below the Commission's 1.5 per cent target. Of the priority measures identified in the internal market strategy review, all but two (directive for an internal market in natural gas, and the European company statute) had not been fully implemented. Market fragmentation, however, remained high: one in eight of the 1459 single market directives had not yet been implemented in all Member States.

On a brighter note, three-quarters of the 4,000 companies consulted by the Commission regarded the consolidation of the internal market as favourable or very favourable for their businesses. Overall, they thought markets were more open to trade, but they still faced extra costs in meeting national standards and securing product approval, and encountered obstacles such as state aid, tax distortions, and VAT obligations. Mechanisms for dealing with cross-border breaches of contract remained ineffective, and there was dissatisfaction with the regulatory framework and the application of single market rules.

The level of infringement cases remained high, and the amount of time taken to close disputes lengthy, despite some improvement – 40.9 per cent of cases closed in 1998–99 compared with 36.8 per cent in 1997–98. Belgium, Germany, France, Italy and Austria were the worst offenders. The number of cases relating to Arts. 28–30 of the EC Treaty (removal of quantitative restrictions and measures having equivalent effect) outstanding on 31 December was 318, and the number of new complaints received in 2000 151. Other internal market measures included:

- a Commission internal market strategy for services (*COM* (2000) 888) in response to the call by the Lisbon European Council to remove remaining barriers;
- a Commission reform package to overhaul the regulatory framework for telecommunications;
- a Commission review of the first three stages of the SLIM exercise, which called on the Member States to simplify their rules;
- a Commission analysis of services of general interest in response to a European Council request;
- a welcome by the Nice European Council of the Commission's intention to consider, with the Member States, ways of ensuring greater predictability and legal certainty in the application of competition rules;
- a Commission report on the operation of Directive 98/34/EC on the provision of information on technical standards and regulations between 1993 and 1998. In 2000, it received 752 notifications of draft technical regulations, bringing the total number received since the directive came into effect to 7,257;
- with regard to foodstuffs, a directive on cocoa and chocolate products on the harmonization of vegetable fats other than cocoa butter; in pharmaceuticals, a directive on the approximation of provisions on good practice regarding clinical trials on medicinal products for human use; and, in the motor vehicles sector, measures relating to speedometers, the emission of pollutants, and road noise;
- the publication of a guide, *Exercising your rights in the single European market*, as part of Commission efforts to improve dialogue with consumers and business;
- a Commission report on the application of the regulation on the export of cultural goods and a directive on the return of cultural objects unlawfully removed from their country of origin;
- continued efforts by the Commission to apply measures relating to public procurement announced in March 1998, and new initiatives calling for an overhaul of the legal framework concerning the award of public contracts with particular regard to water, energy and transport;
- a Commission proposal, following its 1997 Green Paper and 1999 communication 1999, on a Community patent, to create a new industrial property right alongside existing national and European patent systems. It also proposed harmonizing some aspects of copyright related to the information society.

- Commission progress reports on the implementation of the action plan on financial services – an area highlighted by the Lisbon European Council. Among several financial services measures, the Commission followed its 1997 Green Paper on pensions with a proposal in October on institutions operating occupational schemes in order to ensure a high level of protection for beneficiaries;
- political agreement between Member States in November on a 'fiscal package', including the controversial proposal on harmonizing taxation on savings income with transitional arrangements for Belgium, Luxembourg and Austria. The target date for the implementation of the directive is 2002. The Nice European Council asked the Commission and the Presidency to hold talks with the US and other countries with the aim of introducing similar measures at an international level.
- a Commission proposal to improve the VAT system by simplifying, modernizing, and standardizing the rules governing implementation in the Member States, and stepping up administrative co-operation to combat fraud.

Economic and Monetary Union

Since the changeover to the euro on 1 January 1999, the European Central Bank has conducted monetary policy throughout the euro-zone, setting interest rates in line with the goal of price stability, as set out in the EC Treaty. In November, these were: 3.0 per cent for refinancing operations, 4.0 per cent for marginal lending, and a 2.0 per cent deposit rate.

The co-ordination of economic policy between the participating states – 11 in 2000, with Greece due to become the twelfth member on 1 January 2001 – has assumed a new importance. Consistency is achieved by the pursuit of broad economic guidelines that set down detailed recommendations for each Member State. The guidelines were proposed by the Commission in April, recommended by the Council in June, and adopted by the Feira European Council. The guidelines aim to improve economic performance through:

- the pursuit of sound, growth-oriented macroeconomic policies, based on monetary policies directed towards preserving price stability, budgetary consolidation, and wage increases compatible with price stability and job creation;
- effective management of public finances;
- promotion of the knowledge-based economy;
- reform to ensure the effective operation of product markets, to stimulate and integrate capital markets, and to revitalize labour markets;
- sustained economic development.

The guidelines were informed by the Commission's review of the EU economy in 1999 (which replaces the annual economic report), its report on the implementation of the 1999 broad economic policy guidelines, and its review of structural reform in the Member States, conducted as part of the Cardiff process. The Commission reported that implementation had been good overall, but that little progress had been made on lowering state aid, reforming social security systems, and modernizing work organization. In September, the Commission proposed 27 structural indicators for employment, innovation, research, economic reform and social cohesion in response to European Council requests.

The guidelines are crucial elements of the multilateral surveillance regime in the euro-zone where Member States share a common monetary policy and exchange rate, but retain responsibility for the other areas of economic policy. It was decided in 2000 to strengthen this regime by convening a spring meeting of the European Council each year to discuss economic and social issues. Ecofin was invited by the Heads of State and Government (HOSG) to co-ordinate more closely with other Council formations to ensure the effective implementation of its conclusions. In accordance with the Stability and Growth Pact, designed to promote budgetary discipline, the Council, following Commission recommendations, adopted opinions on the stability programmes presented by the Member States.

Throughout the year, the European Central Bank (ECB), the Commission and the Council prepared for the final changeover to the euro at the beginning of 2002. The ECB, in co-operation with the Member States, examined the practicalities involved in introducing new banknotes and coins. The Council emphasized the importance of adjusting coin-operated machines, and approved a scheme for handling counterfeit coins. The Commission adopted a communications strategy for the final phases of economic and monetary union to ensure that the general public, SMEs and non-participating countries are fully informed, and launched a series of awareness campaigns.

Competitiveness, Employment and Enterprise

At Lisbon, the HOSG made a series of commitments to strengthen employment in the Union in the face of globalization and the new knowledge-driven economy. While underlining its strengths, political leaders highlighted several weaknesses in the European economy, including high unemployment (15 million Europeans or 9 per cent of the workforce), low rates of labour participation by women and older workers, long-term structural employment with marked regional imbalances, an underdeveloped services sector, and a widening skills gap. The new strategic goal required:

- preparing the transition to a knowledge-based economy and society by better policies for the information society and R&D, stepping up the process of structural reform for competitiveness and innovation, and completing the internal market;
- modernizing the European social model (see below);
- sustaining the healthy economic outlook and favourable prospects for growth by following the appropriate macroeconomic policies (Economic and Monetary Union, above).

A Knowledge-Based Economy

The HOSG meeting at Lisbon called for: an information society for all to increase growth, competitiveness and employment, and to improve quality of life; a European area of research and innovation; and a friendly environment for starting up and developing innovative businesses, especially SMEs. With respect to the first, two Commission documents, a draft action plan, '*e*Europe 2002: an information society for all', and 'Strategies for jobs in the information society', adopted in December 1999 and February 2000 respectively, largely prefigured the commitment undertaken at Lisbon. A further action plan, adopted by the Commission in May, was approved by the June European Council, and a progress report endorsed in December. Other measures concerned use of the internet.

A major Commission initiative on research, adopted in January, proposed a frontier-free approach to create jobs and increase competitiveness, which was endorsed by the Lisbon European Council. Following a Council resolution in June, the Commission published guidelines for research activities to be carried out over 2002–06. Several other initiatives were also launched.

The Commission's communication, 'Challenges for enterprise policy in the knowledge-driven economy', adopted in April and endorsed by the Council in May, proposed a comprehensive set of measures to encourage business innovation. It included a multi-annual programme directed at the needs of SMEs adopted by the Council in December. In the same month, the Council welcomed a Commission initiative on innovation as a factor in competitiveness launched in September, as well as European scoreboards for innovation and enterprise policy. The Feira European Council approved the drafting of a European Charter for Small Enterprises.

Employment

The Lisbon European Council highlighted the importance of education and training, and an active employment policy, and stressed the importance of involvement by the social partners. It called for adaptation to the demands of the knowledge society and enhancement of lifelong employment opportunities. The Commission responded with its 'eLearning – designing tomorrow's education' initiative. It also proposed an action plan promoting the transnational mobility of persons active in education, training and youth, which was approved by the Nice European Council. The HOSG called on the Member States to implement practical measures to increase and democratize mobility in Europe.

With respect to active employment, the Lisbon European Council called for an elaboration of the Luxembourg process – the medium-term approach begun in 1997, whereby employment guidelines are drawn up at European level and translated into national employment action plans – with a view to: improving employability and reducing skills gaps; giving higher priority to lifelong learning; increasing employment in services; and furthering equal opportunities. The overall aim is to increase the workforce from 61 per cent to 70 per cent by 2010 and to raise female participation from 51 to more than 60 per cent.

The Commission put forward a comprehensive action plan in June in its Social Policy Agenda (*COM* (2000) 379). Three ambitions were envisaged:

- *realizing Europe's full employment potential* through the creation of more and better jobs, anticipating and managing change and adapting to the new working environment, exploiting the potential of the knowledge-based economy and promoting mobility;
- *modernizing and improving social protection*, promoting social inclusion, strengthening gender equality and reinforcing fundamental rights and combating discrimination (see below);
- *preparing for enlargement*, promoting international co-operation, and making the social dialogue contribute to meeting the challenge.

The new agenda called for stakeholder participation and action at European, national, regional and local levels; a list of specific measures was outlined. The European Council endorsed the plan in December.

Following approval by the Helsinki European Council, the Council adopted recommendations on the implementation of Member States' employment policies in February and a decision on guidelines for Member States employment policies for 2000 in March. After examining the national employment plans in September, the Commission adopted three documents:

- the joint employment report 2000, which registers improvements, but notes that unemployment remains unacceptably high and identifies problems in the labour market;
- a proposal on employment guidelines for 2001 that calls on the Member States to set national targets for raising employment to 70 per

cent by 2010, to develop a set of common indicators, and to strengthen the role of the social partners; and
- the recommendation that the 1999 recommendations be maintained
  largely unchanged or amended to include provisions relating to lifelong learning and participation by the social partners.

The package was approved by the Nice European Council.

Further measures included a Commission proposal to promote labour
market co-operation between Member States and an 'acting locally for
employment' campaign to examine how actors at local level can create or
maintain jobs. The Commission continued to support the EURES network,
which encourages the exchange of good practice in employment strategy.

Structural Funds and Regional Policy

A new legislative framework for the structural funds for 2000–06 was agreed
in 1999 in the context of *Agenda 2000*. The main priority in 2000 was drawing
up the programming documents for the new period. The Commission adopted
Community support frameworks (CSFs) and single programming documents
(SPDs) for regions eligible under Objective 1 – those where the level of
development has been less than 75 per cent of the EU average over the last three
years. Nearly 70 per cent of the funds have been earmarked for these regions
– the home of nearly a fifth of the Union's population. The areas to be covered
by Objective 2 funds – assistance for regions undergoing structural change –
were also designated by the Commission. The main beneficiaries under
Objective 3, which supports the adaptation and modernization of education,
training and employment policies and systems, are Germany, France, Italy and
the UK, who together will receive two-thirds of the €3,316.671 million
available.

Guidelines covering the four Commission initiatives – Intereg (EDRF)
relating to inter-regional, cross-border co-operation to encourage sustainable
development; URBAN (ERDF) directed at the economic and social regener-
ation of cities to promote sustainable urban development; Leader (EAGGF
Guidance Section) to support rural development, and EQUAL (ESF) to
promote new means of combating discrimination and inequality in the labour
market – were also adopted. Commitments in 2000 came to €391 million
(Intereg and URBAN), €69.9 million (Employment), and €80.2 million
(Leader II).

New cohesion policy regulations were introduced to take account of the
euro. Management procedures were also simplified to increase the effectiveness of assistance. Commitments for cohesion projects in 2000 totalled
€2,406.352 million. Spain was the major beneficiary, receiving €1,548.624

million (64 per cent), followed by Portugal (16.52 per cent), Greece (9.71 per cent) and Ireland (9.41 per cent).

Industrial and Competition Policies

Industrial policy in 2000 focused mainly on SMEs in the knowledge-based economy (see above). Further measures relating to particular sectors included a forward programme for steel, adopted by the Commission in January, and the modification of the system for trading processed agricultural products in November.

The Commission continued its overhaul of Community competition law. Following its 1999 White Paper on the rules implementing Arts. 81 and 82, the Commission adopted proposals to replace the centralized system of notification and authorization of agreements with directly applicable exemption systems under which the Commission and national courts and competition authorities will have parallel powers to apply Art. 81. The controversial proposal also includes a provision establishing for first time that, where trade between the Member States is affected, only Community law applies, and recommends strengthening the Commission's investigative powers in order to ensure the rapid detection of infringements. Further measures introduced by the Commission included regulations on the application of Art. 81 (3) to certain agreements concerning R&D and specialization agreements, and guidelines on the applicability of Art. 81 to horizontal co-operation.

The Commission followed the 1999 reform of rules relating to vertical restraints by producing guidelines designed to enable firms to assess the validity of their vertical agreements themselves. Notable decisions on restrictive agreements included the imposition of fines on five companies in the synthetic amino acids sector found to have fixed lysine prices worldwide. The decision to grant an exemption until 31 December to manufacturers and importers of domestic washing machines in the EC, following an undertaking by the companies to cease the production and import of energy inefficient washing machines, represented the first use of Art. 81 (3) to improve the ecological performance of products.

The Commission adopted two regulations exempting, subject to certain conditions, state aid to SMEs and aid for education and training from the need to seek prior agreement as stipulated under Art. 88(3). It also approved Member State regional aid maps for 2000–06, aimed at concentrating aid in the regions with most serious development problems, while reducing the general level of aid in the EU – an apparently realizable objective, given its finding that the total volume of state aid fell by 11 per cent between 1996–98 and 1994–96. In June, the Commission extended the scheme for state aid to the motor vehicle industry for one year. During the year, the Commission received 869 new notifications and registered 133 un-notified cases. In 623, it raised no objections. Of the 76 where proceedings were begun, 17 final decisions were positive, 38 negative, and 11 conditional.

With respect to mergers, the Commission approved a simplified investigation procedure to reduce the burdens on the notifying parties to agreements that pose no threat to the competition rules. In a report on the merger regulation that was presented in June, the Commission found that too many mergers with cross-border effects fell below the turnover threshold set in the regulation. During the year, the Commission received 345 notifications and made 345 final decisions. Most were cleared during the first stage, but 19 went into the second stage, in addition to the nine notified in 1999. In three of these cases, the Commission issued unconditional authorizations. Twelve were authorized subject to conditions, and two banned; in six, the operation was abandoned, and in five, the decision deferred to 2001. Notable decisions concerned the merger operations between Glaxo Wellcome and SmithKline Beecham, creating the largest pharmaceutical company in the world (conditional authorization), American Online Inc. (AOL) and Time Warner Inc. (conditional authorization), and MCI WorldCom Inc. and Sprint Corp (prohibition).

Other Developments

The year 2000 was the first year of the new financial framework for trans-European networks that runs until 2006. Activities were largely operational.

In transport, safety was a main priority. The Commission submitted a communication of the safety of seaborne oil trade in March, following the sinking of the tanker, *Erika*. It put forward a package of measures to improve the safety and efficiency of road transport, and proposed the creation of a European Aviation Safety Agency. Agreement was reached on a joint text on rail transport liberalization and a directive to protect the marine environment from operational pollution by ships. The Commission launched an information campaign on air passenger rights, and continued to pursue the development of the integrated European satellite navigation system, Galileo.

The adoption in November of a Green Paper on the security of the supply of energy launched a debate on energy sources and energy policy priorities. The Nice European Council invited the Commission and the Secretariat of the Council to carry out a detailed study. Following the request made by the Lisbon European Council to liberalize the markets in gas and electricity, the Commission adopted a communication on electricity. With respect to gas, most Member States incorporated Directive 98/30/EC into national law before the August deadline. The Parliament and the Council adopted a multi-annual framework programme (SAVE II) for 1998–2002 to improve energy efficiency. Further initiatives aimed to develop a coherent EU response to the increase in oil prices, and to promote an EU strategy on nuclear safety in central and eastern Europe.

The Commission adopted guidelines to cover research activities for the sixth framework programme to run 2002–06. Several thousand research proposals were received in the context of the fifth framework programme 1998–2002 under its four themes: quality of life and living resources; user-friendly information society; competitive and sustainable growth; and energy, environment and sustainable development. The Commission published an assessment of the framework programmes, carried out by an independent expert panel, the conclusions of which will inform preparations for the next programme.

In education, two new programmes were adopted: Socrates II (2002–06) aimed at strengthening the European dimension of education and the promotion of co-operation and mobility in education, and Youth (2002–06) to help young people contribute to the building of Europe; and the second phase of the Leonardo da Vinci programme (2002–06), which supports vocational training, was launched. The Commission adopted measures concerning the evaluation of the quality of school education, education-related co-operation with third countries, and, following Lisbon, 'eLearning – designing tomorrow'.

The Parliament and Council adopted the 'Culture 2000' programme to run until 2004 to support co-operation in artistic and cultural sectors. Sport also featured on the culture agenda in the wake of the Commission's report to the Helsinki Council, and culminated in the adoption of a declaration on sport at Nice. The final year of the MEDIA II programme saw the total number of audiovisual projects receiving finance rise to 907, while the Council agreed to implement the MEDIA Plus programme to encourage audiovisual production.

Important initiatives were launched in health and consumer protection. The most important was the Commission White Paper on food safety that elaborated an integrated 'farm to table' strategy (*COM* (1999) 719) and proposed the creation of a European Food Authority, an independent body responsible for risk assessment, crisis management, and disseminating scientific information. The Nice European Council endorsed the strategy in December. Other proposals related to foodstuff hygiene, labelling of foodstuffs containing genetically modified organisms, and applying the precautionary principle to health and environment matters. In the area of public health, in May, the Commission drew up a strategy for implementing the Amsterdam Treaty provisions (Arts. 3 and 152 EC Treaty).

II. Social Policy

Social policy was a major preoccupation after Lisbon. At their meeting in March, the HOSG called for the modernization of the European social model to increase the Union's competitiveness, while emphasizing that the developed systems of social protection that characterize Europe must underpin the transformation to the knowledge economy. On the premise that 'people are Europe's main asset and should be the focal point of the Union's policies', governments highlighted the need to invest in people and to develop an active and dynamic welfare state to ensure Europe's place in the knowledge economy, and expressed concern that the emergence of the new economy should not exacerbate existing unemployment, social exclusion and poverty. The Commission's new Social Policy Agenda was designed to confront the social challenges arising from the transformation of Europe's economy, as well as creating more and better jobs (see above). Emphasis was placed on the dual role of social policy as a productive factor, and a means to protect individuals, reduce inequalities, and enhance social cohesion.

The Agenda, which was approved by the European Council in December, identified specific actions to implement the six strategic guidelines:[1] encouraging the creation of more and better jobs; anticipating and capitalizing on change in the working environment by creating a new balance between flexibility and security; fighting poverty and all forms of exclusion and discrimination to promote social integration; modernizing social protection; promoting gender equality; and strengthening the social aspects of enlargement and external relations. Responsibility is shared between the Commission, the Council, the social partners, and the Member States. On the basis of reports from the Commission and the Council, and a regularly updated scoreboard, the European Council will examine how effectively the Agenda is being put into effect each spring, starting at its meeting in Stockholm in March 2001. Social partners are invited to play a full part in implementation and monitoring, and will participate in an annual meeting prior to the spring European Council.

During the year, reports were presented by the Commission on social protection in Europe, and by a high-level group (later replaced by the European Social Protection Committee) on social inclusion and the sustainability of pension schemes. The Commission also presented a strategy for modernizing social protection, stressing the importance of gender issues and the need for effective fiscal co-ordination, proposals for co-operation between Member States to combat social exclusion, and a report on emerging social issues, such as ageing and the changing role of women in economic and social life, as well

---

[1] See Presidency Conclusions, Nice European Council Meeting, 7–9 December 2000, Annex 1.

as a communication on how access to areas of social life for people with disabilities can be improved. The Council adopted a directive on equal treatment irrespective of racial or ethnic origin (part of a package proposed by the Commission in November 1999, and intended to put into meaningful effect the new powers conferred on the Community by the Treaty of Amsterdam under Art. 13 of the EC Treaty); a directive establishing a general framework for equal treatment in employment aimed at combating discrimination on the grounds of religion or belief, disability, age or sexual orientation; and a Community action programme to combat discrimination with a budget of €98.4 million for 2001–06. The European Monitoring Centre on Racism and Xenophobia, located in Vienna, was inaugurated in April.

Equal opportunities were addressed by the Commission's proposed strategy on gender equality for 2001–05. The Council adopted a programme to assist the organization of awareness campaigns, supported by a budget of €50 million over a five-year period. The Commission also proposed an amendment to the existing directive on equal treatment in access to employment, vocation training and promotion, and working conditions, which takes account of recent rulings by the European Court of Justice, as well as establishing for the first time that sexual harassment in the workplace constitutes discrimination on the grounds of sex. It reported on equal opportunities for men and women in the European Union, and continued to co-finance projects that exchange information and good practice on equal opportunities (€6 million on 60 projects).

In the area of labour law and industrial relations, the organization of working time directive was extended to cover sectors and activities that had previously been excluded. The Commission reported on the implementation of the original directive in December. European peak organizations, meanwhile, as well as 15 social partner representatives, expressed their support for the strategy adopted at Lisbon. As part of this strategy, initiatives covering training and the modernization of work organization were taken by social partners in telecommunications, civil aviation and transport.

III. Finances

The 2001 budgetary procedure saw the introduction of activity-based budgeting, as set out in the Commission's White Paper on Reform, *COM* (2000) 200. The integrated debate on political and budgetary guidelines – the annual policy strategy – is then translated into an activity-based budget. Quantitative guidelines were agreed for each of the 29 policy areas identified by the Commission, and budgets agreed to cover the human, administrative and operational resources needed to achieve them. Following a detailed review that set its tasks and functions against the resources at its disposal, the Commission decided to scale down or abandon certain activities, and to request, in a letter of amendment to the budgetary authority, an additional 717 posts, as well as funds to dismantle technical assistance offices and transfer their responsibilities to the Commission services.

In accordance with the changes agreed as part of *Agenda 2000* and following the Inter-institutional Agreement of May 1999, the budgetary authority adopted a regulation on budgetary discipline and a decision on own resources in July. A key objective of the first is to ensure that agricultural expenditure remains below the agreed ceiling. The second increases from 10 to 25 per cent the proportion of traditional own resources kept by the Member States to cover collection costs from 1 January 2001 and reduces the maximum call-in rate for the VAT resource from 1 to 0.75 per cent from 1 January 2002 and then to 0.5 per cent from 1 January 2004. There will be a corresponding increase in the proportion of the GNP resource, which better reflects Member States' capacity to contribute than the VAT resource. The windfall gains derived by the UK from the percentage changes to traditional own resources and the forthcoming enlargement are neutralized, and the financing of the UK rebate modified to reduce the contribution made by Austria, Germany, the Netherlands and Sweden by 75 per cent.

The Commission adopted the preliminary draft budget for 2001 in May. The total of €96,924 billion in commitment appropriations and €93,874 in payment appropriations included an increase in agricultural expenditure of €3.127 billion – 7.6 per cent more than in 2000 – as a result of the decisions taken at the Berlin European Council in March 1999. The remainder accounted for an increase of only €517 million or 1 per cent in commitment appropriations and €1.359 billion or 2.8 per cent in payment appropriations. The draft budget established by the Council set commitment appropriations at €95.86 billion and payment appropriations at €92, 498, rejecting the Commission's proposed revision of the financial perspective – raising the external aid ceiling, designed to finance aid to the western Balkans and reclassifying aid for Cyprus and Malta – increasing the margins available (except Heading 2), and making cuts in all headings. The Parliament raised both figures after its first reading, increasing agricultural expenditure, structural funds appropriations, internal policies, external action and administration, reducing the proposed amounts associated with the management of the pre-accession programmes, and setting up reserves of various sorts.

After Parliament's first reading, the Commission adopted letters of amendment in September, following the review of its tasks and functions as outlined above, and in October updating the estimate of agricultural expenditure – €900 million lower than in the preliminary draft – and expenditure on fisheries agreements, as well as adjusting the revenue – €900 million higher – arising from the redefinition of VAT bases and the new GNP figures in 2000. The outstanding issues between Parliament and Council were resolved at a conciliation meeting prior to the Council's second reading in November. Parliament, Council and Commission reached a global agreement that settled most of the differences. As a result the flexibility instrument for Serbia (€2000 million in commitment appropriations) was mobilized, an entry of €839 million made for the Balkans, €450 million allocated for the enterprise and entrepreneurship programme for 2001–05, the overall increase in payment appropriations for 2001 limited to 3.5 per cent compared with the 2000 budget, the letter of amendment in relation to agricultural expenditure adopted to include €60 million for BSE tests, and a re-budgetization for 2002 and the following years of €1.6 billion in commitment appropriations for Community initiative programmes agreed. A second meeting was convened in early December before the Parliament's second reading to finalize the details.

The 2001 budget was declared adopted after Parliament's second reading in mid-December. It totals €96,238 billion in commitment appropriations and €92,569 billion in payment appropriations, representing increases of 3.1 and 3.5 per cent respectively in relation to 2002. A margin of only €1.113 billion is left beneath the ceilings for commitments, bearing in mind that Heading 4 has already been overshot due the mobilization of the flexibility instrument. Appropriations for payments correspond to 1.08 per cent of Community GNP and are €2,323 billion beneath the ceiling of 1.11 per cent.

Parliament granted the Commission discharge for the clearance-of-accounts decisions for the years 1993, 1994, and 1995. In relation to 1997, it noted that the Commission had implemented the changes recommended by the Parliament to improve the system of financial management. In July, Parliament granted discharge for the 1998 financial year and for the sixth, seventh and eighth European Development Funds, acknowledging the Commission's efforts to improve its management.

The Commission continued its efforts to improve budgetary arrangements, financial control, and the fight against fraud. In October, it adopted a comprehensive plan aimed at recasting and simplifying the financial regulation. A series of internal changes to its financial control system were introduced as part of the reform programme: an internal audit service was created in April; the existing internal monitoring systems within individual directorates-general were reviewed and changes introduced so that each has its own internal audit capacity; a charter was drawn up on the responsibilities of authorizing officers, standards for internal monitoring, and general guidelines on financial circuits and the role of financial units; and a central finance department was set up in May in the Directorate General for the Budget as an advisory service for the

Table 1: European Community Budget, 2000 and 2000, Appropriations for Commitments

Heading	2000 Budget (€)	Financial Perspective 2001 (€)	Budget 2001 (€)	% Change 2001 over 2000
1. AGRICULTURE				
Agricultural expenditure (excl. rural dev't)	36 889 000 000		38 802 700 000	+5.2
Rural dev't and ancillary measures	4 084 000 000		4 495 000 000	+10.1
TOTAL 1	40 973 000 000	44 530 000 000	43 297 700 000	+5.7
Margin			1 232 300 000	
2. STRUCTURAL OPERATIONS				
Objective 1	20 781 000 000		20 832 000 000	0.2
Objective 2	3 668 000 000		3 613 000 000	1.5
Objective 3	3 505 000 000		3 575 000 000	+2.0
Other structural measures	161 000 000		164 000 000	+1.9
(outside Objective 1 areas)				
Community initiatives	1 743 000 000		1 683 000 000	3.4
Innovative measures and tech. assistance	161 000 000		138 000 000	14.3
Cohesion fund	2 659 000 000		2 715 000 000	+2.1
EEA financial mechanism	p.m.			
TOTAL 2	32 678 000 000	32 720 000 000	32 720 000 000	+0.1
Margin			0	
3. INTERNAL POLICIES				
Research and technological development	3 630 000 000		3 920 000 00	+8.0
Other agricultural operations	52 500 000		54 575 000	+4.0
Other regional policy operations	15 000 000		15 000 000	0
Transport	20 500 000		25 205 000	+23.0
Other measures concerning fisheries and sea	66 450 000		61 050 000	8.1
Education, vocational training and youth	481 500 000		491 320 000	+2.0
Culture and audiovisual media	113 100 000		120 100 000	+6.2
Information and communication	104 000 000		103 050 000	0.9
Social dimension and employment	144 615 000		148 370 000	+2.6
Energy	36 800 000		33 800 000	8.2
Euratom nuclear safeguards	16 700 000		17 700 000	+6.0
Environment	157 700 000		116 200 000	26.3
Consumer policy and health protection	22 500 000		22 500 000	0
Aid for reconstruction	3 698 000		1 260 000	65.9
Internal market	147 445 000		159 280 000	+8.0
Industry	p.m.			
Labour market and technological innovation	214 493 000		127 000 000	40.8
Statistical information	31 400 000		32 600 000	+3.8
Transeuropean networks	688 000 000		665 000 000	3.3
Area of freedom, security and justice	98 500 000		113 150 000	+14.9
Fraud prevention & expenditure in support	5 650 000		5 000 000	11.5
of internal policies				
TOTAL 3	6 050 551 000	6 272 000 000	6 232 160 000	+3.0
Margin			39 840 000	
4. EXTERNAL ACTION				
European Development Fund	–		–	
Food aid and support measure	463 406 000		455 000 000	1.8
Humanitarian aid	472 590 000		473 000 000	+0.1
Co-operation – Asia	446 284 000		446 000 000	0.1

Table 1: *(Contd)*

Heading	2000 Budget (€)	Financial Perspective 2001 (€)	Budget 2001 (€)	% Change 2001 over 2000
Co-operation – Latin America	335 914 000		336 250 000	+0.1
Co-operation – southern Africa and S. Africa	123 540 000		122 000 000	1.2
Co-operation – third countries in the Med. and the Middle East	1 127 923 000		896 320 000	20.5
EBRD	470 139 000		469 280 000	0.2
Co-operation – the Newly Independent States and Mongolia	502 630 000		839 000 000	+66.9
Other Community operations – the CCEE, the NIS, Mongolia and western Balkans	362 722 000		389 540 000	+7.4
Co-operation – the Balkan countries	100 373 000		102 000 000	+1.6
Other co-operation measures				
European initiative for democracy and human rights	276 105 000		273 440 000	1.0
International fisheries agreements	81 444 000		71 842 000	11.8
External aspects of certain Community policies				
Common Foreign and Security Policy	47 000 000		36 000 000	23.4
Pre-accession strategy for the Med. countries	15 000 000		19 000 000	+26.7
TOTAL 4	4 825 070 000	4 735 000 000	4 928 672 000	+ 2.1
Margin			193 672 000	
5. ADMINISTRATION				
Part A (excluding pensions)	2 503 392 410		2 598 831 297	+3.8
Other institutions (excluding pensions)	1 656 005 362		1 687 136 540	+1.9
Pensions (all institutions)	564 311 000		618 327 000	+9.6
TOTAL 5	4 723 708 772	4 939 000 000	4 904 294 837	+3.8
Margin			34 705 163	
6. RESERVES				
Monetary reserve	500 000 000		500 000 000	0
Guarantee reserve	203 000 000		208 000 000	+2.5
Emergency aid reserve	203 000 000		208 000 000	+2.5
TOTAL 6	906 000 000	916 000 000	916 000 000	+1.1
Margin			0	
7. PRE-ACCESSION AID				
Agriculture	529 000 000		540 000 000	+2.1
Pre-accession structural instrument	1 058 000 000		1 080 000 000	+2.1
Phare (applicant countries)	1 579 710 000		1 620 000 000	+2.6
TOTAL 7	3 166 710 000	3 240 000 000	3 240 000 000	+2.3
Margin				
Total appropriations for commitments	93 323 039 772	97 352 000 000	96 238 826 837	+3.1
Margin			1 113 173 163	
Total appropriations for payments	89 440 586 295	94 893 000 000	92 569 368 837	+3.5
Margin			2 323 631 163	
Appropriations for payments as % of GNP		1.11		

Source: Commission (2001) General Report on the Activities of the European Union (Luxembourg: OOPEC).

Table 2: Budget Revenue

	2000 (€ m)	2001 (€ m)
Agricultural duties	1 102.2	1 180.0
Sugar and isoglucose levies	1 162.7	1 006.3
Customs duties	12 300.0	13 657.5
Own resources collection costs	–1 456.5	–1 584.4
VAT own resources	32 554.6	33 467.2
GNP-based own resources	43 049.8	45 452.1
Balance of VAT and GNP own resources from previous years	–	–
Budget balance from previous year	–	–
Other revenue	674.1	695.0
Total	89 386.9	93 873.6
Maximum own resources which may be assigned to the budget (% GNP)	1.27	1.27
Own resources actually assigned to the budget (% GNP)	1.11	1.07

Source: Commission (2001) General Report on the Activities of the European Union, (Luxembourg: OOPEC).

other services. Responding to a request by the Helsinki European Council in December 1999, the Commission adopted in June a communication setting out a general strategy for combating fraud. It identified four challenges that confront the Community and the Member States: developing a coherent framework of anti-fraud legislation; defining a new culture of operational co-operation with the Member States; adopting an inter-institutional approach to prevent and combat corruption; and enhancing the judicial dimension. The Council welcomed the document in July. OLAF, the European Anti-Fraud Office, which began operation in June 1999, submitted its first annual report in June. Its Supervisory Committee (composed of independent persons) and the Council in December expressed concerns about the unit's effectiveness. In November, the Commission adopted its annual report for 1999 on protecting the Community's financial interests and the fight against fraud. In 1999, the Member States notified a total of 1, 235 cases of fraud and 4,912 irregularities. OLAF opened 252 new investigations. Structural measures accounted for 80 cases of fraud and 618 irregularities, involving €120 million. The increase in relation to 1998 – 407 cases in total – reflect the greater effort of Member States directed towards detecting fraud.

V. Agriculture and Fisheries

Agriculture

The year 2000 saw the implementation of the reforms agreed at the Berlin European Council in March 1999 as part of *Agenda 2000*. The new policy introduces a number of changes – replacing guaranteed prices with direct support for farmers, simplifying market organization, reducing institutional prices, integrating environmental goals, and introducing a rural development framework as part of a new second pillar of the CAP – designed to update the European model of agriculture in response to a more liberal trading environment and the challenge of enlargement.

Ten regulations[2] and a decision on the level of allocations for the reform of the agricultural sector – an average €38 billion annually for market policy and €4.3 billion for rural development – adopted in March 1999 came into effect in 2000. These changes affected arable crops (intervention price cut by 15 per cent in two equal steps from 2000–01), beef and veal (a 20 per cent decrease in prices in three equal steps), milk and milk products (review in 2003 with quota arrangements to lapse in 2006), rural development (a coherent programme to enhance competitiveness and maintain employment), wine (a new common market organization) and the financial framework (designed to ensure greater security in the administration of the EAGGF). Additional reforms agreed outside *Agenda 2000* concerned olive oil and tobacco. Further measures continued the process of simplification. As a result of the reforms, the annual price setting exercise now only covers a few sectors. The Council adopted the relevant regulations in June and July. The regulations follow the same multi-annual approach as *Agenda 2000* and fix prices and amounts for the six sectors for an indefinite period.

Bovine spongiform encephalopathy (BSE) continued to be a major concern. In June, the Commission agreed a new surveillance system, starting on 1 January 2001, to improve detection of the disease using rapid post-mortem tests and annual monitoring by the Member States. Also in June, the Commission harmonized rules for removing animal tissues most likely to present a BSE risk from the feed and food chain from 1 October. Emergency measures were taken at the end of the year, following the discovery of the first cases of infected cattle in Germany and Spain. At a special Agriculture Council in December, ministers agreed to impose a temporary ban on meat and bone meal (except fishmeal) for all farm animals for six months from 1 January 2001, and to withdraw specified risk material. They also decided that the Commission should review the recent measures taken by Member States in the light of the

[2] *OJ* L 160, 26.06.99, *OJ* L 179, 14.07.99.

opinion of, and consultation with, the Scientific Steering Committee, and propose to the Standing Veterinary Committee either that the measures be lifted or that they be applied across the whole Community. In the same month, the Commission agreed a 'purchase for destruction' scheme, whereby farmers are compensated for the destruction of cattle older than 30 months, unless tested BSE-negative.

Fisheries

The Commission presented its mid-term review of the fourth phase of the multi-annual programmes (MAGP IV), which set limits on fleet capacities, and called for more substantial reductions in the light of continued overcapacity. The Council discussed the report in June and November. A majority of Member States agreed with the Commission view that reliance on Total Allowable Catches (TACs) and quotas alone would not resolve the imbalance between fishing capacity and effort, and the available resources. The issue will be examined as part of the wider reflection on the Common Fisheries Policy (CFP), on which the Commission is preparing a Green Paper for 2001. The Commission also reported on consultations with representatives of the fishing industry and other interested groups that will inform the process.

Policing the implementation of Community rules on conserving and managing resources, and establishing a closer dialogue with the industry and other interested parties, were further concerns. In June the Council adopted measures on the collection and management of fisheries data necessary for the Common Fisheries Policy, and on financial contributions from the Community towards Member State expenditure on the collection of data and financing studies for carrying out the policy. The Commission adopted a report on the implementation of the CFP 1996–98, which will inform discussion of future action. A Council Regulation in March increases decision-making transparency by involving the fishing sector and groups affected by the CFP.

In December, the Fisheries Council set the TACs for 2001. Following independent scientific advice indicating the severe collapse of cod, whiting and hake stocks, the Council adopted drastic reductions on the TACs for the stocks most at risk and agreed that the Commission would put in place multi-annual rebuilding plans early in 2001. TACs were reduced by 50.5 per cent for cod in the west of Scotland, 41–55 per cent for northern hake, and less than 27 per cent for haddock also in the west of Scotland. The reductions were, in all cases, substantially smaller than those proposed by the Commission, and the Council postponed until next year the setting of a TAC for deep-water species, proposed by the Commission for the first time. Discussion of the application of the precautionary principle to fisheries conservation will continue. Other developments included a Commission decision to launch a diplomatic initiative to try to break the deadlock in negotiations for a new fisheries agreement with Morocco – the EU's most valuable.

VI. Environmental Policy

Progress took place on a number of fronts in the environmental policy domain during the year, but the inability of parties to the Kyoto Protocol to reach agreement at The Hague in November was a black spot. Preparations for the sixth environmental action programme, the multi-annual framework for environmental action in the medium term, proceeded in the wake of the publication in November 1999 by the Commission of its assessment of the implementation of the fifth action programme and guidelines for the future (*COM* (1999) 543). Extensive consultation was undertaken.

Efforts continued to integrate environmental considerations in other Community policies, following commitments undertaken by the European Council at meetings since 1997, as well as new provisions in the Treaty of Amsterdam. Progress towards this objective as part of the Cardiff process was reported in the areas of economic and monetary policy, internal market, enterprise, agriculture, fisheries, energy, transport and development co-operation.

Legislative measures adopted concerned emissions, biotechnology, waste management, the protection of air quality, and water. These included:

- an amendment to the regulation on the deliberate release of genetically modified organisms into the environment;
- conciliation on a proposal for a regulation allowing voluntary participation by certain organizations in Community eco-management and audit scheme (EMAS);
- a directive on the incineration of waste, enlarging the scope of and strengthening existing arrangements;
- a directive on monitoring carbon dioxide emissions from new passenger cars;
- a regulation on a revised Community eco-label award scheme intended to promote on a voluntary basis products likely to reduce any harmful impact on the environment;
- a directive on end-of-life vehicles;
- a Council common position on the proposal to amend a directive on measures to be taken against air pollution by emissions from motor vehicles;
- a directive setting limit values for benzene and carbon monoxide;
- a directive establishing a framework for Community action concerning water policy, providing for co-operation between the Member States to prevent the further decline in water quality;

- Council common positions on a proposed directive relating to ozone in ambient air, on a proposal for a directive setting ceilings for sulphur dioxide, nitrogen oxides, volatile organic and ammonia; and a proposed amendment of the directive on large combustion plans and to establish national emission ceilings for various gases and dusts;
- a decision establishing a Community framework for co-operation in marine pollution.

In March, the Council welcomed the Commission's 1999 proposals for a strategy for endocrine disrupters and called upon the Member States and the Commission for its implementation and for the application of the precautionary principle.

The Commission launched several initiatives in 2000. Foremost, was a White Paper on environmental liability, an area where the Commission considers action to be imperative for the implementation of the principles enshrined in Art. 174 of the EC Treaty, in particular, the 'polluter pays' principle. The paper proposes coverage of three types of damage: injury to persons and damage to their property, damage to biodiversity, and contamination of sites. A second concerned pricing policies to ensure the sustainability of water resources. The Commission proposal outlines how the environment should be taken into account in water-pricing policies. It also adopted a Green Paper on the environmental issues relating to PVC, and invited interested parties to submit their views. It published reports on freedom of access to information on the environment and a proposal aimed at correcting the shortcomings in the existing directive and the Auto Oil II programme. Other proposals concerned the management of waste from electrical and electronic equipment, and the extension of a directive on the emission of gaseous and particulate pollutants from internal combustion engines in non-road mobile machinery.

The adoption by the European Parliament and the Council of the financial regulation for LIFE III in July was a major event. A total budget of €641 million has been agreed for the period 2000–04, allocated between the three parts of the programme as follows:

- LIFE-Environment (incorporation of environmental concerns into industrial and land-planning activities) 47 per cent;
- LIFE-Nature (nature conservation) 47 per cent; and
- LIFE-Third Countries (a new element enabling the co-funding of technical assistance and environmental demonstration projects in their countries) 6 per cent.

The participation of Estonia, Romania, Latvia, Slovenia, and Hungary in the programme was agreed.

With respect to nuclear safety, the Council adopted a regulation on agricultural imports from third countries following the accident at Chernobyl. Commission action under the Euratom Treaty included the verification of the application of safety standards protecting the health of the public and workers, the publication of documents on the application of directives on the dangers of ionizing radiation, the delivery of 12 opinions on plans for the disposal of radioactive waste, and two visits to verify the operation and efficiency of facilities for monitoring levels of radioactivity in the environment.

Follow-up to the Kyoto Protocol on global warming was a central preoccupation throughout the year. In March, the Commission adopted a Green Paper on the trading of greenhouse gas emissions within the EU, in which it explored the use of such a scheme and the role it could play towards meeting the Community's commitments under the Kyoto Protocol. The same month, it adopted a communication on EU action necessary to reduce greenhouse gas emission, emphasizing the difficulty faced by the Union in attaining a reduction of 8 per cent between 2008 and 2012, in comparison with 1990, given increasing emissions. The Commission outlined several possibilities in its climate change programme and called for wide consultation. Later in the year, it published a report on a mechanism for monitoring the emission of carbon dioxide and other greenhouse gases. The Council set out the EU's strategy for The Hague conference (the sixth Conference of the Parties to the United Nations Framework Convention on Climate Change) in June and November. Though progress was made by the parties on technical issues, two major political issues – the use of 'carbon sinks' to reduce greenhouse gas emissions, and the balance between domestic action in industrialized countries and the use of the 'Kyoto mechanisms', namely, emissions trading, joint implementation, clear development – could not be settled. EU ministers decided not to accept the proposals made by the US and other parties and, in the absence of an agreement, the parties decided to suspend the conference. The Nice European Council expressed regret at this failure, appealed to parties to resume their efforts, and signalled its intention to organize meetings with other signatories.

References

Commission of the European Communities (2001) *General Report on the Activities of the European Union* (Luxembourg: OOPEC).

Presidency Conclusions, Lisbon European Council, 23 and 24 March 2000; Santa Maria da Feira, 19–20 June 2000; Nice, 7–9 December 2000.

Journal of Common Market Studies
Volume 39, Annual Review
September 2001

Climbing Up (and Sliding Down) the Euro Learning Curve

ALISON COTTRELL

UBS Warburg

Ever the contrarian, the euro spent much of 2000 defying expectations of a revival, preferring instead to motor along the same downhill gradient it had followed through 1999 (Figure 1). By mid-September, the single currency had lost 28 per cent of its launch value against the US$, 16 per cent against the UK£, and almost 22 per cent on a trade-weighted basis.

For central bankers and finance ministers, sustained depreciation on this scale was a dual source of concern. First, it exacerbated the upward pressure already being applied to import prices by a surging oil price, sparking fears that inflationary expectations and wage demands might follow suit. Second, it raised concerns that ongoing official complaints about the euro's 'unjustified' decline, accompanied by repeated predictions of an imminent recovery which inexplicably refused to materialize, might call into question policy-makers' ability and credibility. If such doubts took hold, euro selling might turn speculative, tipping a sliding currency off the cliff edge.

While a potential price–wage spiral was a headache, it was the risk of imploding credibility which did most to give tired European central bankers sleepless nights. And it was not just Europe's central bankers who were developing dark circles under their eyes. Concern that what many commentators already routinely referred to as the euro's 'inexorable' slide might, in fact, prove precisely that, was shared by policy-makers elsewhere who recognized

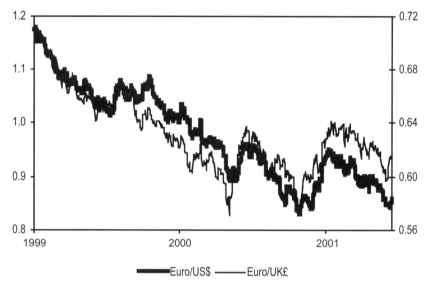

Figure 1: Euro Exchange Rates against US Dollar and Sterling

Source: Datastream.

the impact an outright loss of confidence in the new currency would have on their own financial markets, exchange rates and economies.

The markets therefore approached the 23 September G7 meeting with antennae tuned even more finely than usual for any hint of a shift in exchange rate policy. Aware that verbal support for the euro had now lost much of its effectiveness; that looming US elections had persuaded markets that the window for new currency initiatives was closing fast; and that post-G7 therefore risked seeing a further down-leg in the euro which might turn into a rout, the authorities acted.

On the eve of the meeting, the US Federal Reserve, the Bank of Japan, the Bank of England, the Bank of Canada, and the European Central Bank joined forces to buy euros, surprising the markets and even, perhaps, themselves. The US, in particular, had previously appeared sceptical of such action. Warnings from US corporations as to the impact of euro depreciation on earnings were, however, beginning to come thick and fast, unnerving the stock market. US congressional and vice-presidential incumbents had no wish to go the polls without the Dow on their side. Like old age, the appeal of intervention only became apparent after contemplating the alternative.

That the currency managed in late 2000 to get back on to its knees (if not quite its feet) had, however, less to do with co-ordinated intervention than with a US economy which unexpectedly began to surprise on the downside. A reassessment of the outlook for US growth, and hence for US interest rates, lifted the euro back over US 90c and pushed it into 2001 with a spring in its step, albeit a short-lived one.

As an explanation of euro weakness, forecast growth differentials (or, more accurately, forecast potential output differentials) stand up better than most. The idea that a surging US stock market underpinned the US$ – an argument always sensitive in any case to the equity index chosen – died many deaths in 2000. While falling US equity prices may, indeed, prompt investors to look for pastures new in European assets, those same investors may just as easily conclude that a sneezing US presages a global bout of 'flu, and the resulting 'safe haven' flows support rather than dampen the US$.

Home-grown factors, such as the EMU area's initial policy mix, proved equally unco-operative as euro-scapegoats. More expansionary fiscal policy and tighter monetary policy should, on paper, have been euro-supportive, but left the single currency in 2000 distinctly unimpressed. And while there is undoubtedly room for improvement in the communications skills of central bankers and politicians, to attribute the entirety of the single currency's anaemia to Wim Duisenberg's verbal dexterity hints at an attempt to explain retrospectively what was not adequately forecast in advance. Certainly, policy coherence and presentation matter; but had the euro-zone economy performed more impressively last year than it did – and at 3.4 per cent, it did not do badly – Duisenberg could have recited poetry at his monthly press conferences, and the euro appreciated regardless.

Why, then, did the late 2000 turnaround in economic prospects not give the euro a more substantial boost? Primarily because a shift in relative growth on the back of a US downturn is a different animal to one reflecting European acceleration. If the US economy is slowing (let alone contracting), investors will wonder not whether Europe might be pulled along in the same direction, but how far it will be dragged. They will then ask if it might be harder for a more sluggish Europe to follow in the US's productivity-boosting footsteps, and ponder the difference a slowdown might make to the bloc's appetite for structural reform, deregulation, policy co-ordination and enlargement. At best, euro enthusiasm will be capped; at worst, investor confidence in the global outlook could be so shaken as to trigger a (euro-detrimental) flight-to-quality.

If sustained euro appreciation is unlikely to come through climbing on the shoulders of a sinking US, achieving it on the euro-zone's own merits will require demonstration that reform is, indeed, underway in a bloc that is changing technologically, geographically and demographically. While this is not an impossible challenge, it is one to which policy-makers have, on the whole, so far failed to rise.

Extra 'encouragement' may, however, stem from the fortuitous coincidence of the euro's introduction and the spread of the internet. The single currency forces businesses to re-evaluate the way they operate within the single market; the internet offers new ways to exploit that market. Add the two together and the impact on Europe's competitive temperature is akin to global warming, producing a climate in which businesses will be even keener to ensure that governments (themselves forced to compete more aggressively to retain mobile employers and tax-payers) are left in no doubt as to the policies needed to boost competitiveness.

A strengthening euro requires governments able both to combine macro-ambition with micro-imagination, and to convince an observant and sceptical market audience that the European leopard has indeed changed its spots. Three years into EMU, and with the economic and social step-change of the introduction of euro notes and coins imminent, Europe's politicians are still climbing up a very steep learning curve.

Journal of Common Market Studies

Volume 39, Annual Review
September 2001

Legal Developments

JO HUNT
Cardiff University

Introduction

While 2000 saw proportionately more cases dispatched by the Community
Courts (the European Court of Justice (ECJ) and the Court of First Instance
(CFI)) than 1999, there was no diminution in the number of cases being lodged,
nor in the duration of proceedings.[1] Thankfully, concerns voiced by the ECJ
that the time taken to dispose of cases is coming close to denying an acceptable
level of judicial protection in the Union and, further, potentially compromises
the rule of law,[2] were taken seriously in the deliberations leading to the
conclusion of the Nice Treaty.[3]

A range of Treaty amendments have been agreed which will, if implemented, bring significant changes to operation of the Community judicature. These
should contribute to ensuring the effectiveness of those institutions.[4] Most
significant is the decision to grant jurisdiction to the CFI to hear certain

---

[1] The ECJ brought 526 cases to a close, 503 new cases were lodged before it, and the average time taken
for proceedings remained 21 months for references from national courts for preliminary rulings, 24 months
for direct actions and 19 months for appeals. The CFI disposed of 334 cases, 398 were lodged, and the
average duration of proceedings remained 27months (ECJ Press Release No 12/2001, available on «http:
//www.curia.eu.int»).

[2] ECJ (1999).

[3] Most of the preliminary work on identifying an agenda and achieving political agreement on amendments
was in fact undertaken by a 'Friends of the Presidency Group' specifically constituted for this purpose.
The Courts' own contributions to this process are available on the curia website.

[4] For a more detailed consideration of the impact of the Nice Treaty on the Courts, see Shaw (2001).

categories of Art. 234 (ex 177) EC Treaty references.[5] While having the potential to relieve pressures from the ECJ, the provision also contributes to raising the status and profile of the CFI which, under the Nice Treaty, ceases to be described as merely 'attached' to the ECJ. The Treaty also provides for the establishment of a third level of Community court – judicial panels, which may be created to deal with specific issue areas – the first[6] of which is to be a panel for cases brought by staff of the EU institutions, currently heard by the CFI.

Away from the IGC process, agreement was reached on a number of amendments to the Courts' Rules of Procedure, designed to accelerate the administration of justice. New, simplified procedures enable the ECJ to dispatch swiftly, by reasoned order, Art. 234 references involving questions which it deems to have been answered by previous rulings.[7] In addition, a new expedited procedure allows the Courts to dispense with certain administrative formalities in cases of urgency.[8] Future reform of the Rules of Procedure will be facilitated post-Nice, as the Treaty provides that these Rules may be amended by a qualified majority vote in Council, rather than the unanimity as is currently required.[9] It is apparent, though, that the Courts would have liked these changes to have gone further, bringing them greater autonomy in the regulation of their activities.

The Nice IGC also, of course, saw political agreement on the EU's Charter of Fundamental Rights. While non-legally binding, it is to be expected that this document will be a future source of inspiration for the ECJ in its development of a body of human rights law, and there will no doubt be more to report on the Court's use of that document in the review for 2001.[10] What follows below is a overview of some of the most legally and/or politically significant judicial pronouncements during 2000, maintaining the general format employed in previous reviews.

---

[5] This jurisdiction will be operationalized following a decision of the Community institutions, Art. 225(3) EC Treaty. The ECJ will have the power to intervene and review cases so disposed.
[6] Although a *de facto* judicial panel already exists, the Alicante Board of Appeal of the Office for Harmonization in the Internal Market (OHIM), dealing with the Community trademark.
[7] Amendments entering into force 1 July 2000, *OJ* 2000L122/43, and used for the first time in Case C-89/00, *Bicakci*, judgment of 19 September 2000.
[8] Amendments dated 28 November 2000, in force 1 February 2001, *OJ* 2000 L122/1.
[9] Fundamental principles concerning the operation of the Court, contained in the Treaty will still require amendment through an IGC, and amendment to the statute of the Court which contains basic rules on the Courts' procedure continues to require unanimity, although there has been some movement of rules from the statute to the rules of procedure.
[10] In his opinion on the rights of contract workers under the Working Time Directive, A.G. Tizzano suggested that the Charter provides 'reliable and definitive confirmation' of the fundamental nature of the right to paid annual leave, Case C-173/99 *BECTU*, Opinion of 8 February 2001.

I. The Development of the Competence
and the Powers of the EU and its Institutions

External Competence

Parfums Christian Dior and *Assco*[11] concerned Art. 50 of TRIPS (the WTO Agreement on Trade Related Aspects of Intellectual Property Rights), a 'mixed' agreement entered into jointly by the Community and the Member States. The questions referred sought to establish the extent of the ECJ's interpretative jurisdiction in relation to TRIPS, and the possible direct effects of Art. 50(6) TRIPS, which sets procedures in relation to the 'provisional measures' which may be invoked to protect intellectual property rights. The ECJ's decision reaffirms and extends its earlier judgment in *Hermès*,[12] with the ECJ now explicitly accepting jurisdiction to interpret TRIPS in relation to matters which have not yet been legislated on by the Community. The ECJ maintained its refusal to accord direct effects to the WTO Agreement and its Annexes, though it confirmed the national courts' obligation to interpret national law protecting IP rights covered by TRIPS 'as far as possible in the light of the wording an purpose of Article 50 TRIPS'. However, this 'indirect effect' for TRIPS arises only in situations where the Community has legislated.

Internal Competence

Germany's successful challenge to the validity of the Tobacco Advertising Ban Directive[13] is perhaps the one decision of the ECJ to have aroused the most popular comment during 2000. The decision certainly shows a Court committed to ensuring the observance of the law in the face of political pressures from the number of Member States supporting the Parliament and Council. Germany sought annulment of Directive 98/43/EC[14] on the grounds that an incorrect legal base (100a, now 95 EC Treaty) had been used. The ECJ agreed with the German government that the grounds for the use of Art. 100a, which provides a basis for approximating measures which have as their object the establishment and functioning of the internal market and the elimination of distortions of competition, could not be made out. While reaffirming the Community's commitment to human health policies, the ECJ made it clear that the Community lacked the competence to introduce harmonization measures designed to protect and improve human health, as this is excluded under the provisions on public health (Art. 124(4), now 152(4) EC Treaty), declaring that 'other articles of the Treaty may not ... be used as a legal basis in order to circumvent

[11] Joined Cases C-300/98 and C-392/98, *Parfums Christian Dior SA* v. *Tuk* and *Assco Geruste GmbH* v. *Willhelm Layher GmbH,* judgment of 14 December 2000.
[12] Case C-53/96, *T. Hermès International* v. *FHT Marketing Choice BV* [1998] ECR I-3603.
[13] Case C-376/98, *Germany* v. *European Parliament and Council* [2000] ECR I-8419.
[14] *OJ* 1993 L307/18.

the express exclusion of harmonisation'.[15] A significant aspect of the Court's robust ruling is the literal and limited reading it ascribes to Art. 95 EC Treaty, observing that 'to construe that Article as meaning that it vests in the Community legislature a general power to regulate the internal market would be ... incompatible with the principle embodied in Article 3b (now 5) EC Treaty that the powers of the Community are limited to those specifically conferred upon it'.[16]

Inter-institutional Relations

In *Commission and Parliament* v. *Council*,[17] the applicant institutions sought to overturn a Council regulation on the grounds that the Council had opted for a legal base which excluded the Parliament from the right to participate in co-decision. The Commission alleged that the Council had committed a breach of an essential procedural requirement by introducing the regulation on identification and registration of bovines for the purposes of product labelling[18] on the basis of Art. 43 (now 37) EC Treaty, despite an earlier submission from the Parliament, accepted by the Commission, that the measure should be introduced under Art. 100a (now 95) EC Treaty, read in conjunction with Art. 124 (152) EC Treaty on the protection of public health. Following a thorough consideration of the aims and objectives of the regulation, the ECJ held that it had been correctly introduced under Art. 43, declaring irrelevant 'the fact that an institution wishes to participate more fully in the adoption of a given measure'.[19] No discussion of the possibly enhanced democratic legitimacy of the involvement of Parliament under an alternative legal base was entered into by the ECJ.

II. Development of Principles of Substantive EC Law

Free Movement of Goods (Arts. 28–30 Non-tariff Barriers including Intellectual Property Considerations)

In *TK-Heimdienst*[20] the ECJ considered the 'selling arrangement' exemption to Art. 28 introduced in *Keck*.[21] Heimdienst supplied goods in contravention of an Austrian law restricting the right of butchers, bakers and grocers to sell

---

[15] At para. 79.
[16] At para. 83.
[17] Case C-269/97, judgment of 4 April 2000.
[18] Council Regulation EC No 820/97 of 21 April 1997 (*OJ* 1997 L117/1).
[19] At para. 44.
[20] Case C-254/98, *Schutzverband gegen unlauteren Wettbewerb* v. *TK-Heimdienst Sass GmbH* [2000] ECR I-0105.
[21] Joined Cases C-267 and 268/91, *Keck and Mithouard* [1993] ECR I-6097.

door to door to those permanently established in the relevant administrative district, or a neighbouring municipality. Was this obstacle to trade protected under the 'selling arrangement' exemption? The ECJ made clear that selling arrangements do not automatically fall outside the scope of Art. 28, and are only permissible if they affect in the same manner, in law and in fact, the marketing of domestic products and those from other Member States. This is not the case with a rule of the type at issue here, requiring as it does traders established in other Member States to bear the additional costs associated with acquiring another permanent establishment in a specified geographical territory.

Belgium v. *Spain*[22] presents an exceedingly rare example of inter-state litigation under Art. 227 (formerly 170) EC Treaty. In a previous judgment rendered in the context of an Art. 234 procedure, *Delhaize*,[23] the ECJ had ruled that Portugal's rules restricting the allocation of the '*denominacion de origine calificada*' (DoC) to Rioja wines bottled in the region of production were capable of being caught by Art. 29 (formerly 34) EC Treaty. The bottling requirement was to be considered a measure having an equivalent effect to a quantitative restriction on exports (MEQR), as it restricted the bulk export of 'DoC' Rioja, while there was no such restriction on bulk sales of 'DoC' Rioja in the region of production and bottling. The Court was unconvinced by the attempted justifications presented. Despite the ruling in *Delhaize*, Portugal took no steps to amend the rules on bottling requirements, and the Belgian government brought an action before the ECJ for a declaration that by maintaining these rules in force, Portugal had failed to fulfil its Community law obligations. The ECJ found once more that the national rules could constitute a MEQR, but then departed from the result in *Delhaize*, by ruling that the measures could indeed be justified under Art. 30 (former 36). On this occasion, the Portuguese government successfully adduced evidence in support of the argument that the rules were required to protect industrial and commercial property. This decision serves as a useful reminder of the proper allocation of responsibilities under Art. 234 – in *Delhaize*, the Court had usurped the role of the national court when it ruled that the Art. 30 justification had not been made out.[24]

In *Commission* v. *France*,[25] which again concerned the Art. 30 exemption in relation to the protection of industrial and commercial property, the ECJ held that while Community law recognizes that proprietors of design rights may exercise those rights in relation to the manufacturing, selling and importing of goods infringing their rights, protection in relation to intra-Community transit

[22] Case C-388/95 [2000] ECR I-3123.
[23] Case C-47/90, [1992] ECR I-3669.
[24] See, further, the case note by Spaventa (2001).
[25] Case C-23/99 [2000] ECR I-7653.

of goods does not form part of the specific subject matter of industrial property rights in relation to designs. Thus France could not detain motor parts produced in Spain and destined for the Italian market.

Free Movement of Workers

Angonese[26] is a significant decision in a number of respects, notably because for the first time the ECJ has explicitly confirmed the horizontal direct effect of Art. 39 EC Treaty. Angonese, an Italian national was excluded from consideration for employment at a private Italian bank in Bolzano, on the grounds that he did not have the necessary certificate of bilingualism, evidenced by possession of a certificate only available locally. While declaring that language requirements may be open to justification, the ECJ ruled that it was not acceptable under Art. 39 EC Treaty for the employer to rely exclusively on the candidate's possession of a particular certificate to ascertain linguistic competence. The novelty of the case lies in their application to a private undertaking, and, apparently, in the context of a wholly internal situation – Angonese being an Italian national seeking employment in Italy. Indeed, in his opinion, AG Fennelly had submitted that, on the facts, there was an insufficient connection with Community law in this case.[27] The Court did not address this point in any depth, and proceeded to examine the substance of the case. In so doing, the Court has extended yet further the reach of Community law, some may say without justification.

In *Graf,*[28] the applicant, a German national, contended that Austrian legislation denying compensation to workers for termination of their contracts when the worker ends the contract him/herself was contrary to Community law, as it dissuaded the worker from exercising the right to leave the country of origin to work in another Member State. Finding the rule to be non-discriminatory, the ECJ also submitted that it was not such as to affect access to the labour market of another Member State. The national legislation could not be seen as deterring a worker from ending a contract of employment in order to take up employment in another Member State, the entitlement to compensation being dependent on an event 'too uncertain and indirect' to affect the worker's decision (that is, termination of the contract by the employer). As with its decisions in relation to goods,[29] the Court is clearly taking the opportunity to forestall 'misuse' of the market access (non-discriminatory hindrances to free movement) approach in relation to workers, and placing limits on its application.

---

[26] Case C-281/98, *Angonese* v. *Cassa di Risparmio di Bolzano SpA* [2000] ECR I-4139.
[27] AG Opinion of 25 November 1999.
[28] Case C-190/98, *Graf* v. *Filzmoser Maschinenbau GmbH* [2000] ECR I-493.
[29] As in the case of *Keck, supra.* n. 21.

Free Movement of Services

More sport-related free movement questions were dealt with – this time concerning judo.[30] Having not been selected by the Belgian federation to compete at an international tournament in France, Delière sought to challenge the European Judo Union's rules which limited participation to members selected by national federations (despite the fact that the competition is not one between countries) on the grounds that they limited the right to provide services. Delière was brought within the personal scope of Community law through a particularly broad interpretation of the concept of 'service provider': the ECJ's rationale being that through participation in high-level tournaments, the competitor is enabling the organizer to put on events which may be attended by the public, may be transmitted by television companies, and which may be of interest to advertisers and sponsors. Nevertheless, it was suggested that Art. 49 (ex 59) EC Treaty did not preclude such rules, on the grounds that they were necessary in the interests of the organization of the competition.

Competition Law

In *Bayer*,[31] the CFI overturned a Commission decision fining the company 3 million ECU for infringement of Art. 81(1) (ex 85(1)) EC Treaty. The Commission's decision was based on there having been an agreement between Bayer and its French and Spanish wholesalers to limit re-exports of the drug Adalat to the UK (where there was a ready market, prices for the drug being considerably higher than in the exporting states). As Bayer argued, and the CFI accepted, the Commission had failed to prove the existence of an agreement between the parties. Whilst Bayer decided to reduce the amount of Adalat supplied to French and Spanish wholesalers in an attempt to limit the drug's re-exportation to the UK (a practice which was leading to large losses in turnover for Bayer UK), this decision could not be seen as an agreement between Bayer and the wholesalers, who objected to the change in policy. The necessary concurrence of wills between the parties did not exist, there being no proof of acquiescence, explicit or tacit on the part of the wholesalers. Nor could the continued existence of commercial relations between the parties be seen as evidence of there being an agreement between them. The Commission, which considers that the CFI has raised the burden of proof for finding an agreement, has filed an appeal with the ECJ.

---

[30] Joined Cases C-51/96 and C-191/97, *Delière* v. *Ligue Francophone de Judo and others* [2000] ECR I-2549.
[31] Case T-41/96, *Bayer AG* v. *Commission* [2000] ECR II-3383.

In *Deutsche Post* v. *GZS and Citicorp*[32] the ECJ considered whether Deutsche Post's practice of charging full internal postal rates for forwarding to German addresses mail posted in large quantities in other Member States could constitute the abuse of a dominant position under Art. 82 (ex 86) EC Treaty. The mail in question was sent by the Dutch- and Danish-based European Service Centres of a number of banks, who were already paying full international postal rates to the Post Offices in which the mail was initially posted. In addition to the charges imposed on the banks, Deutsche Post was also in receipt of 'terminal dues' collected from other states' postal administrations for the delivery of international mail. Finding that the exclusive rights granted to Deutsche Post in relation to German postal services were for services of a general economic interest under Art. 86(2) (ex 90(2)),[33] the Court proceeded to examine whether charging full internal postal rates on forwarded mail was necessary to enable Deutsche Post to perform its service of general interest (if so, Deutsche Post would be taken outside the scope of Art. 82). The Court held it was necessary, and therefore lawful in the absence of Deutsche Post's receipt of terminal dues covering the actual cost of processing. Were it to demand full internal rates in addition to terminal dues, however, Art. 82 would be infringed. The judgment is particularly significant in respect of the Court's readiness to examine the question of necessity on the grounds of profitability in relation to only one aspect of Deutsche Post's general service, and not examining the possibility of cross-subsidization from other areas of its activities.[34]

In the context of the ice-cream war between Masterfoods and HB Ice Cream concerning the distribution of freezer cabinets only to retailers agreeing to stock them exclusively with HB products, the ECJ issued a judgment[35] clarifying the respective roles of the national courts and the Commission in the enforcement of EC competition rules. Where the Commission has taken a decision on the legality of agreements or practices under Arts. 81 and 82 EC Treaty, the duty of sincere co-operation requires that the national court must not take an opposite view to that decision. While the Commission decision may be open to annulment before the Community courts, until such an event occurs the Commission decision remains a binding Community act. In the event that an action for annulment is brought at the same time as national proceedings, the national court may decide to stay the action until final judgment is delivered, or request a preliminary ruling.

---

[32] Joined Cases C-147 and 148/97 [2000] ECR I-825.
[33] Following Case C-320/91, *Corbeau* [1993] ECR I-2533.
[34] See the case note by Bartosch (2001).
[35] Case C-344/98, *Masterfoods* v. *HB Ice Cream Ltd*, judgment of 14 December 2000.

Sex Equality

German constitutional provisions which impose a general ban on women serving in the armed forces in positions involving the use of firearms have been declared incompatible with Community law. Last year's judgment in *Sirdar*[36] which, controversially,[37] affirmed the principle that organizational defence issues could fall within the scope of EC law (and specifically secondary legislation on equal treatment[38]) cleared the way for the ECJ's decision in *Kreil*.[39] Whilst Art. 2(2) of the Equal Treatment Directive allows for the exclusion of one sex from certain jobs where by reason of the nature of the position sex is a determining factor, and whilst Member States are recognized as having 'a certain degree of discretion' when adopting measures they consider necessary to guarantee public security, a blanket ban on the employment of women from *all* arms-bearing units was found to be disproportionate. Particular exemptions may be admissible in relation to specific units (as with the Royal Marines in *Sirdar*), but a general exclusion is not.

Two judgments on positive discrimination are worthy of note. *Badeck*[40] concerned a challenge to German state laws which seek to eliminate under-representation of women in the public service by means of 'advancement plans' which lay down that more than half of the posts to be filled in sectors where women are under-represented must be awarded to women. Following *Marschall*,[41] it was clear that there would have to be some 'saving clause' for such provisions to be compatible with EC law,[42] as any system which gives absolute and unconditional priority to women is precluded by Community law. In this case, there was such a clause, in the form of five 'social aspects' which would be taken into account when deciding between male and female applicants with equal qualifications (including preference for those with serious disability, and the long-term unemployed), thus allowing the necessary objective consideration of reasons specific to the individual candidate. Rules setting targets for the percentage of women appointed to temporary academic posts to be at least equal to the percentage of women graduates, higher degree holders and students in that discipline also found no objection from the ECJ, as they were held not to fix an 'absolute ceiling' but instead a ceiling set using 'an actual fact as a quantitative criterion'. In addition, rules which sought to eliminate under-representation in relation to access to training, selection for

---

[36] Case C-273/97, *Sirdar* v. *the Army Board* [1999] ECR I-7403.
[37] See the case note by Langer (2000).
[38] Council Directive 76/207/EEC, OJ 1976 L39/40.
[39] Case C-285/98, *Kreil* v. *Germany* [2000] ECR I-0069.
[40] Case C-158/97, *Badeck* v. *Landesanwalt beim Staatsgerichthof des Landes Hessen* [2000] ECR I-1875.
[41] Case C-409/95, *Marschall* v. *Land Nordrhein-Westfalen* [1997] ECR I-6363.
[42] Article 2(4) of Directive 76/207/EEC permits Member States to 'promote equal opportunity for men and women, in particular by removing existing inequalities …'.

interview, and on representation on employee bodies were all suggested to be compatible with Community law. This judgment appears to confirm a shift towards a more substantive conception of equality, as apparently endorsed by Art. 141(4) EC Treaty (ex 119), introduced by the Amsterdam Treaty. The ECJ clearly considers 141(4) to be broader than Directive 76/207's provisions, as it observed that, if it found the German rules to be precluded by Art. 2(4) of the directive, it would move to consider their status under 141(4) – although such a consideration was in fact found to be unnecessary.

A consideration of national positive action provisions in the light of both Directive 76/207 and Art. 141(4) was, however, deemed necessary in the case of *Abrahamsson,*[43] which concerned Swedish rules on selection procedures in relation to university appointments. These rules afforded preference in appointment to 'sufficiently' qualified candidates of an under-represented sex over candidates of the opposite sex who would otherwise have been selected. This was subject to the condition that 'the difference in their respective qualifications is not so great that the application of the rule would be contrary to the requirement of objectivity in the making of appointments.' Ms Fogelqvist had been appointed to a chair at Gothenburg University, in preference to the better qualified Mr Anderson, though in the selection board's opinion, the difference between them was not so great as to breach the objectivity requirement. The Court had no difficulties in finding that such a rule was precluded by both secondary and primary EC law, on the grounds that it allowed for no objective assessment of the specific personal situations of the candidates (as provided for in *Badeck),* and instead granted an automatic preference to the sufficiently, though not best qualified candidate from the under-represented sex.

Turning to discrimination on the grounds of pregnancy, the ECJ held in *Mahlburg*[44] that an employer's decision not to appoint a pregnant woman on the grounds that national statutory prohibitions on pregnant women working with dangerous substances prevented her from being available for work from the outset of her contract constitutes direct discrimination under Directive 76/207. As with the earlier decision in *Webb,*[45] the Court was mindful to stress the fact that the position was one of an indefinite, rather than fixed-term period, raising the possibility that direct discrimination in the latter situation potentially may be justifiable.[46]

---

[43] Case C-407/98, *Abrahamsson and Anderson* v. *Fogelqvist* [2000] ECR I-5539.
[44] Case C-207/98 [2000] ECR I-3201.
[45] Case C-32/93, [1994] ECR I-3567.
[46] This point is set to be considered in Cases C-438/99, *Jiménez Melgar* and C-109/00, *TeleDanmark,* to be heard in 2001.

Worker Protection

The exemption from the protection of health and safety legislation (including the Working Time Directive[47]) of sectors of the workforce engaged in 'certain specific public activities'[48] does not apply to primary health care workers, the ECJ held in *SIMAP*.[49] Having established this point, the Court then proceeded to examine whether time spent 'on call' constituted working time within the meaning of the directive. If it were found to be so, these periods could be taken into consideration when calculating the maximum working week, and minimum rest periods provided for under the directive. While the directive defines working time as any period when the worker is '… at the employer's disposal', the ECJ drew a distinction between periods on call spent at the place of work, and those where the worker is away from it, but contactable. Only the former are to be considered 'working time' for the purposes of the directive.

Environment

Sydhavnens Sten[50] involved the question of the compatibility of Danish measures on the processing of non-hazardous building waste with Treaty rules on the free movement of goods and on competition. An agreement authorizing three Copenhagen-based undertakings the exclusive rights to process all building waste produced with the Municipality of Copenhagen was recognized by the ECJ as potentially infringing Art. 29 on the free movement of exports. Exemptions under Art. 30 (health and life of humans, animals and plants) were not available, nor could environmental grounds contained in Art. 174(2) EC (ex 130r(2)) be used, on the basis that the materials were non-hazardous – though significantly this suggests that a derogation from free movement on the latter grounds may be permissible in different factual circumstances. Considering separately the question of the infringement of competition law, the ECJ looked at the issue of granting special and exclusive rights for the processing of waste, and suggested that these could in principle be justified as necessary for the performance of a task of general economic interest (Art. 86(2) EC Treaty). It may, however, be assumed that this cannot form the basis of an exemption from the free movement provisions.

When selecting sites for designation as 'Special Areas of Conservation' (SAC) under the Habitats Directive,[51] Member States must have regard only to environmental factors. Despite the directive's Art. 2(3) which provides that 'measures taken pursuant to this directive shall take into account economic,

---

[47] Council Directive 93/104/EC, OJ L307/18.
[48] Art. 2(2), Council Directive 89/391/EEC, OJ 1989 L183/1.
[49] Case C-303/98 [2000] ECR I-7963.
[50] Case C-209/98, *Entreprenørforeningens Afflads* v. *Københans Kommune* [2000] ECR I-3743.
[51] Council Directive 92/43/EEC, OJ 1992 L206/7.

social and cultural requirements', these should not be factored into the decision to identify an area as an SAC. To do so would jeopardize the objective of bringing together a coherent ecological network, the ECJ has ruled.[52]

III. Enforcement and Effectiveness of Community Law

Individual Enforcement – Direct Effect

In *Linster*,[53] the applicants sought to challenge at national level the legality of the legislature's decision to authorize motorway construction on the basis that the terms of the Environmental Impact Assessment Directive[54] had not been respected. The referring court was unsure as to whether it had the power to review the legality of the national legislation against the directive, particularly as the directive had (unlawfully) not yet been transposed, and there had been no prior ruling on its direct effect. The Court found it unnecessary to consider the issue of the directive's direct effect, declaring that the national court could nevertheless rule on the compatibility of the national law with the directive, by reviewing whether the national legislature had kept within the limits of the discretion granted to it by that directive. This decision contributes to the view that there are two distinct approaches pursued by the ECJ in relation to the enforceability of unimplemented directives within national law. On the one hand, where the applicant is seeking the *substitution* of a national rule with one contained in a Community directive, in order to rely on the rights contained therein, the standard requirements of direct effect must be made out. On the other, where the applicant is simply seeking the *exclusion*, or the non-application of the national rule which does not accord with the terms of a directive, the same requirements as to the direct effect of that directive are not demanded.[55] The approach is clearly one motivated by a desire to ensure the *effet utile* of Community law.

The 'exclusion' doctrine was again apparently applied by the ECJ in the case of *Unilever Italia*,[56] this time in the context of an action between private parties. Unilever had a contract to supply olive oil to Central Food, which the latter refused to accept as it was not labelled in accordance with Italian labelling regulations. These technical regulations had been notified to the Commission by the state, as it is obliged to do under Directive 83/189,[57] but

[52] Case C-371/98, *R* v. *Secretary of State for the Environment ex parte First Corporate Shipping* [2000] ECR I-9235.
[53] Case C-287/98, *Luxembourg* v. *Linster* [2000] ECR I-6917.
[54] Directive 85/337/EEC, OJ 1985 L175/40.
[55] This distinction is explored by A.G. Leger in his opinion in *Linster*, though was not addressed in these terms by the ECJ. See further on this distinction, Lenz (2000).
[56] Case C443/98, *Unilever Italia* v. *Central Food* [2000] ECR I-7535.
[57] *OJ* 1983 L109/8.

had been put in place before the end of the three-month standstill clause demanded by the directive. Despite Advocate General Jacob's arguments to the contrary,[58] the ECJ found the situation in *Unilever* to be comparable to that in the *CIA*[59] case, where the ECJ called for the disapplication of national technical standards introduced without the fulfilment of the directive's notification requirements. By this ruling, the ECJ has again blurred the boundaries of horizontal direct effect, as the enforcement of the directive will clearly have an impact on the rights and obligations of private parties. While the judgment may be justified on the grounds that it contributes to ensuring the supremacy of Community law, it may be criticized for the degree of uncertainty it introduces to commercial transactions. Traders must it seems be on their guard to ensure that national regulations have indeed been properly introduced before they can, with any confidence, rely on them in their contractual relations.

State Liability

In the context of a case concerning an Italian dentist's claim that a German state dental association unlawfully refused to recognize the equivalence of his qualifications and experience, the ECJ in *Haim*[60] confirmed that a public law body, legally independent of the state, may incur *Francovich* liability for breaches of Community law.

Article 228 – Fining for Breach

For the first time the ECJ has made use of its powers to fine a Member State for failing to comply with a previous judgment finding that it is in breach of its Community law obligations.[61] This power, introduced into the EC Treaty by the TEU was exercised in relation to Greece, following its continued failure to rectify its breaches of Community law in relation to the disposal of waste. The fixing of a fine of €20,000 for each day that Greece continues to be in breach was held by the Court to be the most appropriate way of ensuring that Community law was applied uniformly and effectively. The criteria for assessing the level of fine include the duration of infringement, the degree of seriousness (including the effects of non-compliance on public and private interests), urgency and the state's capacity to pay. The Court will soon be called upon to exercise this power again in a case against France on night work by

---

[58] Opinion delivered 27 January 2000.
[59] Case C-194/94, *CIA Security* v. *Signalson and Securitel* [1996] ECR I-2201.
[60] Case C-424/97, *Haim* v. *KVN* [2000] ECR I-5123.
[61] Case C-387/97, *Commission* v. *Greece* [2000] ECR I-5047.

women,[62] and against Greece, again, in relation to the recognition of diplomas.[63]

IV. Protection of Individual Rights

Fundamental Rights and General Principles of Law

In *Emesa Sugar* order,[64] Emesa applied for leave to submit written observations in response to the Advocate General's Opinion, relying on Art. 6(1) ECHR (right to a fair and public hearing) and drawing parallels with decisions of the Court of Human Rights involving the right to present submissions following the opinion of the Belgian Procureur Général.[65] Recognizing a general jurisdiction to review the compatibility of the actions of Community institutions with the provisions of the ECHR as general principles of law, the ECJ also made reference to the power of review granted to it by Art. 46(d) TEU. Unsurprisingly, the ECJ refused to grant Emesa's application, as the 'case-law of the ECHR does not appear to be transposable to the Opinion of the Court's Advocate General'[66] due to the status and role of the latter. This case has aroused further concerns about the development of conflicting lines of authority from the ECJ and the ECHR, and brought about renewed calls for the accession of the EC to the ECHR.

In *Schröder*,[67] meanwhile, the ECJ set down a principle of constitutional significance for the EU polity. Referring to the dual economic and social aim pursued by Art. 141 (ex 119) EC Treaty, the Court stated that 'it must be concluded that the economic aim pursued by Art. 119 of the Treaty, namely the elimination of distortions of competition between undertakings established in different Member States is secondary to the social aim pursued by the same provision, which constitutes the expression of a fundamental human right'.[68] It will remain to be seen what implications this recognition of the hierarchically superior nature of the right to non-discrimination will have, particularly in relation to economic justifications to indirect discrimination, which have in principle been accepted by the Court.[69]

---

[62] Case C-224/99, pending.
[63] Case C-197/98, pending.
[64] Case C-17/98, *Emesa Sugar* v. *Aruba* [2000] ECR I-665.
[65] ECtHR, judgment of 20 February 1996, *Vermeulen* v. *Belgium* (Reports 1996, p.224).
[66] At para. 16.
[67] Case C-50/96, *Deutsche Telekom* v. *Schröder* [2000] ECR I-743.
[68] Case C-50/96, *Deutsche Telekom* v. *Schröder* [2000] ECR I-743, at para. 57.
[69] Case 170/84, *Bilka-Kaufhaus* [1986] ECR 1607.

Access to Documents

In a judgment notable for the restrictive reading the ECJ gives to the grounds for exemption from the right to access to Community documents, the ECJ has ruled that the Commission is not entitled to rely on the court proceedings exemption in Decision 94/90[70] automatically to refuse access to documents issued to national courts in response to the latter's questions on the application of the competition law provisions. In *van der Wal,*[71] the ECJ overturned the decision of the CFI which had upheld the Commission's refusal to grant access to such documents to the applicant, a Dutch competition law specialist. The Netherlands government intervened to support van der Wal in the appeal before the ECJ. The ECJ declared that the CFI erred in law in finding that documents drawn up for a case before a national court became part of the national court's files, such as to make the issue of access a matter for the national court alone. The ECJ drew a distinction between general opinions issued by the Commission, and those drawn up on the basis of specific information provided by the national court, and including economic or legal analyses of those facts. In the latter case alone the Commission can take into account national court rules on access to documents, refusing access only where the national court, having been consulted, objects to disclosure.

In *Kuijer,*[72] one of the grounds explicitly pleaded by the applicant before the CFI was that the Council, in refusing the request for certain documents relating to immigration and asylum matters, had breached the fundamental principle of access to documents. Finding for the applicant on other grounds, the CFI declared that it was therefore unnecessary to consider this plea, and thus the existence of such a fundamental right, thereby exempting itself from pronouncing on a question of constitutional significance. The explicit recognition of this right as a general principle of law would do much to enhance the position of individual within the EU legal order.

Judicial Review (including Locus Standi of Non-privileged Actors)

Before the ECJ had heard the German government's challenge to the Tobacco Advertising Directive, a group of companies came before the CFI, seeking to have the same directive annulled on the same grounds. They were not successful.[73] Unlike privileged applicants under Art. 230 (ex 173) EC Treaty, undertakings and individuals must show that they have a direct and individual

---

[70] Decision on public access to Commission documents, *OJ* 1994 L46/58.
[71] Joined Cases C-174/98 P and C-189/98 P, *Netherlands and van der Wal* v. *Commission* [2000] ECR I-0001.
[72] Case T-188/98, *Kuijer* v. *Council* [2000] ECR II-1959.
[73] Joined Cases T-172, 175 to 177/98, *Salamander and others* v. *Parliament and Commission* [2000] ECR II-2487.

concern in the challenged act. The CFI ruled that they had no direct concern, as the directive did not affect their legal situation. On a strict reading of Art. 249, the CFI held that as directives oblige Member States to take action to give them effect, the directive, independently of national measures transposing it, had no effect on the applicants' own legal situation. To recognize such effects would be tantamount to recognizing the immediate horizontal direct effect of directives. Nor did the economic consequences they were suffering give rise to a 'direct interest', the CFI finding that even if the consequences were a direct result of the directive, they influenced the applicants' factual, not legal situation. The CFI also rejected the applicants' plea that a finding of inadmissibility would violate their rights to an effective remedy. There was, noted the CFI, the possibility of bringing an action before the national court and challenging the validity of the measure through an Art. 234 reference,[74] and of bringing an action for damages against the Community institutions under Art. 288 (ex 215) EC Treaty. Even if the preliminary ruling procedure was 'less effective' than a direct action, as the applicants contended, that was not grounds for the CFI to change the Treaty's system of legal remedies.

V. Overall Evaluation and Conclusion

In 2000, the ECJ delivered a number of high-profile judgments which attracted the attention of the popular press – most notably in relation to the tobacco advertising ban. In that judgment, the Court demanded a degree of compliance with the letter of the Treaty to which the ECJ has itself been criticized for being somewhat less than faithful. There were again this year instances of the ECJ interpreting the law in a more teleological than literal manner, *viz.* its decisions in relation to the effects of directives, such as that in *Unilever Italia.* The objective the Court is pursuing in these cases is clear, that of ensuring the *effet utile* of Community law, and of securing respect for the supremacy of Community law. In this regard, the ECJ has also shown that it is prepared to use the power to fine Member States, and decisions such as *Commission* v. *Greece* should serve as an effective warning to Member States.

Finally, the amendments to the Courts' rules of procedure, and an increase in their budgetary allocation are to be welcomed, as they will increase the capacity for the Courts to function effectively and efficiently. More prospectively, the provisions in the Treaty of Nice, if activated, should contribute to that objective as well.

---

[74] As was undertaken by Imperial Tobacco and others in Case 74/99, *R* v. *Secretary for State for Health* [2000] ECR I-8599. The ECJ, referring to its decision in *Germany* v. *Parliament and Council* held that it was unnecessary to answer the questions posed by the national court. A challenge to the admissibility of the action had been rejected by A.G. Fennelly in his opinion [2000] ECR I-8419.

References

Bartosch, A. (2001) Case note on Joined Cases C-147& 148/97, *Deutsche Post CmLRev.* Vol. 38, pp. 195–210.

Court of Justice of the European Communities (1999) 'The Future of the Judicial System of the European Union' available on «http://www.curia.eu int».

Court of Justice of the European Communities (2000) Contributions to the IGC, available on «http://www.curia.eu int».

Court of Justice of the European Communities and the Court of First Instance, case law from 2000, available on «www.curia.eu.int».

Langer, J. (2000) Case note on Case C-273/97, *Sirdar* and Case C-285/98, *Kreil CmLRev.* Vol. 37, pp. 1433–44.

Lenz, M. (2000) 'Horizontal What? Back to Basics'. *ELRev.* Vol. 25, No. 5, pp. 509–22.

Shaw, J. (2001) 'The Treaty of Nice: Legal and Constitutional Implications'. *European Public Law,* Vol. 7 No. 2, forthcoming.

Spaventa, E. (2001) Case note on Case C-388/95, *Belgium* v. *Spain CMLRev.* Vol. 38, pp. 211–19.

Journal of Common Market Studies   Volume 39, Annual Review
September 2001

External Policy Developments

DAVID ALLEN

and

MICHAEL SMITH

Loughborough University

1. General Themes

Introduction

There was no one dramatic event during 2000 to rival the Kosovan adventure of 1999. Nonetheless, there was, as ever, much to occupy the time of the numerous individuals and institutions charged with the formulation and implementation of the EU's external dimension. Both Chris Patten for the Commission and Javier Solana for the Council busied themselves with the implementation of the numerous commitments made in Helsinki at the end of 1999. Individually and together, they also produced a number of reports and reflections on the overall management of EU external relations that drew attention to the need to prioritize external EU objectives, streamline and clarify the relevant decision-making procedures and ensure a greater coherence, consistency and efficiency in the delivery of EU foreign policy using both Community and Union instruments.

Although the external relations provisions of the Treaty of Amsterdam only came into effect in May 1999, much of 2000 was taken up with the negotiation of the Treaty of Nice which was agreed in December. The new Treaty makes only minor amendments to the articles dealing with the CFSP: it provides for the abolition of most of the WEU (Art. 17); recognizes the fact that the Political

Committee has now become the Political *and Security* Committee; and that it has a key role in the evolving system of EU crisis management (Art. 25). The Nice Treaty also provides for the limited use of the closer co-operation procedures in the implementation of CFSP joint actions and common positions (Clauses J, K, L and M), even though, during 2000, no use was made of the Amsterdam 'constructive abstention' procedures. Nice also provides for a small extension of exclusive Community competence (Art. 133.5) and the use of qualified majority voting (QMV) (Art. 133.4) with regard to the trade in services, although unanimity in the Council will remain for all areas where it is required for the adoption of internal rules. The Member States have preserved their specific interests in certain aspects of the trade in services by creating a 'mixed competence' category in the Treaty (Art. 133.6) to include trade in cultural and audiovisual services, education services and social and human health services, as well as (under Art. 300) transport services. The Community is given exclusive competence over the 'commercial aspects of intellectual property' meaning that all other aspects are in the 'mixed competence' category – hardly a triumph for those who advocated the communitarization of all trade in services and intellectual property.

During 2000, the Commission further developed its plans to devolve more responsibility to its overseas delegations and to make better use of local staff as opposed to seconded personnel. New Commission delegations were opened in Macedonia and Croatia, Bosnia (upgraded from a representative office) and Indonesia (upgraded from a representation). The delegations in Cape Verde and Togo were downgraded to offices and attached to the delegations in Senegal and Benin respectively. At the end of the year, the Commission was accredited to 161 countries and international organizations, 128 with diplomatic status.

Foreign and Security Policy

The CFSP proper was once again rather overshadowed by the activities surrounding the further development of the European Security and Defence Policy (ESDP) under the overall guidance of Javier Solana, the Secretary-General of the Council and the High Representative for foreign and security policy (SG/HR). In the course of the year, the new interim institutions (political and security committee, military committee) were established and military staff seconded to the Council Secretariat. By the end of the year, their permanence was confirmed by the Nice arrangements. If the actual Treaty amendments were relatively minor, the *Report on the European Security and Defence Policy* produced by the French Presidency was much more substantial. The report, which builds on a similarly comprehensive document produced by the Portuguese for the Feira European Council, provides a good summary of the state of the ESDP at the end of the year. It outlines procedures for the development of military capabilities (Annex I) and the strengthening of civilian crisis management capabilities (Annex II). They follow the establishment of a civilian crisis management committee in June and the successful holding of a 'Capabilities Commitment Conference' in November, when the Member States and others pledged sufficient forces and equipment to begin the process of making credible the achievement of the Helsinki 'headline goals' of deploying 50–60,000 troops in the field within 60 days and sustaining them for one year. The Report goes on to cover in some detail the establishment of permanent political and military structures (Political and Security Committee (COPS) – Annex III; Military Committee – Annex IV and the Military Staff – Annex V), the arrangements for the consultation and participation of the non-EU European NATO members and the EU applicant states in EU crisis management (Annex VI), arrangements for EU–NATO consultation and co-operation (Annex VII), arrangements for consultation with other potential partners such as Russia and Canada, the inclusion in the EU of all appropriate functions of the WEU (other than Art. V), conflict prevention, and a mandate for the ongoing activities for the Swedish Presidency designed to make the ESDP 'quickly operational' in 2001.

During the year, despite an apparently good personal relationship between Commissioner Patten and SG/HR Solana, 'institutional tensions' between the Commission and the Council Secretariat were alluded to by both of them as they sought to make the foreign policy process more efficient and coherent. Solana was successful in persuading foreign ministers to set aside some time each year to establish EU external priorities before the EU budget was set. It was also agreed that country studies would be developed in a bid to improve the links between EU pillars one and two and the external activities of the Member States. Both Patten and Solana expressed criticism of the newly-introduced common strategies. Both were jointly charged by the European Council with the difficult task of improving the implementation of the EU's policy towards the western Balkans (although even here it was noted that it was Solana who was formally put in charge of this exercise, albeit with a mandate to work closely with the Commission). Patten resisted pressure from within the Commission to 'muscle into' the strictly military aspects of the ESDP. This strengthened his arguments about the need to give the civilian aspects of ESDP, where the Commission does have a clear role, equal attention, although they did not prove strong enough to convince the Council to agree to his request for the establishment of a rapid reaction facility. While the Commission, the Council Secretariat and the Council Presidency were collectively required to work together in the 'new troika', their representatives were all also anxious to stake their individual claims to a role in the management and implementation of the CFSP. At the end of the year, the agreements reached at Nice did little more than confirm the arrangements for the CFSP and the ESDP that had been provisionally agreed in Helsinki; they did little to suggest how they might eventually work in practice. For its part, the European Parliament demonstrated unease (and naivety) when faced with Solana's determination to keep military documents secret and preferably housed, along with his limited staff, in a separate and secure building in Brussels. It was perhaps fortunate for those involved that the EU did not experience a significant international crisis in 2000. The suspicion remains that the evolving decision-making and implementation machinery, while increasingly elegant on paper, might prove unwieldy in practice. There is clearly much for the Swedish and Belgian Presidencies to address in 2001: the EU and NATO need to refine and clarify their relationship further; the EU Member States have some embarrassing gaps to fill in their collective military capability; and the EU's role in the overall European order requires more work on EU political and military relations with non-EU European NATO members (15+6), with them and the other EU candidates (15+15), and with other significant 'European' states such as Russia and the Ukraine. Once the military and civilian crisis management mechanisms are in place, it will be also be necessary to consider the ESDP in the broader context of the CFSP it is meant to complement and serve (it was, for instance, noticeable that the EU Member States were not able to make any collective statement about their position on controversial American proposals for Ballistic Missile Defence). This will require further consideration of the role of the Commission, the Council, the Council Secretariat, Coreper, COPS, and the Member States in the making and delivery of EU external policy.

During 2000, the EU adopted one more common strategy (towards the Mediterranean) but suspended plans for another towards the western Balkans, adopted ten joint actions and repealed one, and defined 16 common positions and amended two. The joint actions included six on the western Balkans, one on Georgia, one on Africa (Great Lakes) and one relating to the European code of conduct on arms exports. The joint action that was repealed concerned the export of dual-use goods which, interestingly, the European Court of Justice had ruled should be the subject of action under the EC Treaty not the CFSP provisions of the TEU. The common positions related to the western Balkans (five on the Federal Republic of Yugoslav (FRY), one on the Stability Pact), Africa (Angola, Ethiopia and Eritrea (three), Sierra Leone and Rwanda), Asia (Afghanistan and Myanmar (two)) and the Non-Proliferation Treaty regime. The EU and the Presidency issued 146 CFSP statements all of which are listed in the European Commission's 2000 *General Report on the Activities of the European Union* (points 760 –88) and some of which are referred to in Part II (below).

External Trade and the Common Commercial Policy (CCP)

As in previous years, the evolution of the EU's external trade policies during 2000 reflected a combination of internal and external forces. Within the Union, and more particularly within the European Community (EC), there were a number of intersecting trends. As Trade Commissioner, Pascal Lamy undertook an activist role, not only in terms of particular relationships (see below) but also in terms of the principles and practice of trade policy itself. Key general objectives of EU policies included the promotion of the 'knowledge economy' through emphasis on e-commerce and the establishment of new regulatory frameworks, and the defence of the 'precautionary principle' in a number of areas with trade policy implications, such as environment and food safety. As can be seen from these examples, the principles of trade policy were intimately linked to other areas of EU policy-making. Within a broader external focus, Lamy, during 2000, placed considerable emphasis on the development of new trade policies for the poorest countries in the global system, espousing the principle of 'zero tariffs, zero quotas' for 48 of the least developed countries and pursuing it in the face of some resistance from both some EU Member States and other industrial countries.

At the same time as these and other external principles were framed, the Intergovernmental Conference (IGC) saw a debate about just what EU trade policies should cover. The Amsterdam Treaty had left the issue of competence on trade in services and other areas in limbo, and the Commission, not unnaturally, saw the run-up to Nice as an opportunity to make its case for extended competence once again. The autumn of 2000 saw a continuing tussle between the Commission and, particularly, the French about how much of trade in services, intellectual property issues and investment the Commission might claim. With the Presidency so committed, it was largely left to the intervention of the Finns to bring about a still uneasy compromise in the Treaty, whereby the Community was given additional competence but with some exclusions (largely reflecting French priorities). Whether this is sustainable, and how far it will affect the negotiating clout of the Community and the Commission, is, of course, still an open question.

In more specific CCP activities, this was a relatively quiet year. The use of anti-dumping and anti-subsidy measures continued to increase, in line with a global trend, and in tension with efforts to regularize the regimes for trade in textiles and other sectors, which reflected the legacy of the Uruguay Round in the early 1990s. The Community continued to exert pressure in the handling of customs fraud, and became concerned more than ever with the impact of counterfeiting on the trade in industrial goods, partly because of internal pressures from, for example, the engineering industry. As always, the Community found itself entangled in a large number of World Trade Organization

(WTO)-related disputes, details of which are given below where relevant, and gained a number of significant successes in terms of WTO panel rulings. There was continued wrestling with the definition of 'market economies', which has significant implications for the treatment of trade with countries such as China and, as noted above, the trade impact of the 'precautionary principle' made itself felt, not least because of the conflicting views in major trading partners such as the USA.

While these tensions made themselves felt in the context of the WTO, they were in many ways dwarfed by concern over the future of the WTO itself in the wake of the 'battle of Seattle' (see last year's *Review*) and the failure to launch a new trade round. In the aftermath of the Seattle fiasco, there was a good deal of 'the politics of blame', with the EU and the US in particular engaged in mutual recriminations. But during the year, Lamy and the trade DG came to play an increasingly influential role in attempts to relaunch a new round. Lamy made active efforts to recruit support for a new round based on a comprehensive agenda (which would favour the EU because of the opportunity to trade off concessions in some areas, such as agriculture, against gains in others, such as competition policy). The Commissioner's efforts attracted support from Japan, and less enthusiastically from a number of Asian countries but, as the year wore on, it became clear that the mood was against a 'jumbo' round. Although no final determination had emerged by the end of the year, it appeared that the EC would have to accept a 'lean' agenda with the exclusion of some areas such as environment, investment and competition policy. Another noteworthy aspect of Lamy's efforts was his emphasis on the need to consider the capacity of less-developed countries to implement any agreements reached in the WTO – which in turn linked with his focus on the least developed countries in trade terms (see above). Meanwhile, important sectoral negotiations got under way in the WTO on agriculture and services. Not surprisingly, the former especially saw the EU 'targeted' by others, and in both cases there had been little progress by the end of the year. The stickiness of global trade talks led some countries during 2000 to conclude new-style bilateral deals (e.g. the US and Singapore), but the Community in general held to its support for global frameworks.

Finally within that context, it is important to note the continuing issues arising from global financial institutions. While not formally part of trade policy, these have implications for the contribution of the Community to global economic management. During 2000, there were continuing tensions about the representation of the euro-zone in global financial institutions; the need for co-ordinated management of currencies in the wake of the introduction of the euro preoccupied some policy-makers, not least because of the euro's decline on the currency markets. There was a co-ordinated intervention in defence of the euro during July, but later in the year support for this type of action, especially from the United States, was less forthcoming. During the early part of the year, the broader institutional leadership issues focused on the nomination of candidates for the Director-Generalship of the International Monetary Fund (IMF), in which the Germans doggedly insisted on getting their candidate accepted even after their first one was rejected. Eventually, and after a good deal of EU–US tension, Horst Köhler was nominated.

Development Co-operation Policy and Humanitarian Aid

At the end of 1999, an interim agreement was signed for a new partnership with the ACP (Lomé) states. Negotiations were finally concluded in February and the new agreement was signed in Cotonou, Benin, in June (it was to have been signed in Fiji but the overthrow of the Democratic Government prevented that). The Cotonou agreement (see the 1999 *Review* for further details) is to run for 20 years, which represents a compromise between the EU, who wanted a 15-year deal, and the ACP, who wanted it to run for 30 years. The first five-year tranche of financial aid (the ninth European Development Fund (EDF)) will run from 2000–06 and will be worth €13.5 billion to which must be added the €9 billion unspent funds from previous EDFs. In the Lomé context, the EU applied Art. 366a (Art. 97 of the new Cotonou agreement) to three states, Côte d'Ivoire, Haiti and the Comoros. In each case consultations were opened because of a breach of the rule of law and democracy, but in no case was EDF money withheld. In 2000, €3.612 billion was awarded to the ACP states under the sixth, seventh and eighth EDFs – further testament of the need for the EU to speed up its procedures for spending, as opposed to allocating, money.

During the year, the Commission published several reports examining both its development aid priorities and its procedures for the delivery of aid. It was agreed in November that, in future, the main priority would be poverty reduction and the integration of the developing world into the global economy. The Commission's report was challenged by a number of development NGOs but was accepted without significant modification by the Council. The Commission and its external delegations also subjected their procedures to internal scrutiny and decided (in a 58-point action plan designed to improve co-ordination, consistency and coherence and thus transparency and efficiency) to streamline them, partly by speeding up and simplifying the Brussels procedures, partly by giving a greater co-ordination role to overseas delegations and partner countries, and partly by better relating collective EU policies to those pursued by the Member States with the introduction of comprehensive country studies. It was also agreed that the prominence of EU programmes would be enhanced by the adoption of the generic name *EuropeAid* along with a logo. In the UK, EU aid delivery procedures were heavily criticized by Clare

Short (Secretary of State for International Development), who described them as 'the worst in the world' and who noted that, despite the desire to eliminate poverty, only one-quarter of EU aid went to the very poorest states while the remaining three-quarters went to the much better off 'near abroad'. As part of his own efforts to enlist the support of the third world for a new round of trade talks in the WTO context, Pascal Lamy, the Trade Commissioner, has proposed the removal of trade restrictions for 'Everything but Arms' for EU imports from the 48 poorest states in the world.

In 2000, the EU also extended €463 million in food aid to developing countries plus an additional €96 million to the World Food Programme, €200 million to development projects run by non-governmental organizations, €131 million to rehabilitation and reconstruction operations in the developing countries and €527 million in humanitarian aid through a reformed European Community Humanitarian Office (ECHO). The two largest recipients of ECHO funding were the ACP states who received €140 million and the western Balkans who received €100 million. It should, however, be noted that, while further ECHO funds were allocated to the victims of Hurricane Mitch in 2000, much was made of the fact (by those critical of the EU's implementation procedures) that, although a total of €200 million plus had been allocated to this cause, no money has yet actually been spent! The Community continued to support north–south projects to combat drugs and drug abuse (€5.6 million) and allocated €93 million (for 2000–06) to promote the environmental dimension of development and €249, also for 2000–06, to promote the conservation of tropical forests in developing countries. The Commission is also justifiably proud of its participation in the global campaign against anti-personnel land mines, most of which are produced in developed countries but laid in developing countries. In March, it published a list of the various operations mounted by the EU in this context as part of a campaign to establish a special budget heading and an enabling general regulation to underpin EU policy.

II. Regional Themes

The European Economic Area (EEA) and EFTA

This was generally a quiet year in relations with the EEA and EFTA. Regular meetings of the EEA Council took place in May and September, and the Joint Parliamentary Committee met in May and November. Work continued on adapting and transposing legislation, and on improving transparency. More significant were two bilateral relationships: those with the Nordic EEA members and with Switzerland. During the spring, Norway offered 3,500 troops as a contribution to the proposed Rapid Reaction Force, no doubt partly as a means of maintaining its access to the European Security and Defence Policy (ESDP) process as a non-EU NATO member. Norway and Iceland continued to be involved in Schengen co-operation, which was now within an EU context as a result of the Treaty of Amsterdam, and they began negotiations with the aim of agreeing mechanisms for asylum applications. In the case of Switzerland, the major focus of interest was the referendum in May on the bilateral agreements negotiated between the EU and the Swiss government during the previous years (see earlier *Reviews*). These agreements covered seven areas of policy: free movement of persons, transport, agriculture, aviation, public procurement, standards/testing and research. The referendum produced a 67 per cent 'yes' majority, which was taken as a good omen for the possibility of a future re-opening of accession negotiations that had been stymied since the early 1990s. Later in the year, there was a move by some groups in Switzerland to initiate a referendum on the immediate resumption of those negotiations. It was not a move welcomed by the Swiss government, which wanted to preserve some freedom of manœuvre.

Western Balkans

In many ways, 2000 was quite a good year for the EU in the western Balkans as it developed the stabilization and association process within the context of the Stability Pact for south eastern Europe, which it had initiated and helped launch in 1999. In Croatia, the defeat of the Croatian National Union and the election of the coalition headed by Ivica Racan and, in Serbia, the defeat of Slobodan Milosevic by Vojislav Kostunica opened the door for improved relationships with the EU. There were, though, worrying signs towards the end of the year that there might be renewed problems in Kosovo and Macedonia, while the reform process seemed to be faltering in Bosnia.

The Lisbon European Council charged Javier Solana and Chris Patten, together, with the task of taking control of EU policy towards the western Balkans. Both made numerous visits to the area during the year as they sought to rationalize EU decision and delivery procedures and eliminate duplication. In the period before the fall of Milosevic, the EU became internally divided over the continuation of sanctions against Serbia, with France keen to review them and the UK determined to maintain them. Compromise attempts to target the regime rather than the population led to an increase in the visa restrictions on Milosevic supporters, but a relaxation of the ban on commercial flights and the sale of oil. When Kostunica took over in September, the EU was quick to lift all the remaining sanctions (even though the US sought to maintain them until Milosevic was handed over for trial at The Hague) and to offer €180 million emergency aid to Serbia for energy, medicines and food, as well as €20 million for refugees. In a gesture of support, Kostunica was invited to attend the European Council meeting in Biarritz. In Kosovo, the EU is the largest donor and aid (€354 million) has, since February, been managed through the European Agency for the Reconstruction of Kosovo. There has been much criticism of the fact that the new agency, which took over from the Task Force for the Reconstruction of Kosovo (TAFKO) based in Pristina, is based in Thessalonika in Greece – a classical and illogical EU compromise!

The fall of Milosevic also added greatly to the positive atmosphere that was generated at a special 'EU–Balkans' summit held at President Chirac's instigation in Zagreb in late November. The Zagreb summit brought together the EU heads of government and the leaders of Albania, Croatia, Bosnia, the FRY, the Former Yugoslav Republic of Macedonia (FYROM) and Slovenia, as well as the President of the Commission. At this meeting the first of the new stabilization and association agreements designed to pave the way to eventual EU membership was initialled with FYROM, and approval was given for the opening of negotiations for a similar agreement with Croatia. It seemed as if the long-term, essentially 'civilian' EU plan for the resolution of the Balkan problem was beginning to bear some fruit.

In March, in the context of the Stability Pact, the EU and the World Bank hosted a pledging conference for south eastern Europe at which €2.4 billion was committed – €1.1 billion from the EU, of which €531 million was from the Commission. In December, as part of the effort to streamline the delivery of EU aid, the Council legislated to bring all EU assistance to the western Balkans under a single legal framework. Community Assistance for Reconstruction, Development and Stability (CARDS) will replace the old PHARE and OBNOVA programmes and will cover the period from 2000–06 supplying €4.6 billion to the area, of which €2.3 billion is for Serbia.

Russia and the Soviet Successor States

The EU held two summit meetings with Russia, in Moscow in May and Paris in October. The meeting in May was the first opportunity to appraise the new Russian leader, Vladimir Putin. Although the Helsinki European Council had decided to take further action against Russia over its activities in Chechnya, the Council showed great reluctance to support further sanctions as proposed by the Commission (under some pressure from the European Parliament). By June, even the €58 million worth of aid to Russia that had been withheld after Helsinki was released. The Member States were anxious to get off to a good start with Putin and they were also keen that Russia did not rock the ESDP boat. For their part, the Russians expressed an enthusiasm for an active role in the ESDP (which they, like the US, perhaps saw as potentially disruptive of NATO), while the EU tried to encourage them to offer the support of their considerable diplomatic weight (over Serbia for instance) rather than their creaking and potentially disruptive military machine.

The EU is also engaged in some delicate negotiations with Russia over the future supply of gas and oil. The Russians are keen to build a new pipeline, effectively cutting out the transit of the Ukraine in favour of a route through Poland and the Czech Republic. This proposal impacts on Polish –Ukrainian relations and on EU relations with each of them. The EU's desire for securing oil and gas supplies increases as the peace process in the Middle East falters and as the oil price rises, but the Ukrainians (whose energy policy the EU is also keen to influence) fear a significant loss of pipeline revenue, while the Poles remain determined to maintain even-handed relations with all their neighbours.

The EU also held a summit with the Ukraine in Paris in September. While the Ukrainians were anxious to explore the possibility of future membership, the EU was more concerned to maintain the focus on the provisions of the partnership and co-operation agreement already in place. It may well be that Ukrainian demands for a 'road map' for eventual membership may be held at bay with an EU proposal for a free trade area, as was the case with a similar Russian request in the early 1990s. More immediately, the Commission is anxious to use Euratom (US$ 585 million) and EBRD (US$ 215 million) loans to help finance new nuclear power stations at Khmelnitsky and Rivne to replace those that they have at last persuaded the Ukrainians (with the help of €25 million from the TACIS budget to cover the temporary cost of the power shortfall) to take out of commission at Chernobyl.

EU relations with Belarus remain poor with sanctions still in place because of the absence of democratic reforms.

Finally, the EU is beginning to turn its attention, in the shape of a visit from Chris Patten, to the question of Kaliningrad, which will become a Russian enclave within the EU once Poland and Lithuania become Member States. During 2000, the Portuguese and French Presidencies rather neglected the 'northern dimension', although Romano Prodi attended the Baltic Sea States Council in Bergen in June and the Commission was represented at the Barents Euro–Arctic Council held in Oulu in March. During 2000, some €454 million of TACIS aid was allocated to the area, with €70 million targeted at cross-border co-operation.

The Mediterranean and the Middle East

2000 was not a good year for the EU in the Middle East, despite the fact that a number of Arab states consistently express a preference for a much greater EU involvement in the peace process. A number of factors prevented this during the year, of which the most important was the failure of the Clinton administration to broker a new peace deal before its departure from office and before the Israeli elections. It has always been likely that the EU, as in the western Balkans, would play an essentially economic role once a peace agreement had been reached. However, Israel seems determined to allow no new participants, such as Russia, China or the EU, into the peace process, regarding them all as potentially or actually 'unsympathetic' to the Israeli cause. And while the EU itself remains internally split on many of the relevant issues, President Chirac's meeting with Israeli Prime Minister Ehud Barak in October seems to have set back rather than advanced the EU's chances of exerting any immediate influence on the peace process.

Despite attempts to revitalize it, the Barcelona Process made little real progress in 2000. Although it did prove possible to hold the fourth Euro–Mediterranean conference of foreign ministers in Marseilles in November, events in the Middle East meant that Lebanon and Syria did not attend. Somewhat perversely, Libya did, as a guest. This represented the end of a long year of efforts by Romano Prodi, who was criticized by both Libya and the EU Member States for his constant attempts in 1999 and 2000 to improve the relationship with Libya. In a bid to make the proceedings more palatable to the Arab participants the EU dropped its much-heralded attempts to sign a Charter of Peace and Stability, but the meeting achieved little other than actually taking place. The EU may be anxious to speed up the process of negotiating the new Euro–Mediterranean agreements with its ten partners but, as yet, only Israel and Morocco have been prepared to conclude agreements. Even here there have been arguments about the rights of Moroccans to export agricultural products to the EU at a price which includes the normal duty, over and above their duty-free quotas under the agreement. Relations with the only other signatory, Israel, were also soured by a familiar problem in 2000 when some EU Member States once again raised the issue, dormant for two years, of Israeli exports to the EU from illegal settlements in the Palestinian territories.

The other Mediterranean partners are concerned about the social and industrial implications of opening up their domestic markets to EU imports, with the usual group of EU states proving themselves reluctant to make even the most minor of agricultural concessions. The EU is also concerned about the evolution of trade patterns in the Mediterranean area: while around 50 per cent of the exports and imports of non-EU Mediterranean states go to and from the EU, only about 5 per cent of their total trade is with each other. Despite the lack of real progress, significant funds to the tune of €888 million were committed by the EU to the MEDA programme in 2000 and, following a streamlining of procedures, some €5.35 billion is also promised for the MEDA II programme between 2000 and 2006.

On the bilateral front, problems with Turkey were exacerbated by the EU's need to establish a good working relationship with NATO (of which Turkey is, of course, a long-standing member). Because of Turkish sensitivities over Greece's determination to link the resolution of the Cyprus problem to Turkey's EU membership application, and the European Parliament's need to see progress in Turkey on the human rights front, it was not until the last moment that the EU was able to agree a 'road map' for the progress of Turkey's application. This ensured Turkey's lifting of its veto on the EU–NATO accord, and its participation in the European Conference that was held in Nice just before the European Council meeting in December.

Africa

The first ever Europe–Africa summit was held in Cairo in April bringing together the Heads of Government of the 15 EU states and 52 African states of the Organization of African Unity. Although an action plan was adopted at the conclusion of the meeting, it is difficult to see what added value can be generated by yet another forum that overlaps with both the Euro–Mediterranean Barcelona Process and the Cotonou/Lomé ACP process. As it was, it took delicate negotiations by Javier Solana to prevent the question of Moroccan occupation of the Western Sahara upsetting the arrangements.

The unfortunate saga of EU–South African relations continued in 2000 with several EU states (Greece, Spain, Italy) still refusing to ratify the trade agreement because of essentially petty issues about South Africa's right to produce and export drinks labelled grappa and ouzo. While the Member States claim that they are concerned about the principle rather than the actual practice, which involves imports of minimal and unthreatening value, the South Africans have been given further good reason to doubt the good faith of the EU as a negotiating partner. At the same time, in June, the EU agreed to commit €885 million in aid for reconstruction and development in South Africa for the period 2000–06. As in previous years, the EU made numerous CFSP statements about the many conflicts and threats to democracy that either continued or broke out in Africa in 2000, but backed these up with little substantive action. Some moves, though, were made to prevent the import into the EU of diamonds illegally produced and traded in west Africa, the profits from which were believed to be fuelling the conflict in Sierra Leone.

Asia

The EU's relations with Asia reflect a complex mixture of components: inter-regional and bilateral contacts; global frameworks such as the WTO; and a shifting balance between the commercial and the political expressed in, for example, human rights debates. During 2000, all of these elements were apparent. At the inter-regional level, a major focus of activity was the third Asia–Europe Meeting (ASEM) held in Seoul, South Korea, during October. This was seen as an opportunity to 'relaunch' the ASEM process, which had been sidelined to a degree first by the Asian financial crisis of 1998–99 and then by global trade and economic concerns. The Seoul meeting produced what was effectively a 'road map' for future development, covering a wide range of issues and reflecting a greater sense of stability in the relationship. It also welcomed the 'reconciliation' process between North and South Korea, and reaffirmed a number of areas of public–private co-operation such as the Asia–Europe Business Forum (which itself met during September in Vienna). The other prime focus of EU attention in inter-regional relations was the Association of Southeast Asian Nations (ASEAN), a long-standing partner for the EC but recently subject to tensions caused, especially, by the problem of Burma (see previous *Reviews*). During the year, the Union developed a 'two-track' diplomacy in relation to ASEAN and Burma: first, it tightened its sanctions on Burma (reaffirming its common position and extending sanctions to, for example, the bank balances of Burmese leaders in Europe); second, it was more prepared to accept the participation of Burma in EC–ASEAN meetings (which had not taken place effectively since 1997). This diplomacy, practised through bilateral meetings as well as in the context of the ASEAN Regional Forum which met in July, did produce an inter-regional meeting in December, although this was not attended by a number of EU heads of government. Nonetheless, it could be seen as some progress – and there were even indications that Burma might be willing to accept visits and contacts with opposition leader Aung San Suu Kyi by EU Member States.

China has been both a major bilateral and a highly significant global issue, especially given the Chinese desire to join the WTO and the key role played by the EU in negotiating on that issue. During 2000, the EU, through Pascal Lamy, made intensive efforts to achieve a deal on WTO membership, with the essential proviso that it should be no worse than that achieved by the United States in the previous year (see *Review 1999*). The early part of the year saw both progress and setbacks, but in May a deal was reached which, at that stage, was seen as enabling the Chinese to enter the WTO before the end of 2000. Sticking points during the talks had been EU demands on foreign ownership rights in certain sectors such as telecommunications, and licensing issues especially in financial services. While the deal did not entirely dispose of these problems (for example, licensing of insurance companies caused problems in the later part of the year), it was a considerable achievement. The fact that Chinese entry was then further delayed was not attributable to EU policies alone, since other countries had still to make their bilateral deals, and US–

Chinese relations remained an issue. A range of bilateral disputes continued to characterize EU–China relations more generally, ranging from steel exports to human rights, and with an additional topic in the form of the illegal traffic in persons (particularly stimulated by a number of high-profile cases including the deaths of 58 Chinese in a lorry at Dover).

The year also saw further developments in EU–India relations, following the conclusion of new partnership agreements (see earlier *Reviews*). The first EU–India summit was held in June, and covered a 13-point agenda for co-operation. Effectively, the initiation of this process put India on the same level in EU external policies as Russia, China and Japan, and there were considerable hopes for both economic and political dialogue, despite some tensions over textiles, steel and investment issues.

Other bilateral issues encountered in EU–Asia relations during 2000 were largely a continuation of earlier activities. In respect of Indonesia, the EU withdrew its arms embargo following the establishment of democratic rule during 1999, and committed significant resources to the reconstruction of East Timor. Javier Solana was despatched to the Philippines during May to express EU views on the holding of hostages there. The crises in Fiji and the Solomon Islands also attracted attention, with the Union calling for the restoration of stability and democratic government.

Latin America

As with Asia, EU relations with Latin America contain a mix of inter-regional, bilateral, political and economic issues. It is fair to say that, in 2000, the region occupied rather less of the Union's time than Asia, maybe reflecting its general level of priority as well as the lack of specific crises or negotiating occasions. As usual, a plethora of inter-regional meetings took place early in the year with Latin American groups (the Andean Group, the Rio Group, the San José Group), with the further dimension in 2000 of following up the first inter-regional summit held in Rio de Janeiro during 1999 (see *Review, 1999*). More substantively, negotiations were opened during the spring with the MERCO-SUR group and with Chile on a potential free trade agreement. It was clear that this would be a lengthy negotiation, partly because of problems within MERCOSUR itself caused by economic divergence, and partly because of the need to deal with thorny issues such as agriculture. As a result, the early talks were scheduled to deal with 'non-tariff' items such as intellectual property, anti-dumping and rules of origin.

Bilaterally, the key event of the year was the coming into force of major parts of the EU–Mexico free trade agreement. On 23 March, the EU–Mexico Joint Council adopted a decision to implement most of the agreement from 1 July 2000 and, in September, the Council also adopted an agreement on economic partnership, which entered into force on 1 October. This is likely to be a major influence on the trade and investment decisions of EU companies during the next few years. Elsewhere, bilateral disputes emerged with Chile over discrimination in their drinks taxes and over the handling of swordfish caught by Spanish boats, and with Cuba over the EU's handling of the annual censure vote in the UN on human rights. Fidel Castro was moved to describe the EU Member States as 'a European mafia subordinated to the United States', and also to withdraw Cuba's application to join the African, Caribbean and Pacific grouping within the Lomé/Cotonou framework.

The United States, Japan and other Industrial Countries

If anything, the United States dominated the 'radar screen' of EU external policies during 2000, even more than during recent years. A combination of global negotiations, bilateral disputes, political change and economic fluctuations meant that it was difficult at any point to turn attention away from Washington. At the most general level, the year saw some consolidation of institutional relationships, ranging from Lamy's more cordial relations with the US Trade Representative, Charlene Barshefsky, through more frequent ministerial meetings focusing on political and security issues to the continued and intensified relationships between anti-trust authorities on both sides of the Atlantic. But as the year wore on, this was overshadowed by the approach of the US Presidential election, which meant that Bill Clinton and his administration were increasingly 'lame ducks'. At the end of the year the feeling of transition was underlined by the confusion over the result of the election itself, although there was no marked preference in EU quarters for either George W. Bush, the eventual winner, or Al Gore, the defeated Vice-President.

The institutionalization process was also clouded by a number of broad uncertainties produced by the intersection of developments in the EU and changing US positions. Whereas the EU pursued a revival of the 'millennium trade round' on a broad agenda, the US was more concerned to target the EU in sectoral negotiations in agriculture and services (see above); likewise, the question of China's admission to the WTO saw intersecting interests and a desire to ensure that the EU did not lose out in comparison to the US. While EU firms continued to invest in the US at a record level, this was against a background of a declining euro and a still-strong dollar. Anti-trust collaboration grew, as already noted, but there was a suspicion that a Bush administration would be less inclined to look for an intimate transatlantic exchange of views, or for extensive regulation of big firms. In foreign and security policy, the US continued to support the development of a concrete ESDP, but with two caveats: first, that the EU members should be prepared to pay for substantive capabilities and actions and, second, that ESDP should be conducted in the framework of collaboration within NATO. This latter stipulation was the source of considerable friction not only across the Atlantic (expressed in successive warnings from US Secretary of Defense, William Cohen), but also within the EU, where the French position on 'autonomy' and those of at least some major allies were at odds. At the end of the year also, there was a major crisis in environmental diplomacy, where The Hague Conference dedicated to the implementation of the Kyoto Convention on global warming saw a comprehensive breakdown. In part, this reflected divisions within the EU and elsewhere about the practicability and acceptability of global 'emissions trading' and the use of 'sinks' in the form of forests to absorb hydrocarbon emissions. In part, though, it reflected a fundamental difference of approach between the EU and the US (along with other countries such as Australia), which was likely to become more pronounced under a Bush administration and which might prevent any resuscitation of the negotiations.

As if this were not enough, the year also saw the continuation and, in many cases, the exacerbation of major bilateral disputes between the EU and the US. Bill Clinton and Romano Prodi met in June and pronounced an emphasis on 'telephone diplomacy' rather than 'megaphone diplomacy' on trade and related issues, but this was far from being apparent during the year as a whole. The established disputes over bananas and hormone-treated beef were ratcheted up a notch by the US Congress passing legislation to introduce 'carousel sanctions' on different sets of products every six months (although these were not introduced during the year), and the rejection (by Central American countries as well in the case of bananas) of EU efforts to propose solutions to both cases. The conflict over EU legislation banning aircraft with 'hushkits' from EU airports continued, with the US estimating $2 billion in damages and threatening reference to the International Civil Aviation Organization (ICAO) which might result in EU states losing their voting rights. While there was a deal over thorny issues of data privacy and the acceptability of 'safe harbours' for data in the case of US firms, a number of EU Member States doubted the efficacy of this 'self-regulation', and there were hints of new difficulties over the regulation of e-commerce. And then there were two really big issues, at least potentially. First, in 1999 the WTO had found against the US device of 'foreign sales corporations' (FSCs), and this led the EU to develop plans for $4 billion of sanctions against the US pending Washington's development of revised arrangements (which were only at the last moment passed by the outgoing Congress and signed by Bill Clinton in December). Second, the Airbus dispute reared its head again, in the shape of the launch of the 'A3XX' super-jumbo at the end of the year against a background of US threats to complain to the WTO about subsidies.

Such a brief summary can do scant justice to the richness of EU–US relations during 2000. Compared to this, relations with Japan were almost dormant: the focus at the annual summit in Tokyo and in other fora was on continuing regulatory difficulties in Japan, while the EU developed a form of joint sponsorship with the Japanese for a new and widely-defined global trade round (see above). With Korea, there was a certain amount of tension about the implementation of agreements on shipbuilding signed during June; but the key development was undoubtedly the emergence of 'reconciliation' between North and South Korea, welcomed by the EU. The EU also continued to play its part in the Korean Peninsula Energy Development Organization (KEDO) and set about opening negotiations for its renewal.

Relations with Canada, Australia and New Zealand presented differing pictures. While the links with Australia and New Zealand remained quiet, with the exception of some tensions with Australia over WTO agriculture negoti-ations, those with Canada presented a more interesting picture. The two EU–Canada summits, on 26 June in Lisbon and 19 December in Ottawa, were not simply a reflex of EU–US relations; rather, there could be discerned at least some elements of a distinctive EU–Canada agenda, particularly in the area of conflict prevention, peace-keeping and peace-building. The December sum-mit adopted a four-point plan for co-operation focused on ESDP, justice and home affairs, development assistance and satellite navigation (the latter centred on the Galileo project, a rival to the US-dominated Global Positioning System). Although it would be wrong to overplay these developments, it could be argued that here there is the kernel of a new form of relationship.

Journal of Common Market Studies

Volume 39, Annual Review
September 2001

Enlarging the European Union*

JULIE SMITH

University of Cambridge

Introduction

Considerable progress was made on EU enlargement during 2000. In line with commitments made at the Helsinki summit in December 1999, the Member States held an Intergovernmental Conference to discuss the institutional reforms necessitated by enlargement, and negotiations were opened with six more countries. The Commission presented a 'road map' for progress towards enlargement, which should allow the conclusion of negotiations with the best prepared candidates in the course of 2002, with the prospect of a first group of countries joining the EU by June 2004.

I. Progress in the Negotiations

The so-called 'Helsinki Six' – Bulgaria, Latvia, Lithuania, Malta, Romania, and Slovakia – opened negotiations on 15 February 2000. The intention behind Helsinki was that there should be a 'regatta' approach to the negotiations. In theory any of the 'Helsinki Six' would be able to catch up with some or all of the 'Luxembourg Six' – Cyprus, the Czech Republic, Estonia, Hungary, Poland and Slovenia – which had opened negotiations almost two years earlier.

*The author would like to thank the EU officials and representatives of candidate countries who agreed to be interviewed for this article. Any errors remain her own.

For the purposes of accession negotiations the *acquis communautaire* has been divided into 31 chapters, which are opened and provisionally closed with each candidate individually.[1] There was initially some scepticism about the regatta approach, since each of the Luxembourg Six had already provisionally closed several negotiating chapters before the others had even reached the starting line. In practice, however, the Helsinki Six were able to make relatively faster progress during 2000. This was in part because the negotiations start with the easiest chapters such as small and medium-sized enterprises, external relations and the Common Foreign and Security Policy (CFSP), while the Luxembourg Six were moving on to more difficult chapters.[2] By November 2000, the Commission had received 340 requests for transitional periods in agriculture and 170 requests in other areas. For some of the chapters being opened in 2000 and 2001, including agriculture and the free movement of people, the EU was requesting transitional periods, causing consternation among some of the candidate countries and presaging protracted negotiations in these areas.

By the end of 2000 all the chapters apart from institutions had been opened with the Luxembourg Six. The Czech Republic and Poland had provisionally closed 13 chapters apiece, Hungary and Slovenia 14 each, Estonia 16 and Cyprus 17. Over half the negotiating chapters were opened with the Helsinki Six in 2000. By the end of the year, Malta had already provisionally closed 12 chapters, Slovakia ten, Latvia nine, Bulgaria eight, Lithuania seven and Romania six,[3] with many more chapters due to be opened during the first half of 2001 (Commission, 2000, p. 38). Yet, as the Commission pointed out in its *Strategy Paper*, 'real progress in the negotiations depends more on the quality of preparations made by each candidate than on the number of chapters opened' (Commission, 2000, p. 38).

II. Regular Reports

The Commission's regular reports on the candidate countries published in November 2000 indicated that all the candidate states had made progress towards meeting the Copenhagen criteria. Of the 12 countries already negotiating enlargement, the Commission felt that all continued to meet the political criteria for membership, although some were still struggling to reach the required standards on human rights and minorities (Commission, 2000, p. 17).

[1] Chapters will only be finally closed when the candidates are deemed to have introduced all the necessary arrangements to adopt and implement the *acquis*.
[2] While issues of external relations and CFSP might be difficult for the current Member States to agree on, the existing *acquis* is relatively straightforward.
[3] Details on the number of chapters closed taken from the 'Work Programme for the Swedish Presidency' in *Uniting Europe*, No. 128, 22/01/2001, p. 3.

Whereas there were improvements on the integration of 'non-citizens' in Latvia and Estonia, the situation facing the Roma remained unsatisfactory. While the Commission recognized administrative reforms and strengthening of the judiciary in the candidate countries, it noted that such reforms needed to continue. Corruption continued to be a problem. Romania still had not improved its childcare institutions, one of the conditions laid down when it was allowed to begin accession negotiations.

The economic criteria outlined at Copenhagen fall into two parts: a 'functioning market economy' and the 'capacity to withstand competitive pressure and market forces within the Union'. The two Mediterranean candidates, Cyprus and Malta, were both deemed to fulfil both aspects. The Commission assessment was that the other candidates apart from Bulgaria and Romania had functioning market economies, but to varying degrees needed to continue to work towards becoming sufficiently competitive. Estonia, Hungary and Poland were the front-runners in this respect. Bulgaria had made progress, but did not meet either condition, while Romania was considered to have made unsatisfactory progress (Commission, 2000, pp. 25–6).

As in 1999, Turkey was deemed not to meet either the economic or the political criteria for membership, despite making progress. On a positive note, the government had adopted 'a number of "priority objectives" for reforms and legislation to comply with the Copenhagen political criteria' (Commission, 2000, p. 19). Concern remained about human rights and the treatment of minorities, as well as the role of the army in Turkey's National Security Council, and the Commission did not recommend that Turkey should be allowed to open negotiations. When the EU-15 were producing figures on the weighting of votes and Members of the European Parliament in an enlarged EU, no provision was made for eventual Turkish membership. This was explained in a footnote to the Treaty of Nice and the situation will be rectified once Turkey fulfils the political criteria.

III. *Strategy Paper* and 'Road Map'

Despite significant progress in accession negotiations for the leading candidates in 1999 and 2000, there was an increasing sense of frustration among the candidate states that the EU was unwilling to set a date for enlargement. The front-runners have set themselves the end of 2002 as the date by which they intend to be ready to join the EU. The Helsinki summit pledged that the EU would make the necessary reforms to be 'ready to welcome' the leading candidates by the end of 2002. However, no timetable was given at that stage.

In October 2000, the European Parliament called for the first new Members to join in time to participate in the next European elections, due in June 2004 (European Parliament, 2000). The Commission picked up on this date and the commitments made in Helsinki. In its November 2000 *Strategy Paper*, approved by the Heads of State and Government in December 2000, the Commission outlined a 'road map' for completing negotiations. The twin aims were to fix a timetable for the definition of 'common positions' to be presented to the candidates, and to facilitate the negotiations by creating the possibility of setting aside chapters where there were only a limited number of issues outstanding that could be settled at a later date. The 'road map' also respected the principle of 'differentiation' whereby countries' progress in the negotiations is entirely dependent on their individual preparedness for membership.

The 'road map' gives guidelines for when the candidates should expect to have clear positions from the EU that would permit them provisionally to close (or in the case of the Helsinki Six open and provisionally close) particular chapters. The timetable envisages dealing with most of the chapters by the end of 2001, with the exception of the institutional chapter and those with 'significant budgetary implications', which should be dealt with in the first half of 2002, permitting negotiations with candidates that fulfil all the membership criteria to be concluded by the end of 2002. Since the timetable will be determined by how much progress each candidate has made individually, the question of how many states will enter in the first wave was postponed. Speculation inevitably continued as some predicted a large accession of up to ten countries (all those currently negotiating membership except Bulgaria and Romania), while others suggested that there should be a small enlargement to include well-prepared countries such as Hungary, Slovenia and Estonia. Such a scenario seems a little implausible, perhaps, given the political commitment of Germany to Poland. Moreover, the absence of a political agreement between North and South Cyprus left a continuing question mark over Cyprus's accession to the EU, and over enlargement more generally.

IV. Conclusions

The candidates and the EU-15 all made significant progress towards enlargement in 2000. The conclusion of the IGC with the Treaty of Nice, despite its obvious imperfections, was also a clear indication that the EU was committed to enlargement. By reiterating the European Parliament's hope that the first accessions would take place by 2004, the Nice summit gave a target date for enlargement, offering candidates an incentive to continue with their reforms. Nevertheless, a lot remained to be done, and there was a risk of slippage in the timetable outlined in the 'road map' in the course of 2001 and 2002. The key point remained, however, that for the first time a target date had been set for enlargement. How many countries would be able to accede by that date remained an open question, but one which it was largely up to the candidates themselves to answer by continuing the reform process.

References

Commission of the European Communities (2000) Enlargement Strategy Paper, 8 November. Web version available at «http://www.europa.ue.int/comm/enlargement/report_11_00/index.htm».

European Parliament (2000) Resolution on Enlargement of the European Union, A5-0205/2000 4 October.

Journal of Common Market Studies
Volume 39, Annual Review
September 2001

Justice and Home Affairs

JÖRG MONAR
University of Leicester

Introduction

In justice and home affairs, the year 2000 can be characterized as one of implementation. Not only had the institutions to continue with the implementation of the objectives set by the Treaty of Amsterdam, but also with that of the ambitious agenda set by the Tampere European Council of October 1999. The European Commission played a much more active role in justice and home affairs than in the previous years, but there were also an increasing number of significant initiatives – of varying quality – from Member States. Substantial progress was achieved in the area of judicial co-operation and – especially with the establishment of Eurojust – in the fight against organized crime. However, in some other priority areas – such as asylum policy – there were more new proposals than new measures. Some new ground was covered in the development of the external relations side of the 'Area of freedom, security and justice' (AFSJ). Monitoring progress in matters within the AFSJ was extended through the introduction by the Commission of a 'scoreboard' mechanism. The existing monitoring process on justice and home affairs issues in the candidate countries provided a clearer picture of problems of enlargement in this area.

I. Developments in Individual Policy Areas

Asylum, Immigration and Visa Policy

The creation of a common asylum system had been among the primary objectives set by the Tampere European Council for the development of the AFSJ. This requires a comprehensive approach including not only minimum standards on procedures and conditions of reception, but also action regarding the legal status of refugees, burden-sharing in crisis situations and the improvement of the functioning of the Dublin Convention. After lengthy consultations, the Commission, which continued to struggle with a lack of in-house expertise on some of the issues, came up with a range of proposals. On 24 May, the Commission presented a proposal for a directive on minimum standards for giving temporary protection in the event of mass influx of displaced persons (*COM*(2000) 303). This contained a 'package' of definition in line with the Amsterdam Treaty objectives and minimum standards for temporary protection (including a maximum period of two years) aimed at promoting a balance between the efforts made by Member States, especially through the use of the new European Refugee Fund (see below). On 20 September, the Commission adopted a proposal for a directive on common minimum standards on procedures for granting or withdrawing refugee status. This aimed, *inter alia*, at defining common requirements for inadmissible and manifestly unfounded cases, and common standards on procedural safeguards, reducing the duration of asylum procedures and providing special safeguards for the situation of children (*COM*(2000) 578). The proposal took into account some of the requests formulated by the European Parliament in its resolution of 15 June on the protection of vulnerable groups and harmonization of minimum standards.

On 22 November, the Commission then adopted a communication on a common asylum procedure and a uniform status throughout the EU for persons granted asylum (*COM*(2000) 755). Here, it advocated the adoption of a single 'one-stop-shop' type of procedure aimed at centralizing the examination of all protection needs in a single place in order both to ensure that no form of persecution or risk is ignored and to reduce the time taken to examine a request. The Communication also developed a range of ideas and policy options on the status of asylum-seekers, which included the issues of freedom of movement, conditions of residence and integration. The Commission's ideas touched on core elements of the national asylum systems and generated considerable debate in the Council bodies. In its meeting of 30 November–1 December, the Justice and Home Affairs Council adopted 'Conclusions' on the definition of common minimum conditions for the reception of asylum-seekers, which are intended to serve as guidelines for a Commission directive in the following year. These were adopted on the basis of a French Presidency document and are based on a more restrictive line on minimum guarantees and a lower degree of harmonization than the Commission had aimed at. The outcome indicated that there were still major cleavages among the Member States on the scope of the directive, limitations on the asylum-seekers' freedom of movement and access to employment.

It was also only after protracted negotiations that a substantial step forward was taken on the issue of burden-sharing, with the adoption on 28 September of a decision of the Council on the establishment of a European Refugee Fund (*OJ* L 252 of 6.10.2000). The total financial volume of the fund will be €216 million for the period 2000–04. The funds will be distributed in two ways: fixed equal amounts for each Member State on a degressive scale from €500,000 in the year 2000 to €100,000 in 2004 (totalling €22.5 million); and the remainder proportionally to the total number of refugees which have entered each Member State during the last three years with special mechanisms applying in emergency situations. Negotiations were overshadowed by a sometimes undignified haggling over the distribution of resources. The political compromise that resulted allows negotiations to continue during the period of implementation with the aim of arriving at a 'fair' distribution by 2003 (Council Document No. 11705/00). Projects will be funded on a 50:50 basis (with 25:75 for 'Cohesion Fund' countries) and should focus on conditions of reception, measures of integration and repatriation.

Problems with implementing the mechanisms and applying the criteria for determining which state is responsible for examining an asylum application have undermined the effectiveness of the Dublin Convention. In June 2000, the Commission sent out a questionnaire to the Member States in order to assess the problems. The results are intended to serve as a basis for a new regulation to be adopted in 2001. Despite these problems, the Dublin Convention was strengthened by the adoption on 11 December of the regulation establishing the Eurodac system for the comparison of the fingerprints of asylum applicants and certain other third-country nationals. However, throughout the decision-making process, Eurodac attracted considerable criticism from human rights groups and from within the European Parliament.

On the immigration policy side, the terrible death of 58 Chinese immigrants in a lorry during the crossing from Calais to Dover in June highlighted the need for further EU action in the fight against illegal immigration networks. In this area, the main initiatives came from Member States. On 4 September, France submitted a draft directive and framework decision on defining and strengthening penal laws on the facilitation of unauthorized entry and residence (*OJ* C 253 of 4.9.2000) and, on 20 September, proposed an initiative for a directive concerning the harmonization of financial penalties imposed on carriers transporting third-country nationals lacking necessary admission documents into the EU (OJ C 269 of 20.9.2000). Disagreements over the financial penalties and over the treatment of cases in which a person carried submits an asylum application prevented the Council from reaching a compromise before the end of the year. The Commission added to these initiatives on 21 December with two proposals for framework decisions on trafficking in human beings and the exploitation of children (*COM*(2000) 854). The first includes proposals regarding penalties which should apply to organized crime linked with trafficking of human beings, the second aims at eliminating safe havens for child sex offenders suspected of having committed an offence in another country and also addressing the issue of child pornography on the internet.

Throughout the year, work continued in the context of the CIREFI (Centre d'Information, de Recherche et d'Echanges en matière de franchissement des frontières et d'immigration) on improving action against illegal immigration through the exploration of progress towards common standards and the pooling of resources for investigations into illegal immigration networks. CIREFI submitted a number of practical recommendations on improving co-operation between national authorities, including the further development of the early warning system, and on a better integration of other bodies, such as Europol, the Working Party on Schengen Evaluation and the Chief Police Officers' Task Force, in the common efforts against illegal immigration. These recommendations were endorsed by the Council in December.

Progress on assisting countries of origin and transit remained very limited. In a resolution of 30 March, the European Parliament demanded the establishment of a new budgetary instrument for this purpose on which the Commission promised an initiative only for the next year. On 13 June, however, the Council approved an Action Plan of the High-level Working Group on Asylum and Migration on Albania and the neighbouring region and endorsed a number of implementing measures of the action plans for Afghanistan, Iraq, Morocco, Somalia and Sri Lanka (Council Document No. 8939/00). These action plans were criticized sharply by the European Parliament because of what it regarded as an imbalance between the provisions on punitive action and those concerning integration and the absence of an adequate distinction between immigration and asylum issues (*Bull. EU* 3-2000, 1.4.3). The Parliament had not been consulted in advance on the action plans, nor had it any power to force the Council to introduce changes.

Special attention was again paid to readmission agreements as an instrument for managing migration flows. On 18 September, the Council adopted negotiating mandates for the Commission to negotiate readmission agreements between the Community and Morocco, Pakistan, Russia and Sri Lanka. With this move, the EU took a further step in the generalization of readmission agreements in relations with third countries. The French government tried to strengthen the internal side of the expanding readmission system with the submission on 20 July of a draft directive on mutual recognition of decisions on the expulsion of third-country nationals (*OJ* C 243 of 24.8.2000) aimed at increasing effectiveness in the enforcement of expulsion decisions and better co-operation between Member States in the mutual recognition of such decisions.

While these measures focused primarily on restricting migratory flows, the EU also took substantial action on improving the integration of third-country nationals once inside the Union. On 29 June, the Council adopted a directive on the implementation of the principle of equal treatment between persons irrespective of race or ethnic origin (*OJ* L 180 of 19.7.2000) and, on 17 October, a directive on the establishment of a general framework for equal treatment in employment and occupation (*OJ* L 303 of 2.12.2000). Both are relevant to legally resident immigrants from third countries. In November, on the basis of a Commission proposal, the Council also reached agreement on a Community Action Programme for the years 2001–06 on identifying and spreading best practices in enhancing non-discrimination and fighting racism and xenophobia. In this context, the European Monitoring Centre for Racism and Xenophobia, which was officially opened in Vienna on 7 April, will also have to play an important role. However, improving the status of legal immigrants remains of primary importance. At its meeting of 30 November/ 1 December (Council Document No. 13865/00), the Council identified key points for the negotiations on a future directive on minimum uniform rights to be granted to legally resident third-country nationals. These include access conditions to the status (such as length of presence), the elements of substance of the status (such as economic and social rights), and the need for collateral policies (such as on integration and the fight against discrimination).

There were further signs during the year that Member States might be moving towards a reconsideration of what has so far been a primarily negative attitude towards immigration. Germany, for instance, went through a major public debate on the need to issue 'green cards' to IT specialists in order to compensate for shortages in the German labour market, which risked damaging German industry. In this climate, the Commission adopted in November a communication on a European migration policy (*COM*(2000) 757), which suggested a 'new approach' to immigration with a more flexible and proactive immigration policy. The Commission emphasized that channels for immigration for economic purposes are needed to meet urgent needs for both skilled and unskilled workers, and developed the view that a more open and transparent policy on migration movements with a more effective co-ordination of national policies could help to reduce illegal immigration, irregular work and the economic exploitation of migrants, which is also fuelling unfair competition. The Commission put forward a range of ideas on periodic assessments of appropriate immigration levels by the Member States, the definition of a common legal framework for admission, action on the integration of third-country nationals and the monitoring of migration flows.

Of some importance for both asylum and immigration policy was the breakthrough achieved in the Council of 30 November–1 December on the contents of the regulation listing the third countries whose nationals must be in possession of visas when crossing the external borders of the EU ('black list') and those whose nationals are exempt from the visa requirement ('white list'). The two most controversial issues were the inclusion of Bulgaria and Romania on the 'white list', countries which are seen by several Member States as major countries of origin and transit for illegal immigration. Yet the special status of these countries as accession candidates, and the problems which a 'blacklisting' of Romania (with its substantial ethnic Hungarian minority) would cause Hungary led in the end to their inclusion on the 'white list'. In Romania's case, however, lifting the visa requirement was to be decided subsequently, before the end of June 2001, on the basis of a report by the Commission on Romanian undertakings as regards action against illegal immigration and repatriation (Council Document No. 13865/00).

Judicial Co-operation in Civil and Criminal Matters and the 'European Area of Justice'

The creation of a genuine 'European area of justice' is another flagship project (re-)launched by the Tampere European Council. The most substantial elements of progress were achieved in the more traditional domains of judicial co-operation. The communitarization of former intergovernmental instruments took an important step forward on 29 May with the adoption by the Council of three regulations (EC Nos 1346/2000, 1347/2000 and 1348/2000), which respectively replaced the Convention on Insolvency Proceedings, the Convention on Jurisdiction and the Recognition and Enforcement of Judgments in Matrimonial Matters and in Matters of Parental Responsibility for Joint Children, and the Convention on the Service in the Member States of Judicial and Extrajudicial Documents. This was followed on 22 December by the transformation of the 1968 Brussels Convention on Jurisdiction and the Recognition and Enforcement of Judgments in Civil and Commercial Matters into a Community Regulation (*OJ* L 12 of 16.1.2000). Invoking its 'opt-out' secured in the protocol annexed to the Treaty of Amsterdam, Denmark did not participate in the adoption of the regulation, but it expressed an interest in the conclusion of an agreement allowing it to apply the rules laid down in the regulation – a further example of 'flexibility' related complexity.

The moves towards communitarization of major mutual recognition instruments were in line with the emphasis placed by the Tampere European Council on making mutual recognition the keystone for the further development of the 'area of justice'. On 30 November, the Council adopted – on the basis of a Commission proposal – an action programme of measures on mutual recognition of civil and commercial decisions which defines a number of priority fields for both mutual recognition and enforcement. These include both fields already covered by existing agreements – such as maintenance claims and litigation on small claims – and fields not yet covered by existing agreements – such as the property consequences of the separation of unmarried couples and succession (Council Document No. 13865/00). In this area as well, Member States made use of their right of initiative. On 22 June, France submitted an initiative on the mutual enforcement of decisions on the rights of access to children and, on 26 September, Germany put forward one on co-operation in the taking of evidence in civil and commercial matters.

In the field of criminal law, as well, the principle of mutual recognition was forwarded in a range of new initiatives. On 26 July, the Commission adopted a communication on the mutual recognition of final decisions in criminal matters (*COM*(2000) 495) which provided the basis for a programme of measures adopted by the Council on 1 December. These include action regarding the enforcement of pre-trial orders, the definition of common minimum standards to facilitate the application of mutual recognition (as regards the competence of courts, for instance), and the determination of grounds (and their extent) for refusing recognition. On some issues, however, there were still serious differences among the Member States, such as the question of whether mutual recognition should be generalized or limited to specific offences, or on whether fulfilment of the double criminality requirement as a condition for recognition is maintained or dropped. Co-operation between Member States in criminal law matters was strengthened by the adoption on 29 May of the Convention on Mutual Assistance in Criminal Matters (*OJ* C 197 of 12.7.2000). It supplements the 1959 European Convention on Mutual Assistance and the Schengen Implementing Convention and contains detailed provisions on assistance also in respect of sensitive areas such as the interception of telecommunications and data protection. The Convention includes important rules on specific forms of co-operation, such as temporary transfer of persons, hearing by video and telephone conferencing, cross-border controlled deliveries and covert investigations.

In spite of the strong emphasis placed on mutual recognition, harmonization was not left off the agenda entirely. Member governments, indeed, were especially active with initiatives with strong harmonizing elements. On 11 February, Denmark submitted an important initiative for a framework decision on combatting serious environmental crime (*OJ* C 39 of 11.2.2000), which provides for minimum rules on the elements constituting criminal infringements and applicable sanctions. On 4 September, Germany submitted a draft framework decision on criminal law protection against fraudulent or anticompetitive conduct in relation to the award of public contracts in the common market (*OJ* C 253 of 4.9.2000).

One of the central themes of the 'area of justice' project is better access to justice. On 9 February, the Commission presented a Green Paper on legal aid (*COM*(2000) 51) which highlighted the many practical – and all too often costly – problems encountered by EU citizens in cases of cross-border litigation. In the paper, the Commission proposed a range of measures in areas such as the conditions of eligibility for financial aid, effective access to an appropriately qualified lawyer and the production and distribution of information on cross-border access to justice issues. Initial discussions in the Council suggested that differences between national legal aid systems and financial implications will make it difficult for the Commission to get a substantial directive approved by 2001. In September, the Commission also sent a questionnaire on small claims to the Member States in preparation for a broader consultation process and a later legislative initiative aimed at common procedural rules for small civil and commercial claims, uncontested claims and maintenance claims which should increase transparency in cross-border litigation. On 22 September, it also adopted a draft decision on the establishment of a European judicial network in civil and commercial matters (*COM*(2000) 592) which – partly modelled on the existing European judicial network in criminal matters – is intended to improve judicial co-operation between Member States. It should also provide information on a permanent basis to citizens and companies on access to justice in cross-border litigation.

Another key aspect of the 'area of justice project' is the question of victims' rights. On 20 July, Portugal, building on a Commission communication of 14 July 1999, submitted a draft framework decision on the standing of the victim in the criminal procedure (*OJ* C 243 of 24.8.2000). This is aimed at establishing minimum rules on victims' rights as regards receiving information, access to interpreting facilities, participation in the procedure, protection of personal safety and private life, compensation and the work of victim support groups. In a resolution of 15 June, the European Parliament had also declared itself in favour of substantial EU action in this area.

The Fight against Crime and 'Eurojust'

The EU continued its move towards a more integrated approach towards the fight against crime. The measures in the area of co-operation on criminal law matters (in particular, the Convention on Mutual Assistance in Criminal

Matters) outlined above are seen as one important element of this approach. The Commission tried to open the way to a further broadening of the EU's strategy with its communication on crime prevention of 29 November (*COM*(2000) 786). The Commission argued in favour of comprehensive action based on complementarity between the enforcement side – on which the EU has taken some action – and the prevention side – on which EU action has been extremely limited so far. It also suggested increasing the action on the prevention side in a number of other EU policy areas. These included: social policy, where measures against social exclusion should take crime prevention objectives into account; regional policy, where EC funding should be used for projects contributing to crime prevention; and economic and financial regulation, where the Commission suggested measures aimed, *inter alia*, at more transparency in public procurement and better surveillance of cross-border movements of cash and sensitive goods. The Commission also proposed a draft Council decision establishing a programme of incentives, exchanges, training and co-operation for the prevention of crime (Hippocrates). Although Member States broadly agree on the need for more action on crime prevention, the development of a substantial EU strategy in this area has to struggle with major differences in national strategies, and concerns over subsidiarity and budgetary questions. It should be added that any reorientation of measures in other policy areas – as the 'mainstreaming' of environmental objectives has shown – tends to be a complex and lengthy process.

Some significant progress on the strategy side was achieved, however, in the area of the fight against organized crime. On 27 March, the Council adopted an action programme on 'The prevention and control of organized crime: a European Union strategy for the beginning of the new millennium' (*OJ* 124 of 3.5.2000). This so-called 'Millennium Strategy' replaced the action programme adopted by the Amsterdam European Council in 1997 and takes into account experiences with the implementation of its predecessor. The 'Millennium Strategy' reconfirms most of the existing objectives but also provides a number of detailed new recommendations. These relate, in particular, to preventing the penetration of organized crime in the public and legitimate private sector, additional regulatory action on specific forms of crime (such as computer and financial crime), the improvement of mutual evaluation mechanisms, the strengthening of co-operation on investigative techniques and of the role of Europol, and additional measures on the tracing and seizure of the proceeds of crime and judicial co-operation in criminal matters. The proposed measures make the strategy a comprehensive and multidisciplinary one. However, the tone on some of the more sensitive aspects is hesitant and even evasive. For instance, the strategy only provides that the ongoing work of Europol in the co-ordination of international investigations between the competent authorities and its participation, in a support capacity, in operational actions of joint teams, 'should be continued' without setting any clear objectives. In a resolution adopted on 21 September, the European Parliament criticized both the fact that it had not been consulted on the strategy and the absence of clearer priorities, and suggested further legislative action on the prevention side (*Bull. EU* 9-2000, 1.4.16).

As regards police co-operation, a step forward was taken by the first two meetings of the European Chiefs of Police in April and September at which issues of co-ordination, operational co-operation, best practice identification and training were discussed. Negotiations in the Council on the setting up of the European Police College, one of the projects launched by the Tampere European Council, were (as so often) complicated by differences over its location, programme and status. On 22 December, the Council, on the basis of a Portuguese proposal, adopted a decision establishing the European Police College (for which the official acronym 'CEPOL' was introduced) initially as a network of existing training institutes, leaving the way open towards the establishment of a permanent institution at a later stage (OJ L 336 of 30.12.2000). This means that for a period of at least three years the training courses for senior law enforcement officers, on which the governing board has to decide, will be organized by and at existing national training institutes on what is likely to be some sort of rotating basis. A first course, prefiguring CEPOL's work, was inaugurated in Lyon in November. The primary purposes of the courses will be to increase knowledge of the different national police systems and structures of other Member States, of Europol and cross-border police co-operation, to strengthen the knowledge of international policing instruments and methods and to provide training with regard to the respect of democratic safeguards. The Council decision emphasized the need for CEPOL to develop quickly a relationship with national training institutes in the candidate countries which could, indeed, be a helpful instrument in preparing their police forces for effective participation in EU police co-operation.

The strengthening of Europol as envisaged both by the Treaty of Amsterdam and the Tampere Conclusions made only moderate progress. There was no agreement, for example, on the basis on which Europol could address requests to Member States regarding the conduct and the co-ordination of their investigations in specific areas, so that the Council could only adopt a 'recommendation' on 28 September, calling upon Member States to give 'due consideration' to such requests and 'in principle' to inform Europol about the results of such investigations (*OJ* C 289 of 12.11.2000). Recommendations were also adopted on Europol's assistance to joint investigative teams created by the Member States but an appropriate legal decision has not even been proposed. On 1 December, the Council extended – on the basis of Art. 43(1) of the Europol Convention – the police office's mandate to cover money-laundering, irrespective of the offence from which the proceeds originate (Council Document No. 13865/00).

The Tampere European Council had decided on the creation of a new unit, Eurojust, with the task of facilitating the proper co-ordination of national prosecution authorities and of supporting criminal investigation in organized crime cases. Council delegations, however, varied widely on the notions and concepts that might govern the tasks and powers Eurojust should have. With their focus on a more extensive and active role of the new unit, the discussions in the Council mirrored to some extent those on the role of Europol in the 1990s. After some inconclusive exploratory negotiations, Germany, which had also played a key role in bringing the Eurojust project on the Tampere agenda, submitted a first formal initiative on the composition and tasks of the unit on 19 June (Council Document No. 8938/00). This was followed by a highly innovative procedure, a joint initiative of the 'four Presidencies' (i.e. the current French one plus the preceding Portuguese and the two succeeding Swedish and Belgian), which was submitted on 20 July (Council Document No. 10356/00). There were significant differences between the two texts: the German initiative aimed at avoiding further delays in the setting up of the unit by proposing a very light structure with liaison officers from the Member States. These officers would serve primarily as information exchange agents, providing investigating authorities of other Member States as well as Council, Commission and Europol with information on the relevant substantial and procedural law of their own countries, details regarding specific investigations and judgments in criminal matters and appropriate contact points. The German proposal contained only a rather vague reference to operational actions by the liaison officers in the form of providing support for the co-ordination and conduct of joint investigations. The 'four Presidencies' initiative, however, not only gave the central role to the institution as such rather than to the liaison officers, but also went much further on operational actions, specifying a number of 'powers' that Eurojust should have – such as the possibility of asking a Member State to undertake an investigation or to prosecute specific acts. It also gave Eurojust an assessment function as regards co-operation between the Member States with the possibility of asking Member States' authorities to engage in specific co-ordinating actions. Despite these quite considerable differences, the 'four Presidencies' draft suggested a possible bridge in that it proposed a two-stage approach, with a lighter provisional unit at the first stage and a fully fledged Eurojust with its own tasks, a legal personality and an appropriate infrastructure to follow at the second stage. This two-stage approach was endorsed by the European Commission on 22 November (*COM*(2000) 746), which came out clearly in favour of Eurojust being more than just a documentation and information centre. It also suggested various ways in which it should become actively involved in cross-border criminal investigations.

In the end, a compromise was achieved on the basis of the two-stage approach. On 14 December, the Council adopted a decision setting up a 'Provisional Judicial Co-operation Unit' (*OJ* L 324 of 21.12.2000) consisting of one prosecutor, judge or police officer from each of the Member States in the context of a light structure corresponding to the German proposal. Yet the description of the objectives and tasks, which includes 'stimulati[ing] and improv[ing] the coordination of investigations and prosecution in the Member States' and 'provid[ing] support for the coordination and operation of joint investigative teams', provides for a more active role of its members and the door has clearly been left open for a unit with a role, tasks and legal personality of its own. The Council decision provides for a final decision on the establishment of Eurojust to be taken before the end of 2001. Until then quite a few other difficult issues will need to be considered – apart from tasks and status – such as Eurojust's relationship with Europol, the existing European Judicial Network and the Commission. Europol, itself, favours locating Eurojust close to its own headquarters in The Hague if only for the sake of better practical co-operation, but the provisional unit will, at least for the time being, be located in the Council premises in Brussels.

Various steps were also taken in the fight against specific forms of crime. Against a background of concern over the adequate protection of the single currency against counterfeiting by sophisticated organized crime groups, on 29 May the Council adopted a framework decision on penal sanctions against counterfeiting in connection with the euro which goes beyond the outdated 1929 Convention for the Suppression of Counterfeiting Currency and provides, in particular, that fraudulent making or altering of the euro shall be punishable by prison sentences of no less than eight years (*OJ* L 140 of 14.6.2000). On the same day, the Council reached provisional agreement on a framework decision on the criminalization of fraud and counterfeiting of non-cash payment means (Council Document No. 8832/00). The same Council session also saw the adoption, on the basis of an Austrian initiative, of a decision on measures combatting the production, processing, distribution and possession of child pornography material on the internet (*OJ* L 138 of 9.6.2000). In the area of the fight against drugs, the Feira European Council in June approved the new Action Plan to combat drugs for the years 2000–04, which is based largely on the proposals which the Commission had submitted in May 1999 (see *Annual Review* 1999/2000, pp. 130–1).

The fight against the various forms of cross-border crime and, in particular, organized crime action against money laundering continued to be a priority area. In September, the Council reached an 'in principle' agreement on a French initiative for a framework decision on money laundering, identification, freezing, seizing and confiscation of instrumentalities and the proceeds of crime (*OJ* C 243 of 24.8.2000) This provides for a toughening of penalties, additional rules on value confiscation and the identification of suspected proceeds, as well as improvements in mutual assistance. However, both this text and the revised draft directive on money laundering, which went through its first reading in the Council in September, encountered substantial criticism from the European Parliament which proposed a range of amendments.

II. External Relations

In many areas of justice and home affairs, the efficiency of internal EU action is to a considerable extent also dependent on adequate parallel action in co-operation with third countries. Following a request by the Tampere European Council to draw up specific recommendations on policy objectives and measures for the Union's external action in justice and home affairs, the Council, in co-operation with the Commission, prepared a report on 'European Union priorities' (Council Document No. 7653/00), which was approved by the Feira European Council on 13 June. The report emphasized the worldwide challenges facing the Union in areas such as restoring the rule of law, controlling migratory movements and combatting organized crime, and advocated a more proactive and global approach to the external relations of the AFSJ. A range of priority areas were identified. These included areas directly linked with internal justice and home affairs objectives, such as readmission agreements and other aspects of the external dimension of migration policy, the fight against specific forms of international crime in the context of the Council of Europe, the OECD and the G8, and external action in the fight against drug-trafficking. But they also included possible contributions by the Union in matters of justice and home affairs in the Stability Pact in the Balkans, the Barcelona Process, Common CFSP Strategies (such as on Russia and the Ukraine) and non-military aspects of crisis management. The extensive flagging up of external justice and home affairs action in relation to foreign and security policy objectives was one of the most innovative elements of the report. It parallels a growing tendency in other military security fora, such as the WEU and NATO, to regard ('soft') internal security aspects as an important part of the overall security policy picture. The Council's report also identified a range of primary partners for external action in justice and home affairs. These included both major bilateral and multilateral dialogue or treaty partners – such as the transatlantic partners and the countries of the Lomé (now Cotonou) group – and international organizations and fora, specifically mentioning those involved in the preparation of relevant political guidelines and legal acts – such as the UN and Council of Europe – and those that focus on practical co-operation – such as the UNHCR and the Budapest Group. On the use of instruments, the report recommended, *inter alia*, an increased formalization of EU external interests in justice and home affairs in the form of 'common positions' for matters under Title VI TEU, and the use of EC negotiation instruments for matters under Title IV TEC. It also suggested a greater involvement of diplomatic and consular missions and Commission delegations in third countries and the possible creation of 'flexible financial instruments' – always difficult under EC budgetary rules – to implement specific co-operation objectives.

In addition to this clearly important document on strategy, some concrete progress was also achieved in several areas of external relations. Of particular significance in this context was the signing of the UN Convention Against Transnational Organized Crime and its annexed protocols on combatting trafficking in persons, especially women and children, and the smuggling of migrants by land, air and sea, by the Community and the Member States in Palermo on 12 December. This package of agreements commits signatories to the abolition of bank secrecy and numbered bank accounts if related to criminal activity, the confiscation of goods of illegal origin, measures on the facilitation of extradition, mutual legal assistance, transfer of proceedings, the shielding of legal markets against infiltration by organized crime, the protection of witnesses and against the commercialization of illegal immigration and the sexual exploitation of women and children (see *COM*(2000) 760 and UN document no. A/55/383). Although co-ordinating the EU's position had proved difficult over the two years of negotiation, the Union was in end able effectively to bring some of the key principles and concepts of its internal action into the 'Palermo Convention'. It can therefore be seen as a successful example of a closely co-ordinated external EU justice and home affairs action on the international level.

On the external front of the fight against crime, Russian organized crime is seen as particularly dangerous threat because of its extraordinary growth during the last few years, its aggressive methods and its penetration into central and eastern Europe. On 27 March, the Council adopted an EU Action Plan on a common action for the Russian Federation on combatting organized crime (*OJ* C 106 of 13.4.2000) which is aimed at a significant upgrading of co-operation between the EU and Russia in judicial and law-enforcement matters. It envisages the development of suitable legal instruments, the exchange of technical and strategic information, the development of co-operation between Russian authorities and Europol, and assistance from the EU with the reform of relevant judicial procedures and training measures. The Action Plan takes up some elements of the 1998 Pre-accession Pact on Organized Crime with the current candidate countries but the Union has, quite obviously, much less leverage to bring about corresponding internal action in Russia. Following the entry into force of the agreements with Iceland and Norway on the Schengen *acquis* in June (*OJ* L 149 of 23.6.2000), the association of the two countries made further progress on 28 November with the initialling of an agreement extending the criteria and mechanisms of the Dublin Convention. On 28 September, the Council adopted a decision on the conclusion of an agreement between the Community and Norway on the latter's participation in the work of the European Monitoring Centre for Drugs and Drug Addiction (EMCDDA) in Lisbon (*OJ* L 257 of 11.10.2000). On 1 December, the Council finally took the decision on the application of the Schengen *acquis* to the five 'Nordic' countries (*OJ* L 309 of 9.12.2000), which opened the way towards the inclusion of Norway and Iceland in the operational parts of the Schengen system by March 2001.

III. Monitoring of Progress: Current and Future Member States

The introduction of an increasing number of monitoring mechanisms destined to identify weaknesses, possibilities for improvement and the identification of potentially transferable 'best practices' has been a constant feature of the development of EU justice and home affairs. The Schengen 'collective evaluation' mechanism and EU mutual evaluation system regarding the application and implementation at national level of international undertakings in the fight against organized crime (started in 1999) are among the most notable examples. Following the request by the Tampere European Council, the Commission introduced on 24 March a more political monitoring mechanism, the 'scoreboard', to keep progress on the creation of the AFSJ under constant review (*COM*(2000) 167). The scoreboard will measure action taken by the institutions against the targets set by the Treaty on European Union and the Tampere and Vienna Action Plan guidelines on a bi-annual basis. According to the Commission, it will be more than a purely mechanical indicator and should help to ensure an adequate degree of transparency in the AFSJ project, as well as keeping up the momentum generated by the Tampere European Council and exercising pressure on any identified areas of delay so that those responsible can 'rediscover the political commitment' repeatedly expressed by the European Council. The launch of scoreboard, of which the first issue appeared in March and the second in November, can be taken as an indication of concern within the Commission (and in some capitals) that inertia and hostility towards change, especially among the legal establishments within national administrations, could considerably slow down progress with the build-up of the AFSJ. The use of such a monitoring instrument is not new; it had already been used in the context of the single market programme. But it is an innovation in justice and home affairs and it remains to be seen how much of a political 'incentive' it will turn out to be. Some progress was achieved, however, on the occasion of the bilateral meeting of the subcommittee set up to examine joint efforts in the fight against illegal activities on 5–6 October in Moscow.

As the justice and home affairs chapters were opened during 2000 in the accession negotiations with six of the candidates (Cyprus, Czech Republic, Estonia, Hungary, Poland and Slovenia), both the Member States and the Commission increased their monitoring efforts on the progress made by the applicant countries in justice and home affairs. Whereas the Commission's regular progress reports were, as usual, limited to the broad lines of progress and persisting deficits, the – confidential – reports of the Council's 'Collective Evaluation Group' (set up in 1998) reached a significantly more systematic and sophisticated stage than in the previous year. These reports highlighted a range of problems in many of the candidate countries in sensitive areas such as border control security, the fight against organized crime and illegal immigration, corruption and shortages of data-processing and modern search equipment. The reports included the first on the 'Helsinki group' of candidates, in September on Romania and in December on Bulgaria, Latvia, Lithuania and Slovakia. They indicated a very uneven development of candidates' capability to implement the EU/Schengen and reinforced the impression in most of the Schengen capitals that some 'first wave' countries would be unlikely to be able fully to implement the Schengen *acquis* on accession. This makes it more and more likely that – as in the case of the long delay in Italy's and Greece's full accession to the operational parts of the Schengen system – current Schengen external border controls will remain in place towards the new members from central and eastern European countries for potentially several years beyond the date of accession – a politically sensitive point for the new members. An adequate preparation of the candidates for the rapidly developing and demanding EU/Schengen *acquis* remains a major challenge for both the Union and the candidates. Some new ground was covered during the year with the possibility of candidate countries sending liaison officers to Europol and the adoption of a Council regulation (*OJ* L 253 of 7.10.2000) enabling the EMCDDA to transfer its know-how to applicant countries, but more action and new financial instruments will clearly be needed.

References

Commission of the European Communities (2000) 'Communication ... on a Community immigration policy'. *COM*(2000) 757.

Commission of the European Communities (2000) 'Proposal ... on minimum standards for giving temporary protection in the event of a mass influx of displaced persons'. *COM*(2000) 303.

Commission of the European Communities (2000) 'Communication ... The prevention of crime in the European Union. Reflection on common guidelines and proposals for Community financial support'. *COM*(2000) 786.

Commission of the European Communities (2000) 'Scoreboard to review progress on the creation of an "Area of freedom, security and justice" in the European Union'. *COM*(2000) 167.

Commission of the European Communities (2000) 'Communication ... Towards a common asylum procedure and a uniform status, valid throughout the Union, for persons granted asylum'. *COM*(2000) 755.

Council of the European Union (2000) 'Council Decision ... establishing a European Police College (CEPOL)'. *OJ* L 336, 30 December.

Council of the European Union (2000) 'Council Decision ... establishing a European Refugee Fund'. *OJ* L 252, 6 October.

Council of the European Union (2000) 'European Union priorities and policy objectives for external relations in the fields of justice and home affairs'. Council Document No. 7653/00.

Council of the European Union (2000) 'The prevention and control of organized crime: A European Union strategy for the beginning of the new millennium.' *OJ* C 124, 3 May.

Council of the European Union (2000) 'Council Decision ... setting up a Provisional Judicial Co-operation Unit' *OJ* L324, 21 December.

Journal of Common Market Studies   Volume 39, Annual Review
September 2001

Developments in the Member States

LEE MILES
University of Hull

Introduction

This section of the *Annual Review* examines the main political developments in the Member States that have implications for the European Union (EU) and some of the issues that reverberated in domestic debates in Europe. The year 2000 was, once again, a busy time for the Union, not least in that it culminated in agreement on a new Treaty at Nice in December. However, this section will assess only those areas where the 'Member State' dimension was especially noticeable.

I. Elections and their Consequences

A number of important elections took place during the year and some of them had important consequences for the European Union.

Finland

Finland's reputation within the European Union as the most enthusiastic and pro-integrationist Nordic Member State was further reinforced by the election of Tarja Halonen, the Foreign Minister and member of the Finnish Social Democratic Party (SSDP) as Finland's first female President in a second round of voting on 6 February 2000 (see Table 1). Halonen's election ensures that the

Table 1: Results of Finnish Presidential Election (2nd Round), 6 February 2000

Candidate	Political Party	% of Vote
Tarja Halonen	Finnish Social Democratic Party	51.6
Esko Aho	Centre Party	48.4
Total		100.0

Source: Helsingin Sanomat.

pro-EU Social Democrats hold the office of both the President and the Prime Minister of Finland and is a further boost to the five-party coalition government headed by Paavo Lipponen (elected in March 1999). The Foreign Minister gained 51.6 per cent of the vote in a second round run-off against former Prime Minister, Esko Aho – leader of the main opposition party, the Centre Party (who scored 48.4 per cent of the vote). Halonen's support came mainly from female voters, trade union members and urban voters, and her concentration on human rights issues was well received.

Although the Finnish President no longer holds exclusive competence over foreign policy matters since the 1999 constitutional reforms, the presidential election was of interest from an EU perspective. First, Aho enjoyed an increase in support during the final weeks of the presidential campaign after the former Prime Minister criticized the EU for what he called the other 14 Member States' needless interference in the affairs of Austria following the formation of the new government in Vienna that included the far-right Freedom Party. Aho's criticisms struck a chord with many Finns who are sensitive over their own country's sovereignty. Second, the election of the new President will, most probably, continue Finland's pro-EU, but NATO-sceptic foreign policy, especially since Halonen succeeds Martti Ahtisaari, who was widely praised for his role in negotiating the accords that ended the 1999 Kosovan conflict.

Spain

In the legislative elections of 12 March, the ruling Popular Party (PP) of the Prime Minister, José Maria Aznar, won an absolute majority – surpassing the expectations of pre-election polls. The PP won over 44 per cent of the vote, securing 183 of the 350 seats of Spain's lower house, the Chamber of Deputies (up from 156 in the last parliamentary session). The main opposition party, the Socialist Workers' Party (PSOE) won 34 per cent of the vote (down from 37.5 per cent registered in the 1996 election) and saw its number of seats drop to 125 from a previous 141 (1996). As a result, the leader of the PSOE, Joaquin

Almunia, announced his resignation. The PSOE's allies, the communist dominated United Left (IU) also slumped to 8 seats from 21. The success of the PP can be largely attributed to the economic prosperity experienced under Aznar's four-year term, vindicating in part his decision to allow Spain to become a founder member of the euro. The Prime Minister also maintained a majority in Spain's Upper House, the Senate. Aznar announced (14 March) that he wished to govern by consensus despite his party's absolute majority in the Lower House, and form a parliamentary alliance with the moderate Catalan nationalists (Convergence and Union (CiU)) and Canary Islands Coalition (CC), but without the moderate Basque Nationalist Party (PNV) that had been part of the alliance supporting his government. The new administration was sworn in on 27 April 2000 and the opposition PSOE duly elected a new leader, José Luis Rodriguez Zapatero, at a party conference on 23 July 2000.

During April 2000, Spain and the UK reached agreement over Gibraltar's administrative status, ending a long-running dispute. It unblocked a logjam of stalled EU legislation as well as Britain's application to join part of the Schengen Agreement on the abolition of frontier controls – the latter had been held up because of Spain's refusal to recognize the devolved Gibraltar government as a 'competent authority' in EU affairs, preferring to deal directly with the UK government.

Table 2: Results of Election to Spain's Chamber of Deputies, 12 March 2000

Party	Seats in 2000 (1996)		% of Vote in 2000 (1996)	
Popular Party (PP)	183	(156)	44.6	(38.8)
Socialist Workers' Party (PSOE)	125	(141)	34.1	(37.5)
United Left (IU)	8	(21)	5.5	(10.6)
Convergence and Union (CiU)	15	(16)	4.2	(4.6)
Basque Nationalist Party (PNV)	7	(5)	1.5	(1.3)
National Galician Bloc (BNG)	3	(2)	1.3	(0.9)
Canary Islands Coalition (CC)	4	(4)	1.1	(0.9)
Andalusian Party (PA)	1	(0)	0.9	(0.0)
Catalan Republican Left (ERC)	1	(1)	0.8	(0.7)
Initiative for Catalonia (IC) — Greens (V)	1	(0)	0.5	(0.0)
Basque Solidarity (EA)	1	(1)	0.4	(0.5)
Aragonese Junta (CHA)	1	(0)	0.3	(0.0)
Others	0	(3)	4.8	(4.2)
Total	350	(350)	100.0	(100.0)

Italy

The Prime Minister, Massimo d'Alema, announced his resignation on 17 April after his centre-left coalition government suffered an unexpectedly heavy defeat in Italy's regional elections at the hands of the centre-right opposition led by Silvio Berlusconi. The centre-right obtained 51 per cent of the vote compared to 45 per cent for the centre-left in the elections to the regional councils of Italy's 15 regions. The defeat of the parties of the ruling coalition was largely attributed to the constant internal bickering within the government as well as the performance of Berlusconi in recent months that aided the centre-right's popularity. However, d'Alema was succeeded by Giuliano Amato – hitherto Treasury and Budget Minister and a former Prime Minister (1992–93) – who formed another centre-left administration of eight parties and Italy's 58th post-war government. This ruled out the possibility of holding early general elections – an option not surprisingly favoured by Berlusconi — and enabled Italy to move towards the Nice Intergovernmental Conference (IGC) with some semblance of continuity. However, Amato announced unexpectedly (25 September) that he would not lead the ruling centre-left coalition in the legislative elections due in April 2001 in order to maximize the chances of the centre-left defeating the challenge of the Berlusconi-led centre-right. Thus, it seems that the turbulent throes of Italian domestic politics will continue for the foreseeable future.

Greece

The ruling Panhellenic Socialist Movement (Pasok) led by the Prime Minister, Kostas Simitis, narrowly won a third successive term in office at the 9 April general election – the first time this had been achieved in modern Greece. Pasok defeated the centre-right New Democracy (ND), led by Constantine Karamanlis, by a single percentage point. The population's fragile endorsement of Simitis was primarily due to the government's sound economic record. From the EU perspective, the continuity of Pasok in office was treated positively, especially since the previous Simitis government submitted a formal application for Greece to become the 12th member of the euro-zone on 9 March, with the National Economy Minister, Ioannis Papantoniou, claiming that Greece had met all of the TEU's convergence criteria by February 2000. Indeed, Simitis appointed a new cabinet (12 April) with the task of handling controversial reforms of Greece's debt-burdened pensions system, the liberalization of the energy market and the restructuring of the country's public debt.

Table 3: Results of the Greek General Election, 9 April 2000

Party	Seats	% of Vote
Panhellenic Socialist Movement (Pasok)	158	43.8
New Democracy (ND)*	125	42.7
Communist Party of Greece (KKE)	11	5.5
Alliance of Left and Progressive Forces (Synaspismos)	6	3.2
Democratic Social Movement (DHKKI)	0	2.7
Others	0	2.1
Total	300	100.0

*Note: The total for New Democracy included two Liberal Party members sitting as independents, yet co-operating with New Democracy.

II. Other Political Developments

Austria

In January, the conservative People's Party (ÖVP) led by Wolfgang Schüssel reached agreement with the far-right Freedom Party (FPÖ) headed by Jörg Haider on the formation of a new governing coalition – sparking off international outrage and a nine-month crisis in the EU. The other 14 governments, faced with the reality of having to work with ministers drawn from the FPÖ, protested at the fact that Haider and his party had previously voiced praise of aspects of the nazi regime in Germany. On 1 February, two days before the new Austrian government was to be sworn in, the Portuguese EU Council Presidency stated that ministerial relations between Austria and the EU would be downgraded to their lowest possible level. The Commission, however, was keen to state that contacts with the Austrian government would not be affected and that the initiative was largely bilateral. Some Member States – particularly Ireland and Italy – also expressed their fears that Austrian political isolation might enhance, rather than hinder the domestic popularity of the FPÖ and Austria could respond by obstructing elements of EU business.

Haider announced his intention to resign as party leader of the FPÖ on 28 February as a conciliatory gesture to his government coalition partners, even if it did not necessarily mean a reduction in the influence of Haider on contemporary Austrian politics. Nor did it prevent Prime Minister Schüssel from receiving a frosty reception at the March 2000 European Council summit in Lisbon, with opposition voiced by the French and Belgian governments in particular. Even a visit by the Austrian President, Thomas Klestil, to Brussels in April failed to persuade the other Member States to improve bilateral relations with Austria, leading to several later threats by the Austrian government to withhold its financial contributions to the Union. When the later French EU Council Presidency insisted that the diplomatic sanctions would remain, the Austrians intimated that if the EU did not reinstate bilateral ties then a popular referendum on the issue of sanctions could be held within the year.

The diplomatic sanctions were formally lifted on 12 September after the political will amongst the 14 Member States evaporated once a committee of 'wise men' reported (8 September) that the sanctions could be counterproductive and that the Austrian government was 'committed to common European values' and respect for human rights was 'not inferior to that of other EU countries'. The EU's *volte face* was welcomed by the Austrians. It was portrayed domestically as a vindication that the EU could not meddle significantly in the domestic affairs of Member States. Yet, there were few domestic gains for the FPÖ since the party performed badly in the provincial elections in Styria (October) and Burgenland (December) and suffered from wider allegations of 'dirty tricks' in receiving information on political opponents from confidential police files.

It also represented a political defeat for the Socialist-led French government and perhaps even for the French EU Presidency. There were few on any side that could claim that the policy of diplomatic sanctions had been a success, and the Member States will be wary of adopting such a policy in the future.

Denmark

In a referendum on 28 September, the Danish electorate voted by a narrow but decisive majority against participation in the euro. The result was regarded as a defeat for the pro-euro, centre-left government led by Poul Nyrup Rasmussen who had called the referendum during the previous March. At that time, public opinion polls had suggested that support for the euro was running at around 60 per cent, but support declined over the summer, partly in response to its weak performance on the money markets.

On a high turnout of 87.5 per cent of some 4 million eligible voters, 53.1 per cent voted to retain the existing national currency, the krone, with 46.9 per cent in favour of joining the euro. The decision ensured that Denmark, along with Sweden and the UK, continued as 'euro-refusniks', although the governments of both the latter insisted that they would maintain their previous commitments to holding national referendums in the future, despite the negative result in Denmark.

The 'pro-euro' political forces were drawn from right across the political spectrum. They included the governing Social Democrats (SD) and the Social Liberals (RV), as well as the opposition Liberal (Venstre), Conservative People's (KFP) and Centre Democrat (CD) parties, most of the prominent Danish business and trade union leaders and sizeable elements of the national press. Their campaign centred largely on the perceived economic benefits accruing from EMU membership, the fact that the krone had in fact been tied to the euro (and prior to this the ECU) since 1982, as well the perceived political gains to be had from being a full member of the 'euro-club'. Of course, the Danish debate on the euro was also slightly more unusual since it also focused on whether Denmark should relinquish one of the four 'opt-outs' secured by the government at the Edinburgh European Council summit in December 1992.

The composition of the 'no' camp was similarly wide-ranging. It encompassed the right-wing Danish People's Party (DF) led by Pia Kjaersgaard, the Leftist Socialist People's Party (SFP) and the Red–Green Unity List (ELRG). Most importantly, those rejecting the euro were galvanized by well-funded grassroots movements in the form of the June Movement and the People's Movement Against the European Union. Those rejecting the euro were successful in refuting the economic arguments of the pro-euro camp. They cited the Danish Economic Council's decision in May 2000 that the benefits of Denmark's participation in the euro would be minimal and uncertain, and highlighted the weak value of the euro and the strength of the Danish economy during the year. This went a long way in offsetting the fact that the governor of the Danish central bank, Bodil Nyboe Andersen, had come out emphatically in favour of joining the euro. Furthermore, they argued that Denmark's position in the EU was protected by the existing EMU opt-out from sections of the Treaty on European Union (TEU). In addition, the DF stressed the importance of sovereignty issues, claiming that Denmark's participation in the single currency would lead to a dilution of Danish 'identity', and open the gates to further immigration. It highlighted (once again) Danish concerns about the influence of its larger neighbour, Germany, in any EMU arrangement. Those Eurosceptics drawn from the parties of the Danish left also argued that the single currency posed a threat to Denmark's generous social security system and welfare state provision.

Although Prime Minister Rasmussen accepted responsibility for the defeat of the 'Yes' campaign, he did not offer his resignation, having made clear that he would not seek a repeat of the 1992–93 Maastricht episode when the Danish government sought to secure a speedy reversal of the public's rejection of the TEU by holding another referendum within a year. The results were, however, one of the factors that led to the reshuffle of cabinet posts (21 December 2000), after the belated resignation of the Foreign Minister, Niels Helveg Petersen (RV), who took responsibility for the euro's rejection in September. There were no permanent effects on the Danish economy since its residual strength has been sustained and, in any case, the Danish central bank raised its base rate on 29 September 2000 by half a percentage point to 5.6 per cent to protect the krone's position against the euro.

Germany

On 3 January, a formal investigation was launched into embezzlement charges against the former Chancellor, Helmut Kohl, in what has become Germany's biggest political funding scandal in recent times. Kohl was forced to admit his role in the operation of a system of secret 'slush fund' bank accounts used for illegal (and untaxed) political donations to the Christian Democratic Union (CDU) while his party was in office. He resigned as honorary party chairman on 18 January. The move was seen by many as a humiliating end to the political career of the man once regarded as one of the architects of European, as well as German unity. The parliamentary investigation that had been convened to probe CDU funding during the years of Kohl's chancellorship led the party to be fined DM 41 million for financial malpractice in January.

The legacy of Kohl's grip on the CDU and the party's long tenure in office also meant that most of the existing CDU leadership was implicated in the funding scandal. Kohl's successor as CDU party chairman, Wolfgang Schäuble, also became involved directly in the scandal. Schäuble resigned as CDU party chairman and the party's leader in the Bundestag on 16 February, stating that the party would never recover while those involved were still in charge. This did not prevent the CDU taking a hammering at the polls at state elections in Schleswig-Holstein in early 2000.

Angela Merkel, a former East German physicist who had served as Environment Minister under Kohl, was nominated unanimously as the new CDU party chairman, which was confirmed at the party's national congress on 10 April. However, the scandal was to take on further twists later in the year. Other prominent members of the party were drawn into the affair with, for instance, the CDU premier of Hesse and potential future federal party leader, Roland Koch, facing new media allegations and the party being fined a further DM 7.7 million in December.

The government also got into trouble with the European Court of Justice over disputed state subsidies to Westdeutsche Landesbank (WestLB) which led to the company being forced to repay some €1.1 billion to the government of North Rhine-Westphalia. Nevertheless, the Schröder government did enjoy a number of domestic successes during 2000, including the approval by the German legislature of ambitious tax reforms (July) and the adoption of several measures to deal with neo-nazi groups. The tax changes paved the way for the government to announce the biggest reform of the state pension system since the 1950s in September.

France

The year was also a not particularly good one for President Chirac. In January, he faced concerted domestic opposition from within his own party, Rally for the Republic (RPR), against his proposals for a constitutional amendment to reform aspects of the French judicial system. He ended the year trying to avoid being drawn into one of the country's biggest political scandals since the establishment of the Fifth Republic in 1958. The President also dropped his opposition to constitutional reform relating to a reduction in the length of the presidential term of office from seven to five years, and a bill enabling such a change was introduced during 2000. Parliamentary and presidential elections will therefore be held in 2002.

The year 2000 also seems to have been one when French politicians were more susceptible (than usual) to political scandal. There was, for instance, political fall-out during 2000 from the ongoing 'Elf affair' – a scandal over the corrupt use of funds drawn from the Elf Aquitaine oil group – that led to several high-profile political casualties including, amongst others, the resignation (in March) of Roland Dumas as President of France's Constitutional Court. Moreover, the declining influence of the far-right National Front (FN) was accelerated by the government's decision in April to ban its leader, Jean Marie Le Pen, from sitting in the European Parliament.

Interestingly, Jean-Claude Trichet, the governor of Banque de France was to be investigated by a judicial inquiry for spreading false information to financial markets and for approving falsified balance sheets to cover up losses when he was director of the Finance Ministry's treasury department in the 1990s. Many suspected that this could undermine the EU plan for Trichet to succeed Wim Duisenberg as governor of the European Central Bank in 2002. Moreover, both the RPR and the Socialist Party – the parties of the President and Prime Minister respectively – were tainted by allegations of corrupt party financing late in the year. In particular, the parties were alleged to have taken illegal 'commission' on public works contracts awarded by the Paris administration during Chirac's period as mayor of the capital (1977–95). Chirac appeared on national television on 14 December to deny his involvement in the corrupt party funding activities. To some extent, these domestic events tended to overshadow the efforts of the political elite to extract maximum political benefit from the French Presidency of the EU Council.

III. Policy Developments

While in no way intended to be comprehensive, this section of the *Annual Review* examines those policy areas where the perspectives of, and development in, the Member States have been particularly notable and influential.

Economic and Monetary Union

Alongside the continued evolution of the euro, there were notable domestic developments in each of the four 'euro-outsiders' (Denmark, Greece, Sweden and the UK) during 2000. One of the four, Greece, had always been excluded from the single currency on economic grounds rather than because of political reservations pertinent to the other three countries. Indeed, Greece was able to meet the convergence criteria and subsequently applied to join the euro on 9 March 2000. In the other three states, the primary issue relating to EMU was essentially political and pertained to the timing of domestic referendums on the question of joining the single currency. In the UK and Sweden, there was a softening of governmental positions. The Swedish premier, Göran Persson, secured approval from his Social Democratic Party (SAP) for a 'Yes, but not now' pro-euro position – making a referendum on entry in autumn 2002 a real possibility. In the UK, the Prime Minister, Tony Blair, began a concerted campaign to neutralize the negative press coverage of the euro by Britain's primarily anti-euro oriented national press.

The Danes went the furthest and fastest and, as we have seen, the government duly paid the price in September 2000. The impact of the Danish decision was negligible on the other Member States. Although Eurosceptics in the UK and Sweden hailed the Danish rejection as a vindication of their positions, the British and Swedish governments were quick to highlight the fact that this was a purely Danish issue and they would make their respective decisions on euro participation on an independent basis. Moreover, the day after the referendum, the French and German governments signalled their intention to press ahead with plans for further EU integration on the basis of 'enhanced co-operation', in which the non-participation of some EU members was acceptable even if it facilitated the creation of a multi-speed or tiered Europe.

BSE and Fuel Crises

From the Member States' perspective, there were two pan-European 'crises' that affected most EU countries and illustrated differences between the governments. The first related, as usual, to European agriculture: there was a rise in cases of BSE across the continental Member States by the end of 2000. In January, the European Commission had produced a White Paper on food safety, including the establishment of a new European food safety authority.

In March the German Bundesrat had voted narrowly to approve a government motion removing the German ban on British beef exports imposed in 1996 because of the level of 'mad cow disease' within UK herds. This suggested that, at long last, the shadow of BSE might finally be diminishing since this left only the French government and two maverick German Länder with similar bans in place. Other pressing issues, such as controversies over genetically modified (GM) crops, now seemed to have taken centre stage.

However, it was not to last. By October, there was a growing incidence of mad cow cases in France (73), forcing the government to announce (24 October) the introduction of more intensive testing of cattle dying in suspect circumstances and that the ten-year old EU ban on the use of animal protein in cattle feed had not been respected properly. The first two cases of BSE were detected in German herds in November, provoking massive public concern, an even deeper slump in the already beleaguered sales of beef, and the imposition of bans on French and German beef exports in many Member States – some of which also appeared to have odd cases of the disease emerging. The EU agricultural ministers agreed new measures in December aimed at combating the spread of BSE – to be implemented from 1 January 2001 – ensuring that the BSE issue would remain on the EU agenda well into the next year.

Around the same time as the BSE crisis entered this intensive phase, several of the Member State governments were also confronted by widespread protests against high fuel prices. In the UK, Blair faced possibly his most serious domestic challenge as militant farmers and road hauliers brought the country to a virtual standstill in September. Taking their cue from this British example of 'peaceful people power', similar mass protests appeared in other EU countries such as France, Spain and the Netherlands. This resulted in some government concessions in France, Spain, Germany and the Netherlands as each sought to stave off rather uncomfortable dissent from their domestic electorates. Some European Commission sources questioned their validity under EC competition law.

Nice Treaty

On 14 February, the EU foreign ministers formally launched an Intergovernmental Conference (IGC) aimed at reforming the EU institutions and decision-making processes scheduled to end at the Nice summit under the French Presidency in December 2000. Although the IGC process is covered in other sections of the *Annual Review*, it illustrates the differences between Member States on questions of EU institutional reform. Broadly, the differing perspectives of the Member States can be grouped into three types, each of which was illustrated during the final negotiations on a new EU Treaty at Nice. First, there were differences between the larger EU countries over the representation accorded to Germany in the new working arrangements, since the unified Germany is now by far the largest country in the existing EU-15. Second, there were tensions between the larger states (Germany, UK, Italy, France and perhaps Spain) – wanting a greater share of the votes in the EU Council distributed roughly on the basis of size of domestic population – and the small states wishing to protect their existing provision and fearing that they would be outvoted by the larger states in a revised EU arrangement. Third, there were skirmishes at Nice between the smaller EU countries over the representation accorded to different sized 'small states'. Friction was especially evident between the Belgian and Dutch governments over the their respective allocations in light of the fact that the Netherlands has 5 million more people than Belgium. Broadly, the outcome at Nice can be regarded as a victory for the larger states, although certain concessions were given to the smaller EU countries. There is considerable doubt, however, about whether the agreement at Nice will be sufficient to facilitate the smooth functioning of an enlarged European Union.

IV. Public Opinion

According to *Eurobarometer,* public support for the European Union across the Member States (an average of 49 per cent) in spring 2000 was slightly lower than in autumn 1999 (51 per cent). Yet, once again, this slight decline does not translate into a notable rise in those now opposing their respective countries' membership of the EU, since the proportion that viewed the Union as 'a bad thing' rose slightly but remained a paltry 14 per cent in spring 2000. What perhaps is more interesting is that the values registered by *Eurobarometer* surveys for spring 2000 were similar to those for spring 1999. Indeed, the values registered for those people viewing EU membership as 'a good thing' (49 per cent), 'neither good nor bad' (28 per cent) or as 'a bad thing' (14 per cent) in spring 2000 (*Eurobarometer*, No. 53, pp. 7–9) are virtually the same as those recorded for public opinion some 12 months earlier in spring 1999 (when the figures were 49 per cent, 27 per cent and 12 per cent respectively). This suggests that the impact of the Commission crisis in early 1999, which had led to the resignation of the Santer Commission on 15 March and prompted an average reduction of 5 percentage points in the support levels for EU membership across the Member States from autumn 1998 to spring 1999, had not been recouped by the time of spring 2000.

These EU averages for spring 2000 hide regional variations (see Table 4). Support for EU membership continued to be highest in Ireland (75 per cent), Luxembourg (75 per cent) and the Netherlands (73 per cent). Moreover, Spain (67 per cent), Portugal (64 per cent), Belgium (62 per cent), Greece (61 per cent) and Italy (60 per cent) registered above average values suggesting that over 60 per cent of their populations supported their country's membership of the Union. In Denmark, support for EU membership at 53 per cent was also higher than the EU average, although the country continues to experience significant levels of public opposition (24 per cent). As usual, support for full membership status was lowest in the UK (25 per cent) and opposition levels were highest in Sweden (38 per cent – up 5 percentage points since spring 1999).

The data from *Eurobarometer* suggest that Belgium was the only Member State where public opinion was significantly more favourable (+8) in spring 2000 than six months earlier (autumn 1999). At the same time, the proportion of Belgians actually opposing their country's full membership also increased by 4 percentage points, perhaps suggesting that Belgians have become more polarized on the question of the European Union. Yet, public opinion neither improved nor deteriorated in Spain, the Netherlands, Greece and France. In Denmark and Italy, the proportion of people who saw full membership as 'a good thing' did not change, yet both countries experienced an increase in the number of people who believe their country's full membership status is 'a bad thing' (both increasing by 3 percentage points since autumn 1999).

Levels of support for EU membership dropped most significantly in Austria with the proportion of Austrians supporting full membership falling by 9 percentage points between spring 2000 and autumn 1999 and those viewing it as 'a bad thing' increasing by 7 percentage points. This can be attributed to specific circumstances relating to the Austrians and reflected the public's response to the sanctions imposed by the other 14 Member States against their country as a result of the far-right Freedom Party being part of the conservative-led government coalition. However, a negative shift was also recorded in Sweden (+8 increase in opposition levels) and significant drops in support levels were also recorded in Ireland, Luxembourg, Germany, Finland, the UK and Portugal (although this did not translate into increased opposition levels in the case of the latter three countries).

Turning to related questions assessing the perceived benefits accruing from EU membership across the Member States, almost half of EU citizens (47 per cent) believed that their country has benefited from being a full member of the Union. There was very little change in attitudes from those recorded in autumn 1999 (46 per cent), although the figure of 47 per cent for spring 2000 was some 3 percentage points higher than the EU average recorded 12 months earlier (44 per cent in spring 1999).

Nevertheless, there were striking differences across the Member States (see Table 5). In general it would seem that several groups of Member States continue to have a large proportion of the domestic population that perceives

Table 4: National Attitudes towards EU Membership (% by Member State)

	B	DK	D	GR	E	F	IRL	I	L	NL	A	P	FIN	S	UK	EU15
A good thing	62 +8	53 −1	41 −6	61 +2	67 +3	49 +1	75 −7	60 0	75 −6	73 +2	33 −9	64 −4	40 −4	34 −3	25 −4	49 −2
A bad thing	10 +4	24 +3	15 +3	8 +1	6 +2	14 −2	6 +3	9 +3	6 +3	6 +2	25 +7	5 +1	22 +2	38 +8	24 0	14 +1
Neither good nor bad	23 −11	20 −2	33 +3	26 −2	21 −2	32 +2	13 +5	25 0	15 +3	16 −6	32 +1	22 +3	34 +3	25 −6	29 +1	28 +1
Don't know	5 −1	4 +1	11 +1	6 0	6 −3	5 −2	6 −1	6 −3	4 0	6 +3	10 0	10 0	4 −1	3 0	22 +3	9 −1
Total	100	100	100	100	100	100	100	100	100	100	100	100	100	100	100	100

Source: Eurobarometer 53, 2000, B.11.

Table 5: Perceived Benefits of EU Membership (% by Member State)

	B	DK	D	GR	E	F	IRL	I	L	NL	A	P	FIN	S	UK	EU15
Benefited	60 +10	65 +1	37 0	75 +5	66 +5	49 +3	86 −2	51 +1	69 −3	65 0	34 −11	71 −6	42 +2	26 −2	25 −4	47 +1
Not benefited	25 −3	22 +1	42 +3	13 −2	16 0	29 −2	6 +3	29 +3	19 +7	20 0	48 +16	11 +2	44 +3	56 +7	44 +2	32 +1
Don't know	15 −7	13 −2	21 −3	13 −2	18 −5	22 −1	9 0	20 −4	12 −4	15 0	18 −5	18 +4	14 −6	19 −3	31 +1	21 −2
Total	100	100	99	100	100	100	100	100	100	100	100	100	100	100	100	100

Source: Eurobarometer 53, 2000, B.13.
Notes: Eurobarometer data for late 2000 were unavailable at the time of writing. The second figure in each column represents the change in percentage points from autumn 1999 (EB 52.0) to spring 2000.

their country benefiting from being a full EU member. The first group – the 'Cohesion Four' – include Member States that enjoy generous EU financial assistance stemming principally from the EU Structural Funds, a fact that seems not to have gone unnoticed by the domestic populations. Ireland, for example, continues (see last year's *Annual Review*) to have the highest proportion of the domestic population (86 per cent) that sees their country as benefiting from full membership status and high values are also recorded in the case of Greece (75 per cent), Portugal (71 per cent) and Spain (66 per cent). The second group are the three Benelux countries (Luxembourg, 69 per cent; Netherlands, 65 per cent and Belgium, 60 per cent) that, as founder EU members and small states in the Union, have always appreciated the benefits of being in the Union. The only other EU Member State with over 60 per cent believing that their country benefits from being a EU participant is Denmark. This highlights the fact that although further EU integration may be controversial in Denmark and helps sustain the country's profile as one of the more 'problematic' EU members, this does not prevent most Danes from recognizing the benefits for their country of being in the Union. In any case, Denmark's full membership status is unusual in the sense of having been qualified by the four 'opt-outs'.

In contrast, public opinion continues to be most negative in Sweden and the UK, where only a quarter of the population feel that their country has benefited from full membership. This implies that in these two cases, the questions of EU membership and further European integration remain interlinked and controversial. Indeed, Sweden remains the only country in 2000 where an absolute majority of the population believe that the country has not benefited from membership. In Austria, nearly half of the electorate share this view.

When the situation in spring 2000 is compared with the *Eurobarometer* survey for autumn 1999, then there are also variations among the Member States. There is a significant rise in the number of people believing their country has benefited from full membership status in Belgium (+10). Similar, if less substantial, trends were also evident in Greece (+5) and Spain (+5), although no significant changes were recorded in the Netherlands, Denmark, France, Finland, Germany and Ireland.

There was, however, a notable decrease in Austria in those believing that the country had benefited (down 11 percentage points) and an even more marked rise by 16 percentage points in the proportion of Austrians that now believed that the country had not benefited from EU membership. Again, this can be attributed to a shift in the perceptions of the Austrian public in response to the diplomatic sanctions imposed against their country by the other Member States in 2000. Despite the sanctions being largely bilateral, it has not prevented the Austrian public blaming the European Union for what they see as the interference of other European states in their domestic affairs.

IV. Implementation

The new monitoring procedures implemented by the European Commission since 1998 continue to have a positive effect on the implementation of EC legislation by the Member States. According to the *Seventeenth Annual Report on Monitoring the Application of Community Law*, the number of complaints received by the Commission rose by 16 per cent from 1128 in 1998 to 1305 in 1999 (Commission, 2000). A further 288 cases were detected by the Commission itself. Most of these cases relate to the non-conformity of national measures implementing directives or the incorrect application of such measures, suggesting that the Commission's monitoring procedures have duly improved.

The Commission issued a lower number of reasoned opinions in 1999, falling by 32 per cent in 1999 to 460 (compared to 675 for 1998) and there was also a slight drop in the number of letters of formal notice produced (1075 in 1999 compared to 1101 in 1998). This reflects a return to normal in 1999 after the special efforts made on the part of the Commission during the previous year to reduce delays in the processing of decisions. However, the number of cases referred to the European Court of Justice (ECJ) rose in 1999 to 178, compared with 123 in 1998. Provisional figures for 2000 outlined in the Commission's *General Report on Activities* (Commission, 2001, p. 373) imply that the number of infringement proceedings rose (1317), although the issuing of reasoned opinions remained comparatively stable (460) and referral of cases to the ECJ was also roughly similar (172) to 1999. This suggests that, although the Commission is now quite effective in persuading Member States to tackle implementation delays, the Member States still need coercing into action in some policy fields, such as opening up public procurement, through formal Court procedures.

The figures do not highlight the uneven implementation efforts of Member States. The provisional data on the referral of cases to the ECJ (172 in 2000) on the basis of Member State distribution suggests that the Nordic trio – Denmark (0 cases), Sweden (3 cases) and Finland (4 cases) as well as the UK (4 cases) are the most 'law abiding', while the worst culprits continue (as in 1999) to be France (27) and Italy (24) as well as Greece (23 actions) (Commission, 2000, p. 373).

Indeed, the *Seventeenth Annual Report* covering 1999 concludes that the average level of implementation remained comparatively constant, if slightly

Table 6: Notification of Transposition of European Community Law

Member State	Directives Applicable 31.12.99	Measures Notified	(%)
Denmark	1499	1456	97.13
Spain	1502	1449	96.47
Netherlands	1505	1447	96.15
Finland	1498	1436	95.86
Sweden	1500	1437	95.80
Germany	1507	1439	95.49
United Kingdom	1504	1435	95.41
Austria	1501	1425	94.94
Belgium	1505	1428	94.88
Italy	1504	1416	94.15
Ireland	1499	1411	94.13
France	1505	1412	93.82
Portugal	1507	1407	93.36
Luxembourg	1503	1402	93.28
Greece	1503	1383	92.02
EC average	1508	1426	94.53

Source: Commission (2000, p. 8).

down on the previous year. On 31 December 1999, the Member States had on average notified 94.53 per cent of the national measures needed to implement the directives. This is within acceptable margins according to the European Commission (Commission, 2000, p. 7), since, in absolute terms, the delay affects less than 6 per cent of the directives. However, there is still some concern that the delays could be related to specific market sectors that may have important consequences for the functioning of an integrated economic area.

Denmark continued to occupy the first position in the league table (97.13 per cent of applicable directives transposed). The figures for 1999 show a significant improvement in the performance of Italy which jumped five places in the rankings thanks to a concerted governmental effort in 1999 to tackle the country's reputation as the worst performing Member State (in terms of implementing directives) that it attained in the previous year. However, this also implies that Italy is now tenth out of 15. The country cannot, at this point, be regarded as one of the most diligent Member States. The transposition rate of Greece was identified by the Commission as a 'cause for concern' since it fell from 93.82 in 1998 to 92.02 per cent in 1999 and resulted in the country falling from fourteenth to last place in the league table this year (see Table 6). However, it should be noted that the transposition percentage rate fell for all 15 Member States in 1999 compared to those recorded for the previous year. Some of the directives being transposed in 1999 may have been more ambitious, technical in nature and perhaps even politically controversial – leading to delays in transposition for all Member States.

References

Commission of the European Communities (2000) *Seventeenth Annual Report on Monitoring the Application of Community Law – 1999. COM* (2000) 92 final, 23 June.

Commission of the European Communities (2001) *General Report on the Activities of the European Union – 2000. SEC* (2000) 1000 final, 30 January.

Keesing's Record of World Events (various issues)

European Voice (various issues).

Agence Europe (various issues).

Journal of Common Market Studies

Volume 39, Annual Review
September 2001

Developments in the Economies of the European Union

NIGEL GRIMWADE

South Bank University

I. Overview

The EU economy grew at an average rate of 3.4 per cent during 2000, the best performance for ten years, comparing very favourably with GDP growth of 2.5 per cent in the previous year. A key factor was the improved global situation with real GDP outside the EU growing at a rate of 4.8 per cent. The dominant force in this expansion continued to be the US economy with output growing by 5 per cent. However, it is now apparent that global economic growth peaked in the first half of the year. In the United States, although expansion remained strong in the first half of the year, the rate fell from an annualized 7 per cent in the second half of 1999 to 5 per cent in the first half of 2000 (IMF, 2000). By the end of the year, it was apparent that a marked deceleration was apparent in the US economy, as domestic demand responded to previous rises in short-term interest rates, some decline in share prices and the effects of higher oil prices on real incomes. Real GDP was growing at a rate of only 1 per cent in the final quarter of the year. Given the evidence that demand in the US economy had become excessive even allowing for the rapid increase in potential output, some reduction in US growth was necessary. However, it remains to be seen whether this can be achieved through a moderate fall in GDP growth (a soft landing) or whether a sharp and sudden fall in output will follow (a hard landing), with more serious consequences for the rest of the world. The most recent forecast of the IMF is for a much sharper decline in US growth than was forecast as recently as last autumn: the US growth rate is expected to average only 1.5 per cent in 2001 (IMF, 2001).

The EU economy was also adversely affected by the rise in world oil prices, which rose from about $10 a barrel in 1999 to over $35 in the summer of last year, before falling back to just under $24 towards the end of the year. Estimates by the European Commission are that higher oil prices may have shaved a relatively modest 0.2 per cent from the EU growth rate in 2000 (Commission, 2001). The relatively minor effect of higher oil prices on European growth rates shows how much less dependent the EU economies have become on oil in comparison with the time of the last major hike in world oil prices in the 1970s. The latest Commission forecasts assume that the price of a barrel of Brent crude will average about $24 over the course of the current year. Output growth in all Member States was well above the EU's estimated potential growth rate throughout the year, although the rate fell significantly in the last two quarters of the year. Because output was growing faster than the EU's potential, employment was rising fast and the average unemployment rate fell from 9.2 per cent in 1999 to 8.3 per cent. A further decline to 7.7 per cent is forecast for 2001, despite the fact that output will grow more slowly.

The external sector was also an important source of expansion in the EU economy. Buoyant world demand combined with a weaker euro boosted EU exports, adding significantly to European growth. However, domestic demand also grew strongly, aided by the effect on real disposable incomes of tax cuts in some Member States and job creation in all. With demand growing at a faster rate than potential output, there was some evidence that inflationary pressures were increasing in a number of cases. The EU's harmonized consumer prices index (HICP) rose by 2.1 per cent in 2000, compared with only 1.2 per cent in 1999. However, most of this was caused by the rise in world oil prices and, to a lesser extent, the depreciation of the euro. Core inflation, which excludes energy costs, showed a more modest increase. One reason was that, although there was a marginal increase in the rate of wage inflation, this was offset by a more rapid rate of increase in labour productivity, such that unit labour costs grew more slowly than in the previous year. It is, however, possible that the full effects of higher oil prices on inflation have not yet worked through. If workers seek higher wage settlements in the current year to compensate for the effect of oil prices on real disposable incomes, wage inflation could accelerate.

Faced with evidence that inflationary pressures were increasing in the euro-zone (especially in some of the smaller Member States), the European Central Bank (ECB) raised interest rates in series of small steps. The last of these took the ECB's refinancing rate to 4.75 per cent, closer to, but still below the equivalent rate in the United States. Fiscal policy, however, may have played a moderately expansionary role in the EU during 2000, despite the fact that, overall, the Member States ran a budgetary surplus equal to 1.2 per cent of GDP. This compares with a deficit of 0.6 per cent in the previous year. The budget surplus, itself, was largely due to the one-off proceeds from the sale of UMTS (mobile telecommunication licences). In addition, tax receipts turned out higher than expected due to faster economic growth. As a result, the cyclically adjusted balance was –0.1 per cent, although this was still lower than in the previous year.

Despite this, EU public finances look in a far stronger state than for several years, evidence for the success of economic and monetary union in forcing Member States to implement tough measures to reduce public sector indebtedness. The Commission, however, has warned that further effort will be needed by some governments if they are to meet the commitments they have made under the Stability and Convergence Programme (Commission, 2000). In its *World Economic Outlook*, the IMF, too, has pointed to the danger that the windfall gains from the sale of mobile telecommunication licences are being used to make tax cuts rather than increase budget surpluses (IMF, 2000). They point to the long-term challenge facing the EU as a result of an ageing population that will necessitate a big increase in spending on pensions and health in the not too distant future.

II. Main Economic Indicators

Economic Growth

Table 1 sets out the average annual rate of change of gross domestic product measured at constant prices for the 15 Member States for the period since 1961.

Last year, all the Member States (with the exception of only the Netherlands and Sweden) enjoyed more rapid economic growth than in the previous year. Nevertheless, marked differences exist in the performance of different Member States, which has created a problem for the monetary authorities in the euro-zone. Output grew at a relatively modest rate in Italy, Germany and France, while continuing to expand strongly in the smaller states such as Ireland, Luxembourg, Finland, Spain and Greece. In certain of these countries (Ireland and Luxembourg in particular), there were clear signs of overheating. Outside the euro-zone, growth accelerated in the UK and Denmark, but weakened in Sweden.

In terms of GDP components, domestic expenditure grew at a slightly slower rate than in the previous year. Private consumption was buoyant in the early part of last year, boosted by falling unemployment and higher real disposable incomes, but decelerated towards the end of the year as a result of the loss in purchasing power due to higher oil prices. Fixed investment grew more rapidly, especially in the earlier part of the year, induced by an increase

Table 1: Gross Domestic Product at Constant Prices (Annual % Change, 1961–2001)

	1961 *–73*	*1974* *–85*	*1986* *–90*	*1991* *–5*	*1996*	*1997*	*1998*	*1999*	*2000*	*2001* *(Forecast)*
Austria	4.9	2.3	3.2	1.9	2.0	1.3	3.3	2.8	3.2	2.5
Belgium	4.9	2.0	3.1	1.5	1.3	3.4	2.4	2.7	3.9	3.0
Denmark	4.3	1.6	1.3	2.0	3.2	3.0	2.8	2.1	2.9	2.1
Finland	5.0	2.7	3.3	-0.7	4.1	6.3	5.3	4.2	5.7	4.0
France	5.4	2.2	3.3	1.1	1.6	1.9	3.1	2.9	3.2	2.9
Germany	4.3	1.7	3.4	2.0	1.3	1.4	2.1	1.6	3.0	2.2
Greece	8.5	1.7	1.2	1.2	2.4	3.5	3.1	3.4	4.1	4.4
Ireland	4.4	3.8	4.6	4.7	8.3	10.7	8.6	9.8	10.7	7.5
Italy	5.3	2.7	2.9	1.3	0.7	2.0	1.8	1.6	2.9	2.5
Luxembourg	4.0	1.8	6.4	5.4	3.0	7.3	5.0	7.5	8.5	5.6
Netherlands	4.9	1.9	3.1	2.1	3.1	3.8	4.1	3.9	3.9	3.4
Portugal	6.9	2.2	5.5	1.8	3.3	3.8	3.8	3.0	3.3	2.6
Spain	7.2	1.9	4.5	1.3	2.4	3.9	4.3	4.0	4.1	3.2
Sweden	4.1	1.8	2.3	0.6	1.3	2.1	3.6	4.1	3.6	2.7
UK	3.2	1.4	3.3	1.6	2.6	3.5	2.6	2.3	3.0	2.7
Euro-zone	5.2	2.2	3.4	1.5	1.6	2.4	2.8	2.5	3.4	2.8
EU-15	5.2	2.2	3.4	1.5	1.8	2.6	2.8	2.5	3.4	2.8

Source: Commission (2001).

in business optimism. However, the main generator of output growth in 2000 was external demand. Exports grew at an annual rate of 11.3 per cent in volume terms, more than twice that of the previous year. Although imports also rose rapidly, the net effect was positive. The continuing weakness of the euro appears to have been the main factor bringing this about, in spite of the efforts of the authorities to reverse the decline through exchange rate intervention in the second half of the year. Against the US dollar, the euro fell from roughly 0.95 at the beginning of the year to 0.924 by the end. The one exception to this was the UK economy, where a strong sterling exchange rate hampered growth.

In the last two quarters of the year, however, GDP growth fell sharply. This appears to have been due, mainly, to weaker domestic demand. Household consumption grew more modestly, as consumers responded to the effects of higher energy prices on real incomes, although this was not the case in all Member States. It is possible, too, that the increase in short-term interest rates that took place in the middle part of the year may have contributed to reduced consumer confidence. Falling share prices in the last quarter of the year might also have contributed to the fall in consumer spending through a negative wealth effect. The lower level of average shareholding of households in the EU compared with the US, however, means that Europe is less vulnerable than the US economy to a sudden drop in share prices. The latest forecasts of the Commission (Commission, 2001) expect growth in the EU to fall to 2.8 per cent in the current year, a little above the IMF forecast of 2.4 per cent (IMF, 2001).

Unemployment

As a result of the rapid expansion of output, the EU experienced a substantial increase in the number of people in work. An estimated 2.8 million jobs were created during the course of the year (Commission, 2001). Total employment increased by 1.7 per cent, slightly faster than in the previous year. As a consequence, the average rate of unemployment fell from 9.2 to 8.3 per cent. Continuing efforts by governments to make labour markets more flexible assisted this process. Table 2 shows the average unemployment rate for the EU for the period 1964–2001.

Employment grew fastest in the fastest growing economies, namely, Luxembourg, Ireland and Spain, but was also rapid in slower-growing Mem-

Table 2: Numbers Unemployed as a % of the Civilian Labour Force

	1964 –73	1974 –85	1986 –90	1991 –5	1996	1997	1998	1999	2000	2001 Forecast
Austria	1.7	2.5	3.4	3.7	4.3	4.4	4.5	4.0	3.7	3.4
Belgium	2.0	7.7	8.7	8.5	9.7	9.4	9.5	8.8	7.0	6.5
Denmark	0.9	6.4	6.4	8.6	6.8	5.6	5.2	5.2	4.7	4.6
Finland	2.8	4.8	4.1	13.3	14.8	12.7	11.4	10.2	9.8	9.1
France	2.2	6.4	9.8	11.1	12.4	12.3	11.8	11.2	9.5	8.5
Germany	0.7	4.2	5.9	7.4	8.9	9.9	9.3	8.6	8.1	7.8
Greece	4.2	3.8	6.6	8.3	9.6	9.8	10.9	11.7	11.0	10.5
Ireland	5.7	10.6	15.5	14.5	11.6	9.9	7.5	5.6	4.2	3.8
Italy	5.2	7.0	9.5	10.1	12.0	11.7	11.8	11.3	10.5	9.8
Luxembourg	0.0	1.7	2.1	2.5	3.0	2.7	2.7	2.3	2.2	2.0
Netherlands	1.3	7.1	7.4	6.4	6.3	5.2	4.0	3.3	2.8	2.6
Portugal	2.5	7.0	6.4	5.7	7.3	6.8	5.2	4.5	4.2	4.6
Spain	2.8	11.3	18.9	20.9	22.2	20.8	18.8	15.9	14.1	12.8
Sweden	2.0	2.4	2.0	7.2	9.6	9.9	8.3	7.2	5.9	5.2
UK	2.0	6.9	9.0	9.5	8.2	7.0	6.3	6.1	5.6	5.3
Euro-zone	2.5	6.6	9.3	10.2	11.8	11.5	10.8	9.9	9.0	8.5
EU 15	2.4	6.4	8.9	9.9	10.9	10.6	9.9	9.2	8.3	7.7

Source: Commission (2001).

ber States such as Germany and Italy. Although the unemployment rate fell in every Member State, large differences continued to exist. At one extreme, Spain, Greece and Italy continued to experience rates of unemployment in excess of 10 per cent. At the other, unemployment rates in Luxembourg, the Netherlands and Austria were below 4 per cent. Nevertheless, the gap between the highest and lowest national average was lower than in the previous year. In the fast-growing countries with unemployment rates well below the average rate for the EU as a whole, there is a danger that further output growth will encounter labour shortages. If so, inflationary pressures could become severe. The latest forecasts of the European Commission predict that unemployment will fall further to 7.7 per cent in the current year, despite slower output growth (Commission, 2001). Nevertheless, the rate of employment growth will decline, as output growth slows down, especially as labour productivity is likely to continue rising at the same rate.

Inflation

The EU's harmonized consumer prices index (HICP) increased at a rate of 2.1 per cent in 2000, compared with 1.2 per cent in the previous year, a much more rapid increase in prices than earlier forecasts had suggested (Commission, 2000). Other measures of inflation, the GDP deflator and the private consumption deflator, suggest that the underlying inflation rate was below 2 per cent. As was argued earlier, the main reasons for the rise in the HICP were the sudden hike in world oil prices and the effects of the depreciation of the euro, both of which were one-off occurrences that could be reversed in the current year. Oil prices rose sharply in the summer, as OPEC output failed to increase in step with increased global demand. However, by the end of the year, oil prices had begun to fall, as fears of a global recession and higher global stocks of oil changed the balance on world oil markets. With regard to the exchange rate, the main effect of the decline in the value of the euro (the nominal effective exchange rate fell by 6.1 per cent and 7.2 per cent in the years 1999 and 2000 respectively) was to add to cost inflation in the euro-zone. However, Member States outside the euro were able to enjoy more stable inflation due to the strength of their currencies.

Table 3 shows the average rate of inflation in the EU for the period 1961–2001. The figures from 1996 onwards use the EU's harmonized consumer prices index, while those before are obtained from the deflator of private consumption.

The UK was the only Member State where the average rate of inflation fell despite faster output growth. The strength of the pound sterling was, self-evidently, one of the main contributory factors. Of particular concern for the monetary authorities in the euro-zone was the sharp increase in the rate of

Table 3: Average Annual Inflation Rates (% Change)

	1961 –73	1974 –85	1986 –90	1991 –5	1996	1997	1998	1999	2000 (Est.)	2001 (Forecast)
Austria	4.1	5.8	2.0	3.0	2.8	1.2	0.8	0.5	2.0	1.6
Belgium	3.7	7.4	1.9	2.3	2.3	1.5	0.9	1.1	2.7	1.9
Denmark	6.6	9.7	3.4	2.3	1.7	1.9	1.3	2.1	2.7	2.1
Finland	5.7	10.7	4.3	3.0	1.6	1.2	1.4	1.3	3.0	2.4
France	4.7	10.5	3.1	2.5	1.8	1.3	0.7	0.6	1.8	1.3
Germany	3.4	4.3	1.4	3.3	1.7	1.5	0.6	0.6	2.1	2.0
Greece	3.6	18.2	17.6	13.8	8.3	5.4	4.5	2.1	2.9	2.6
Ireland	6.3	13.8	3.2	2.7	1.4	1.2	2.1	2.5	5.3	4.0
Italy	4.9	15.9	6.1	5.8	4.3	1.9	2.0	1.7	2.6	2.2
Luxembourg	3.0	7.4	2.4	3.0	1.6	1.4	1.0	1.0	3.8	2.2
Netherlands	5.1	6.0	0.9	2.5	1.6	1.9	1.8	2.0	2.3	4.3
Portugal	3.9	22.2	12.2	7.7	3.6	1.9	2.2	2.2	2.8	3.5
Spain	6.5	15.4	6.6	5.6	3.4	1.9	1.8	2.2	3.5	3.2
Sweden	4.8	10.3	6.7	4.7	1.2	1.8	1.0	0.6	1.3	1.5
UK	4.8	11.9	5.4	4.2	3.1	1.8	1.6	1.3	0.8	1.4
Euro-zone	4.6	10.4	3.8	3.9	2.5	1.6	1.1	1.1	2.3	2.2
EU-15	4.6	10.9	4.4	4.2	2.7	1.7	1.3	1.2	2.1	2.1

Source: Commission (2001).

inflation in the fastest-growing economies. Ireland, Luxembourg, Finland and Spain all experienced inflation rates in excess of 3 per cent. Although inflation is expected to decline in all of these countries in 2001, the inflation rate in the Netherlands and Portugal will rise above 3 per cent.

A factor that helped minimize the impact of higher oil prices and the depreciation of the euro on domestic inflation was wage moderation. Despite the sharp increase in inflation, real wages grew at slower rate in 2000 than in the previous year. With labour productivity rising faster than in previous years, this meant that unit labour costs were able to grow at a more modest rate, increasing the competitiveness of EU goods abroad and reducing the pressure of wages on prices. Workers did not seek larger wage settlements as a compensation for higher energy prices, although they may still do so. At the same time, tax cuts announced by several governments diminished the pressure on rising wages by providing workers with an increase in their disposable incomes. Most forecasts for the EU predict that inflation will remain broadly stable in 2001, despite the fact that inflation will increase in some of the faster-growing, smaller Member States (Commission, 2001; IMF, 2001).

Public Finances

In 2000, EU Member States made further progress in reducing the size of their fiscal deficits, building on the progress made in previous years. The EU's general government balance swung from a deficit of 0.6 per cent of GDP in 1999 to a surplus of 1.2 per cent. This compares with the Commission's forecast of a deficit of 0.4 per cent as late as the spring of last year. However, this favourable outcome was due largely to the sale of UMTS licenses, although the impact was greater in some Member States (Germany and the UK in particular) than others. These generated additional fiscal revenues equivalent exactly to the budgetary surplus for the year. As with the proceeds from privatization, these revenues bring no lasting improvement to the state of public finances.

If receipts from the sale of UMTS licences are excluded, the budgetary balance still improved, although not in all countries. The main reason for the improvement appears to have been increased tax receipts resulting from faster growth. This was despite the fact that several Member governments cut taxes by significant amounts during the year. If allowance is made for the effects of fast growth on the budget position, the Member States ran a small budget deficit of 0.4 per cent of GDP, compared with 0.1 per cent of GDP in the previous year. Thus, the overall stance of EU fiscal policy was mildly expansionary, although Member States succeeded in consolidating the progress made in previous years in improving their budgetary positions.

Table 4 shows the trend in general government borrowing expressed as a percentage of GDP in individual Member States over the period 1961–2001.

As part of the EU's Stability and Growth Pact (SGP), Member States are expected to achieve budget positions close to balance or in surplus over the medium term in order to avoid a deficit in excess of 3 per cent of GDP in periods of normal cyclical slowdown. Last year, six countries still recorded a deficit, although in all cases the deficit was lower as a percentage of GDP than in the previous year. If, however, UMTS licenses are excluded, the fiscal deficits of several countries – Germany, Italy, Austria and Portugal – increased last year as a percentage of GDP. In 2001, the number of countries running a fiscal deficit will fall to five, with only Germany forecast to run a larger fiscal deficit than in the previous year. Overall, the EU is forecast to run a deficit of 0.2 per cent of GDP this year, due to a slight fall in GDP growth and the disappearance of most of the proceeds from the sale of UMTS licences.

During 2000, a number of states made considerable progress in reducing the tax burden on individuals and companies. In most countries, tax reform packages were introduced that will eventually reduce the tax burden from 47 per cent of GDP in 2000 to 41.4 per cent in 2002 (Commission, 2000). Measured by the impact on GDP, the biggest reductions have occurred in

Table 4: General Government Net Lending (+) or Borrowing (–) as a % of GDP, 1970–2000

	1970 –3	1974 –85	1986 –1990	1991 –5	1996	1997	1998	1999	2000 (Est)	2001 (Forecast)
Austria	1.4	–2.3	–3.2	–3.8	–3.7	–1.7	–2.2	–2.1	–1.1	–0.7
Belgium	–3.4	–7.8	–7.0	–5.9	–3.1	–1.9	–0.9	–0.7	0.0	0.6
Denmark	4.1	–2.7	1.3	–2.4	–0.9	0.4	1.1	3.1	2.5	3.2
Finland	4.5	3.7	4.0	–5.0	–3.1	–1.5	1.3	1.8	6.7	5.3
France	0.7	–1.6	–1.8	–4.5	–4.1	–3.0	–2.7	–1.6	–1.3	–0.6
Germany	0.2	–2.8	–1.5	–3.1	–2.6	–2.7	–2.1	–1.4	1.5	–1.7
Greece	0.2	–4.9	–12.0	–11.5	–7.5	–4.7	–3.1	–1.8	–0.9	0.0
Ireland	–3.9	–9.9	–5.3	–2.1	–0.3	0.7	2.1	2.1	4.5	3.9
Italy	–5.4	–9.6	–10.8	–9.1	–6.6	–2.7	–2.8	–1.8	–0.3	–1.3
Luxembourg	2.5	1.8	–	1.8	2.8	3.6	3.2	4.7	5.3	4.0
Netherlands	–0.5	–3.4	–4.9	–3.5	–2.0	–1.1	–0.7	1.0	2.0	0.8
Portugal	2.0	–6.9	–4.4	–5.0	–3.3	–2.7	–2.3	–2.1	–1.4	–1.5
Spain	0.4	–2.6	–4.0	–5.5	–3.5	–3.2	–2.6	–1.2	–0.3	0.1
Sweden	4.3	–1.7	3.1	–7.6	–3.5	–1.5	1.9	1.8	4.0	3.9
UK	0.1	–3.6	–0.7	–5.7	–4.4	–2.0	0.4	1.3	4.3	1.0
Euro-zone	–0.7	–3.9	–4.1	–4.9	–4.1	–2.6	2.1	–1.3	0.3	–0.5
EU–15	–0.3	–3.7	–3.3	–5.1	–4.1	–2.4	–1.5	–0.6	1.2	–0.2

Source: Commission (2001).
Notes: The net lending (borrowing) includes in 2000 and 2001 one-off proceeds relative to UMITS licences.

Luxembourg, France, Spain and Austria, although the full effect of these measures will be spread over a number of years. Although the EU has one of the highest tax burdens of any region in the world, these reductions create concern as they imply too great a degree of fiscal loosening at a time of rapid economic growth in the EU (Barber, 2000). More precisely, there is a danger that, unless such measures are accompanied by equivalent cuts on the expenditure side, a number of Member States may fail to meet the requirements of the SGP. Indeed, at the beginning of 2001, Ireland became the first Member State to be cautioned by the Commission for adopting an over-expansionary fiscal policy. This was despite the fact that the Irish government balance is forecast to remain in surplus to the tune of 4.5 per cent of GDP in the current year.

Table 5 shows the trend in general government debt expressed as a percentage of GDP for the period 1980–2001.

The ratio of government debt to GDP for the EU as a whole fell from 67.5 per cent to 64.5 per cent in 2000 and is forecast to fall further to 61.7 per cent in 2001. Nevertheless, several Member States (Belgium, Italy and Greece) continued to experience debt to GDP ratios in excess of 100 per cent, although in all three countries further progress was made during the year in reducing the level of public indebtedness. Despite the improvement made in reducing government borrowing, the need for further consolidation has been emphasized by several organizations in their annual reports on the state of the EU economy (IMF, 2000; OECD, 2000). This is because of the claims that will be made on public finances in the future by pensions and public health as a consequence of the ageing of the EU population.

III. Economic Developments in the Member States

Germany

Last year, Europe's largest economy enjoyed its best performance for over a decade. GDP grew by 3 per cent, compared with only 1.6 per cent in the previous year. The recovery was led by manufacturing, especially those

Table 5: General Government Debt as a % of GDP, 1980–2001

	1980	1985	1990	1995	1996	1997	1998	1999	2000 (Est)	2001 (Forecast)
Austria	36.1	49.2	57.3	68.3	68.5	64.7	63.9	64.7	62.8	61.5
Belgium	78.5	122.2	128.8	128.3	133.8	125.3	119.8	116.4	110.9	104.4
Denmark	36.4	69.8	57.7	65.0	69.3	61.4	55.8	52.6	47.3	43.4
Finland	11.6	16.4	14.5	57.1	57.1	54.1	48.8	46.9	44.0	41.7
France	20.4	31.8	36.3	57.1	54.0	59.3	59.7	58.7	58.0	56.9
Germany	31.7	41.7	43.5	59.8	57.1	60.9	60.7	61.1	60.2	58.6
Greece	27.7	59.8	89.0	111.3	108.7	108.3	105.5	104.6	103.9	99.9
Ireland	72.3	105.3	97.5	74.1	84.4	65.1	55.0	50.1	39.1	33.3
Italy	58.0	82.0	97.3	122.1	123.3	120.1	116.2	114.5	110.2	105.7
Luxembourg	9.2	9.5	4.5	6.2	5.6	3.6	3.2	4.7	5.3	4.0
Netherlands	46.0	70.0	77.1	75.3	77.0	70.0	66.8	63.2	56.3	52.1
Portugal	35.3	67.4	63.4	63.6	63.9	59.1	55.3	55.0	53.8	52.8
Spain	17.0	42.4	43.7	68.0	64.0	66.7	64.7	63.4	60.6	58.1
Sweden	39.6	61.6	42.1	76.0	76.6	73.0	71.8	65.2	55.6	53.4
UK	55.0	54.3	35.2	52.6	52.1	51.1	48.1	45.7	42.9	38.3
Euro-zone	35.2	52.6	58.6	74.7	72.3	74.7	73.1	72.0	69.7	67.7
EU-15	38.4	53.7	54.9	72.1	70.2	71.1	69.0	67.5	64.5	61.7

Source: Commission (2001).

sectors that export a large share of their output. In 2000, exports of goods and services increased by 13.2 per cent, stimulated by faster growth in the world economy and improved international competitiveness. The continuing strength of the US economy and the quicker than expected recovery of the Asian region were important reasons. The weakness of the euro combined with domestic wage moderation improved the competitiveness of German exports in these markets. Improved business confidence, in turn, led to increased equipment investment, which reinforced the favourable effects of the export boom.

As a consequence of rising output, employment levels increased by 1.5 per cent and unemployment fell to 8.1 per cent of the civilian labour force, its lowest level for seven years. Nevertheless, unemployment remains high in comparison with other advanced industrialized countries. Moreover, the national rate disguises a much higher rate in the eastern part of the country. Unemployment in the eastern Länder is roughly twice that of the western part, although there have been signs that employment is beginning to rise in the relatively small but burgeoning manufacturing sector in the east. One consequence of a relatively high national rate of unemployment was that wage inflation remained modest. This helped ensure that, despite faster growth, inflation remained subdued in the first half of the year. However, Germany was adversely affected by the sudden rise in world oil prices in the second half of the year, with the average rate of HICP inflation rising to 2.1 per cent. When present wage agreements expire at the end of 2001, there is a danger that this could lead to wages rising faster as workers seek to restore their purchasing power.

An important development in Germany during the year was the tax reforms announced by the Social Democratic-led coalition. These entailed a major reduction in the level of personal, corporate and capital gains tax, with an estimated impact on GDP equivalent to 1.5 per cent (Commission, 2000). This, however, will be spread over a two-year period, although the effect will be to cause a budget surplus of 1.5 per cent of GDP to move into deficit equivalent to 1.7 per cent of GDP in 2001 (though as pointed out above, the budget surplus last year had been due mainly to sale of UMTS licences, the proceeds from which were equivalent to 2.5 per cent of GDP (Commission, 2000)). The effects of the measures will be to reduce the top personal tax rate from 51 to 48.5 per cent and the top corporate tax rate from 55 to 40 per cent, bringing these rates more closely into line with other European countries (Barber, 2000). It has long been argued that Germany's high taxes have deterred foreign companies from investing in Germany and contributed to its sluggish growth in recent years. Although these tax reductions have been accompanied by measures to reduce public expenditure, the result will be some deterioration in Germany's fiscal position in the next two years.

Despite this impressive growth performance during the year, it is now apparent that the rate of growth fell sharply in the second half, to 0.2 per cent in the fourth quarter of the year (Barber, 2001). The slowdown in the US and some weakening of the recovery in East Asia may have contributed towards this. However, the low level of domestic demand appears also to have been a contributory factor, as wages have failed to keep pace with rising prices. Although tax cuts may have helped to encourage more consumer spending, these have been partly offset by the effects of higher short-term interest rates. One of the difficulties facing the monetary authorities at the ECB is that, while lower interest rates are needed to sustain growth in Germany, in other parts of the euro-zone there are clear signs of overheating.

France

Last year, the French economy repeated the impressive performance of previous years. GDP grew at a rate of 3.2 per cent, compared with 3.1 per cent and 2.9 per cent in 1998 and 1999. As in previous years, private consumption boosted by increased employment was the major factor in the expansion. Employment grew by 2.0 per cent during the year and the unemployment rate fell to 9.5 per cent. The latter compares with an unemployment rate of 12.3 per cent only three years ago. Much of France's success in job creation has been concentrated in the services sector, with a marked increase in the number of temporary contracts (*Financial Times*, 14 June 2000). The introduction of a 35-hour working week in firms employing more than 20 people is also credited with some of the growth in employment, although French employers have questioned how many new jobs have resulted.

Fiscal policy appears also to have played a mildly stimulatory role. Successive budgetary packages introduced by the Jospin government have given an expansionary impetus to the economy. Last year, the government recorded a fiscal deficit equivalent to 1.3 per cent of GDP, only a little below the previous year's deficit of 1.6 per cent. One reason was the tax-cutting measures introduced by the government that added the equivalent of 0.9 per cent of GDP to the economy. During the year, a further programme of tax cuts was announced that is to be implemented between 2001 and 2003, with an impact equal to a further 1.2 per cent of GDP. Unlike in Germany, these tax cuts have not been wholly accompanied by equivalent reductions on the spending side. In its *World Economic Outlook*, the IMF indicated that it considered 'a more ambitious deficit reduction target' to be desirable in France (IMF, 2000).

Italy

Last year, for the second year in succession, Italy had the slowest growth rate of any country in the euro-zone. Indeed, Italy's growth rate for the whole of the period since 1996 has averaged only 2 per cent compared with 2.7 per cent for the EU as a whole. Nevertheless, last year, with GDP growing at a rate of 2.9 per cent compared with 1.6 per cent in 1999, there seemed to be clear signs that Italy's economy was at last growing more quickly. Moreover, growth appears to have been sustained despite the slowing down of the US economy. Official estimates by the Italian government showed output growing at a rate of 0.8 per cent in the final quarter of the year. Export demand appears to have played the major role, helped by the depreciation of the euro. However, domestic demand, especially for investment goods, has also been a major contributor.

As a consequence, employment grew by 1.5 per cent last year and the unemployment rate fell to 10.5 per cent. As in France, the biggest increase appears to have occurred in the service sector with evidence of a growing use of temporary and part-time contracts.

Nevertheless, the Italian labour market continues to suffer from major rigidities that contribute to the relatively high unemployment rate. Bureaucratic administration is widely regarded as a factor constraining growth. Italy's dependence on small and medium-sized companies is regarded by some observers as a further source of weakness. However, for many decades, the greatest burden on the economy has been the large public sector deficit and level of public indebtedness. On this score, considerable progress has been made in recent years as Italy has striven to fulfil the convergence criteria for entering the euro. Last year, the fiscal deficit fell to 0.3 per cent of GDP.

However, as in other Member States, this was helped by a large bonus from the sale of UMTS licences. If sales from UMTS licenses are excluded, the deficit for the year stood at 1.3 per cent of GDP. Next year, the unadjusted deficit is set to rise to 1.3 per cent of GDP, partly as a result of tax reforms announced during the course of last year. More effort may be needed on the expenditure side if Italy is to achieve the objective of balancing the budget in the medium term. In order to make further inroads into the large debt-to-GDP ratio, Italy must run a budget surplus over a number of years. Last year, this stood at 110.2 per cent of GDP but is forecast to fall further to 105.7 per cent in 2001, helped by proceeds from the government's planned privatization programme. In the longer term, a key issue remains the need for a reform of Italy's state pension system, which is widely regarded as unsustainable in the long run and likely to imply a large tax burden for employers (Blitz, 2001). In the absence of any reforms being agreed, future governments will be unable to deliver further tax reductions and achieve their deficit reduction targets.

Spain

Last year, Spain's GDP grew at a rate of 4.1 per cent, its fourth successive year of strong economic growth. This has made it one of the fastest growing economies in the EU. Some slowing down is forecast for this year due largely to weaker domestic demand. As a result of the high level of economic activity, employment grew at a rate of 3.3 per cent a year, only a little below the rate of 3.5 per cent for the previous year. Although Spain still has the highest unemployment rate in the EU, unemployment has been falling fast. Last year, it fell to 14.1 per cent with a further reduction to 12.8 per cent forecast for the current year.

Rapid growth has generated some upward pressure on prices. Last year, Spain had the third highest inflation rate in the EU. As measured by the HIPC, inflation rose from 2.2 per cent in 1999 to 3.4 per cent in 2000 with higher oil prices having an especially major effect because of the relatively high weighting of energy costs in Spain's consumer prices index. Slower growth this year is expected to result in some easing of inflationary pressures. Clearly, however, Spain needs sustained output growth if the objective of bringing unemployment rates down to EU-wide levels is to be achieved.

In 2000, Spain also made further progress in reducing the size of the central government deficit. This fell from 1.2 per cent of GDP to 0.3 per cent and is forecast to move into surplus in the current year. Rising tax receipts stimulated by rapid economic growth have contributed strongly towards this outcome. Receipts from the sale of UMTS licences have also helped, although to a much smaller extent than in other countries. As a result, Spain looks set to achieve a significant reduction in the ratio of public sector indebtedness to GDP in the current year.

United Kingdom

Last year, the UK economy enjoyed an improved growth rate of 3.0 per cent, only slightly below the EU average, and a continuing low inflation rate of only 0.8 per cent. Unemployment continued to fall to 5.6 per cent of the labour force, below the average for the EU as a whole. Despite the strength of sterling, UK exports have held up well, due largely to buoyant demand in the UK's overseas markets. Apart from exports, the main stimulus to growth came from private consumption, stimulated by rising real incomes (as average earnings have grown faster than prices) and declining unemployment. Nevertheless, monetary policy remained relatively tight, while the budget stayed strongly in surplus to the tune of 4.3 per cent of GDP. The latter was due, largely, to a faster increase in tax receipts than the authorities planned for, combined with revenues from the sales of UMTS licences. The European Commission is forecasting a small decrease in the growth rate in 2001, because consumption is expected to grow more slowly. Households are expected to respond to higher real interest rates by restoring their savings ratio. The recent decline in share prices is also expected to weaken consumption further.

Other Member States

Among the smaller countries, *Belgium* saw a sharp acceleration in growth in 2000 to 3.9 per cent compared with 2.7 per cent in the previous year. This was the highest growth rate Belgium has enjoyed since 1988. Growth was broadly based with private consumption, investment spending and exports all contributing. The buoyancy of the EU economy as a whole has been an important factor in the health of the Belgium economy, given Belgium's dependence on trade with the rest of the EU.

On 1 January, 2001, *Greece* became the twelfth member of the euro-zone, after successfully meeting all the convergence conditions required for entry. This followed a year of impressive growth, with GDP rising by 4.1 per cent a year. Domestic demand, especially fixed investment spending, contributed the most to GDP growth. Rapid growth in exports was partly offset by increased imports. Unemployment fell to 11 per cent of the civilian labour force, although this was still the second highest rate in the EU. Inflation rose slightly to 2.9 per cent, despite more moderate wage growth. The main reason was the surge in world oil prices in the final quarter of the year. The public sector deficit fell further to 0.9 per cent of GDP, a major turnaround when compared with government borrowing equivalent to 11.5 per cent in the first half of the 1990s.

Ireland once again enjoyed the highest growth rate of any country in the EU. GDP grew by a very fast 10.7 per cent, quicker even than last year's 9.8 per cent. Private consumption continued growing rapidly spurred on by increased employment, higher real earnings, favourable wealth effects resulting from the boom in the property market and negative real interest rates as domestic inflation increased. Investment spending remained strong, while exports continued rising despite the rise in domestic inflation. The latter, however, remains the principal concern. At 5.3 per cent a year, Ireland's inflation rate is now the highest in the EU. Rising house prices and increased pressure from wages as labour market conditions became increasingly tight were the main reasons for this.

In January of this year, Ireland became the first Member State to be reprimanded by the European Commission for its budgetary policy under the terms of the SGP. This followed the adoption last year of a budget that was considered over-expansionary. The budget provided for substantial increases in expenditure, while, at the same time making large tax reductions. Nevertheless, the budget is forecast to remain strongly in surplus, equivalent to 3.9 per cent of GDP this year. This has led some economists to question the decision taken by the Commission to 'name and shame' the Irish Republic, especially given the fact that Ireland has been Europe's most successful economy for half a decade (see, e.g., Wolf, 2001).

With a growth rate of 8.5 per cent in 2000, *Luxembourg* was the second fastest growing economy in the EU. Over the period 1996–2002, Luxembourg will have enjoyed (if current forecasts prove correct) a growth rate of 6.1 per cent, compared with 2.7 per cent for the EU as a whole. Domestic demand and exports all played a part. As in Ireland, the public sector remained strongly in surplus: the budget balance stood at 5.3 per cent of GDP. Rapid employment growth reduced the unemployment rate to 2.2 per cent. This created some inflationary pressures, with wages rising by 5.1 per cent and consumer prices by 3.8 per cent. The pressures caused by overheating were made worse by the effects of higher energy costs.

Last year, *the Netherlands* economy grew at a rate of 3.9 per cent a year, the fifth successive year of rapid growth. Employment again grew quickly and unemployment fell further to 2.8 per cent of the workforce. This led to some build-up of inflationary pressures with wages rising by 4.1 per cent a year. Although inflation remained relatively moderate with consumer prices rising by 2.3 per cent (the average for the EU as a whole), inflation is forecast to rise further. Higher indirect taxes have added to the effects of rising oil prices in giving a sharp upward push to the price level.

Growth in *Austria* averaged 3.2 per cent last year, somewhat faster than the 2.8 per cent increase in 1999. Rising consumption spending, stimulated by a reduction in income tax and an increase in child benefits, grew strongly. Investment spending and export demand were also strong. After a year of very low inflation, consumer prices rose by 2 per cent in 2000. However, higher excise duties and higher oil prices were the main reasons for this. Despite major cuts in taxes, the fiscal deficit fell to 1.1 per cent of GDP.

At 3.3 per cent, *Portugal* experienced growth only slightly faster than in the previous year, but broadly in line with the EU average. Growth is expected to decelerate to 2.6 per cent this year due largely to a weakening of domestic demand. This follows several years of moderately rapid growth, but which has been accompanied by a steady worsening in the current account balance of payments as imports have grown consistently faster than exports. Last year, this reached the equivalent of 14.2 per cent of GDP.

In 2000, *Finland's* GDP grew at an impressive rate of 5.7 per cent compared to 4.2 per cent in the previous year and the third fastest in the EU. Exports have been the strongest factor in this growth, although this was mainly concentrated in the first half of the year. Private consumption also rose, boosted by a high level of consumer confidence and a strong 'feel-good' factor. As in other Member States, inflation rose sharply to 3 per cent due both to domestic pressures and the rise in oil prices. Public finances remained very healthy with the fiscal surplus rising to 6.7 per cent of GDP.

Outside the euro-zone, *Denmark* enjoyed faster growth in 2000, after a mild slowdown in 1999. GDP grew by 2.9 per cent compared with 2.1 per cent in 1999. Nevertheless, this was still the slowest rate of growth of any country in the EU (with the single exception of Italy) and is forecast to be still lower in the current year. A major problem appears to be the sluggish nature of domestic demand, especially private consumption, which actually fell in 2000. Export demand was relatively strong, aided by the depreciation of the Danish krone, although this was more than offset by increased imports.

Lastly, *Sweden* enjoyed strong growth in 2000 for the third year in succession, albeit a little slower than in the previous year. GDP rose by 3.6 per cent compared with 4.1 per cent in 1999. Domestic and external factors contributed more or less equally towards this. Low interest rates and tax reductions both helped to ensure buoyant domestic demand. Employment grew at a rate of 2.2 per cent and unemployment fell to 5.9 per cent of the labour force. In line with other Member States, inflation rose due largely to higher oil prices. Nevertheless, at 1.3 per cent, Sweden's inflation was among the lowest in the EU.

IV. Conclusion

Overall, 2000 was a good year for the EU economies. At a time when growth was beginning to falter in the United States, and with little sign of a recovery in Japan, growth accelerated in the EU. If, as seems likely, the US experiences a further fall in GDP growth in 2001, the world may look to the EU to ensure a continuing high level of global economic activity. However, this may prove more difficult if the build-up of inflationary pressures in 2000 is enduring. It is true that the rise in world oil prices was the main reason for the rise in consumer prices last year. As this resulted in a one-off increase in energy prices, and assuming that oil prices do not rise further, inflation in the EU will eventually fall. On the other hand, it is clear that there was an increase in inflationary pressures in a number of the smaller Member States in 2000 that was the result of over-heating. This will create continuing problems for the monetary authorities in the euro-zone in determining the appropriate level of short-term interest rates in the current year, in view of the fact that growth may be slowing in a number of the larger Member States (see, e.g., Barber, 2001).

Ironically, the factor that has most helped generate faster growth in the EU in the past year has been the weak euro. Although the weakness of the euro has become a source of concern for policy-makers in the EU, it has done a great deal to boost demand inside the euro-zone and ensure rapid growth in countries where growth appeared to be faltering. It is now widely understood that the decline of the euro was mainly a reflection of the strength of the US economy, which attracted large flows of long-term capital (particularly in the form of foreign direct investment) enticed by the prospect of higher returns. As growth slows down in the US, these inflows can be expected to fall sharply with a consequent downward adjustment in the US dollar and a possible knock-on effect for euro-zone countries. If short-term interest rates are pushed up further in the euro-zone in order to contain the build-up of inflation, there is a danger that growth could fall sharply, particularly in those Member States dependent on exports to the rest of the world. The ECB will need to exercise great skill in determining the appropriate policy response in the light of these conflicting pressures. In the meantime, it is important that the Member States push ahead with structural reforms to ensure that potential output can grow at a faster rate and that sustained growth does not lead to bottlenecks in factor and goods markets.

References

Barber, T. (2000) 'On the Loose'. *Financial Times*, 29 September.
Barber, T. (2001) 'The Juggernaut Slows'. *Financial Times*, 6 March.
Blitz, J. (2001) 'Much has Changed for Italy but Growth Rate Disappoints'. *Financial Times*, 15 February.
Commission of the European Communities (2000) *European Economy* – Supplement A, Economic Trends, No. 10/11, October/November (Brussels: European Commission, Directorate-General for Economic and Financial Affairs).
Commission of the European Communities (2001) *European Economy* – Supplement A, Economic Trends, March/April (Brussels: European Commission, Directorate-General for Economic and Financial Affairs).
International Monetary Fund (IMF) (2000) *World Economic Outlook*, October 2000, Focus on Transition Economies (Washington D.C.: IMF).
International Monetary Fund (2001) *World Economic Outlook*, May 2001 (Washington D.C.: IMF).
Organization for Economic Co-operation and Development (2000), *OECD Economic Outlook* No. 68, December (Paris: OECD).
Wolf, M. (2001) 'Picking on the Wrong Target'. *Financial Times*, 14 February.

Journal of Common Market Studies   Volume 39, Annual Review
                                                    September 2001

The European Union in 2000 at a Glance

GEORG WIESSALA
University of Central Lancashire

- The year of the promotion of reform and new forms of European Governance saw the conclusion of an Intergovernmental Conference (IGC) and the new Treaty of Nice
- 50th Anniversary of the Schuman Declaration and 50th Anniversary of the signing of the European Convention on Human Rights; Human Rights Act (HRA) incorporates the Council of Europe's 1950 ECHR into UK Law
- Presidency of the Council of Ministers: Portugal (January–June) and France (July–December)
- Enlargement negotiations with Bulgaria, Latvia, Lithuania, Malta, Romania and Slovakia officially launched; Accession Partnership with Turkey reached
- Special summit meetings in Lisbon (March) and Biarritz (October), South-east Europe summit in Skopje (October), Danish 'no' vote in single currency referendum
- European Cities of Culture: Avignon, Bergen, Bologna, Brussels, Helsinki, Krakow, Prague, Reykyavik and Santiago de Compostela
- First ever EU summits with India and Africa take place; EU formulates a strategy for its relations with Indonesia
- The Union begins to overhaul its development policy

January

1   Portugal assumes the Presidency of the Council of Ministers for the first half of 2000, continuing the work set by the Helsinki summit in December 1999. Enlargement, reform and job creation are some of the priorities of the Portuguese Presidency.

3   General Election in Croatia. The Croatian Democratic Union of Franjo Tudjman (who died on 10 December 1999) was replaced by a more liberal West-leaning centre-left party. New Prime Minister is Ivica Racan.

4   Following the Commission's reasoned opinion to France of 14 December 1999, the Commission formally initiates a court case against France for failing to lift its ban on UK beef.

12   Commission White Paper on Food Safety.

19   Consultation paper on 'Reforming and Modernising the Commission' is published. It contains 84 measures, to be implemented over the next two-and-a-half years. The three key areas are: financial management and audit, activity-based management and human resources. An Internal Audit Service is to be established on 1 May 2000.

24   EU foreign ministers agree a limited sanctions package against Russia's renewed campaign in Chechnya.

26   Commission paper on reform, decision-making and enlargement before the IGC (IP/00/79) «http://europa.eu.int/igc2000/index_en.htm».

February

2   Commission stresses its concern for human and minority rights, in connection with Austrian developments.

     Commission Communication on *Closer Relations with Indonesia* (IP/00/98; WiE 3/2/00).

2–3 The EU and the ACP states finalize the 20-year successor framework to Lomé IV in Cotonou (Benin). The signing ceremony is on 23 June 2000 in Cotonou.

     The European Parliament's concerns focus on Austria and Jörg Haider's Freedom Party. In a resolution, Parliament condemns Haider's xenophobic and racist statements.

6   Finland elects Tarja Halonen as the country's first female President.

7   In the second round of Presidential Elections in Croatia, Stipe Mesic, Yugoslavia's last President in 1991, is elected.

9   Commission unveils its Work Programme for 2000 and the new Five-Year Strategic Objectives blueprint, focusing on internal reform and good governance, human rights, an enhanced external role for the Union, and a new economic and social agenda for growth and modernization (IP/00/133; WiE 10.2.00).

     Following the October 1999 Tampere summit, the Commission adopts a milestone Green Paper on Legal Aid in Civil Matters (IP/00/130; GR 2000, point 460).

Ole Due presents the Report of a Reflection Group on the future of the judicial system of the EU (IP/00/116) «http://europa.eu.int/en/comm/sj/homesjfr.htm».

14   Special Ministerial Meeting officially launches the 2000 Intergovernmental Conference (IGC) «http://europa.eu.int/igc2000/index_en.htm».

15   Following the decisions taken during the Helsinki European summit on 10–11 December 1999, negotiations with six new applicant counties, Bulgaria, Latvia, Lithuania, Malta, Romania and Slovakia were officially launched.

16–17 Jos Chabert, from Etterbeek, Flanders, is elected President of the Committee of the Regions until 2002, taking over from Manfred Dammeyer, who becomes Vice-President. Chabert emphasizes his determination to strengthen the Committee's political role, ambition and impact.

17–21 The European Parliament (EP) debates, *inter alia*, Vice-President Neil Kinnock's reform initiatives regarding the Commission.

28   The Lomé IV Convention expires.

EU defence ministers agree to pledge troops and equipment to the new Rapid Reaction Force by the end of the year.

March

1   Commission approves White Paper on *Reforming the Commission* «http://europa.eu.int/comm/reform/index_en.htm», see also SPEECH/00/352, 412.

1   Special EU summit on job creation in Lisbon continues discussing the employment strategy first agreed at the Luxembourg jobs summit in November 1997.

8   The Dialogue on Europe public discussion forum is launched.

9   Greece forwards request for membership in the third stage of EMU to the Commission. The Council had issued an opinion on the Greek convergence programme in January 2000.

14   Commission President Prodi presented the Commission's Work Programme for 2000 to the European Parliament. The Programme focused, amongst other topics, on a European Charter of Fundamental Rights, Citizenship and the Environment (SPEECH/00/82).

14   Commission adopts Communication Action against Anti-Personnel Landmines: Reinforcing the Contribution of the EU, containing measures to strengthen the fight against landmines (IP/00/250).

14   Commission report on the Outermost Regions of the European Union.

18   Research Commissioner Philippe Busquin outlines plans for a future European Area for Research, transcending the multi-annual Framework Programmes and counterbalancing US strengths in this area.

21   The GAC approves a punitive sanctions package against Slobodan Milosevic's

Government in Serbia, but shows itself disinclined to sponsor a proposal to condemn China's human rights record at the United Nations Commission on Human Rights in Geneva.

23–4   With European unemployment still standing at around 15 million, the Extraordinary European Council on Employment, Economic Reform and Social Cohesion takes place in Lisbon. Dubbed the 'dotcom summit', it discusses the eEurope Initiative and the eLearning Strategy launched in 1999, against the background of the challenges of globalization, 'e-commerce', the demands of greater social inclusion, the 'information society' and a 'knowledge-based economy'. The summit also debates the role of skilled, non-EU personnel, progress in Security Policy and the situation in the western Balkans (PRES/00/900; IP/00/215, 234, 239, 284; WiE 2.3.00; 16.3.00, 23.3.00, 30.3.00).

April

3–4   First ever EU Africa summit held in Cairo, under the direction of the EU and the Organization for African Unity (OAU). Libya's Colonel Muammar Gadafy attends. The Cairo Declaration and Action Plan emphasize regional integration, social issues, arms policies, terrorism, democracy and human rights «http://ue.eu.int/newsroom/main.cfm?LANG=1».

7   Official opening of the European Monitoring Centre on Racism and Xenophobia in Vienna.

11   Commission follows the recommendations of the Helsinki summit of December 1999 and proposes the establishment of a Rapid Reaction Facility (RRF), to accelerate EU external activities (IP/00/365; WiE 13.4.00).

11   Commission stresses human rights in a new communication on election assistance and observation.

12   According to a Commission report, some UK newspapers are deliberately misleading their readers about the EU, with a 'cavalier disregard for the facts' «http://www.cec.org.uk/pubs/prwatch/pw00/latest.htm and ISEC/06/00)».

24–6   Commission adopts communication on an overhaul of EC development policy (IP/00/410, 480) «http://europa.eu.int/comm/development/document/dev_policy_en.htm».

27   In a move to combat inflation and against the background of a falling euro (€), the European Central Bank (ECB) raises interest rates by 0.25 per cent, increasing the main refinancing rate to 3.75 per cent from 4 May 2000.

May

4   'E-Commerce' Directive adopted (IP/00/442) «http://europa.eu.int/comm/internalmarket/en/media/eleccomm/index.htm».

6–7   Javier Solana, High Representative for the EU Foreign Policy, attempts to resolve a hostage crisis involving some EU citizens on the Philippine island of Jolo.

8   EU finance ministers issue a 'Statement of Common Concern', over the euro's fall against the US dollar.

16   Commissioner Patten announces reforms concerning the EU's development policy (IP/00/480, cf. 26 April).

16   Commissioner Byrne initiates an EU Public Health Strategy to balance Member State health policies (IP/00/484).

The Culture Council adopts a paper on a new EU audio-visual policy, taking into account digital television.

25   The Europe-Direct Information service is launched (IP/00/525, 534) «http:// europa.eu.int/europedirect».

26   EU–Canada summit.

29   A joint statement issued after the EU–Russia summit stresses the potential for common interests and the 'progressive development of relations' and points to areas of future co-operation such as Chechnya, terrorism, money-laundering and trade issues resulting from the EU–Russia Partnership and Cooperation Agreement.

29   The Convention on Mutual Legal Assistance in Criminal Matters is signed at the Council, to facilitate cross-border investigations (WiE, 1.6.00).

Decision to combat internet child pornography and other measures are adopted.

31   Talks during the last EU–US summit involving President Clinton revolve around US plans for a National Missile Defense Plan (NMDP).

June

Screening of the *acquis communautaire* and the drafting of an accession partnership starts with Turkey (IP/00/649, 839).

6   Council of Ministers agrees a directive on anti-racism, as the first measure approved under the anti-discrimination provisions of the Treaty of Amsterdam, with implications for a reversal of the burden of proof in relevant cases.

7   The Commission proposes a directive to ban sexual harassment at work. The proposal interprets sexual harassment as a form of sexual discrimination and brings a 1976 equal opportunities directive into line with European Court of Justice decisions (IP/00/588).

13   European Charter of Small Enterprises adopted.

15   First Report by the European Anti-Fraud Office (OLAF).

19–20 European Council Meeting in Santa Maria da Feira approves Greece's EMU accession and confirms the direction of the accession negotiations. It also adopts a Common Strategy on the Mediterranean Region and approves, amongst other initiatives, the *e*Europe and Anti-Drugs Action Plans.

22   Environment ministers reach agreement on new key environmental legislation, concerning limits to four significant air-polluting substances from 2010.

28   The Commission adopts a new Social Policy Agenda to tackle the challenges of the 'knowledge-based economy' (IP/00/673).

28   During the first-ever EU–India summit, the EU recognizes the bilateral potential for co-operation in the Enhanced EU–India Dialogue. Summit participants debate security, crime and trade issues.

July
1   France takes over the rotating Presidency of the Council of Ministers.

EU–Mexico Free Trade Agreement enters into force and gives EU traders access which has similarities to provisions of the NAFTA framework (IP/00/703).

3–7   Parliament votes 443–64 to grant the Commission a discharge for its 1998 budget and thus ends a protracted dispute over irregularities and fraud.

4   ECJ imposes a fine on a Member State, for the first time, for failing to comply with an earlier judgment.

5   Commission Communication on an '.eu' domain name.

7   Commission proposal to extend the 1980 EC–ASEAN Agreement to new ASEAN members Lao PDR and Cambodia.

14   Commission communication on the reorganisation of the treaties.

18–19 EU–Japan summit reflects on the Deregulation Dialogue and inaugurates a Decade of Japan–Europe Co-operation.

28   Draft Charter of Fundamental Rights is published.

August
1   Commission adopts proposal on the Community patent.

September
Fuel crisis and depot blockades in the UK and Continental Europe.

6   The Commission paper on the Mediterranean, reinvigorating the Barcelona Process, seeks to build on the EU's Common Strategy on the Mediterranean adopted during the Feira Council in June (IP/00/975).

12   EU sanctions against Austria, which were adopted in February, are lifted.

The Commission expresses its 'support in principle', for a Charter of Fundamental Rights of the European Union (IP/00/995).

15   EU–Ukraine summit debates aid and WTO issues, President Leonid Kuchma's plans for reform and a replacement for the Chernobyl reactor, scheduled to close in December 2000.

20   Transport Council holds an emergency meeting in Luxembourg, against the background of Europe-wide fuel tax protests, but makes little progress in agreeing a common stand on the impact of oil prices.

20   Commission adopts Accelerated Action Targeted at Major Communicable Diseases within the Context of Poverty Reduction, to intensify the fight against HIV/AIDS, Malaria and TB (IP/00/1031).

20   Commission initiates the 'Everything but Arms (EBA)' initiative for duty- and quota-free access for all products from Least Developed Countries (LDCs) to Union markets.

24   Presidential elections in the Federal Republic of Yugoslavia is won by Vojislav Kostunica and the democratic opposition to Slobodan Milosevic.

28   JHA Council agrees to invest Europol with the independence to initiate investigations.

28   Danish voters vote 'No' in a referendum on whether to join the single currency.

October

2   Convention drafts the Charter of Fundamental Rights for the European Union.

2   Human Rights Act (HRA) incorporates the Council of Europe's 1950 ECHR into UK law.

9–10 GAC lifts sanctions against Serbia and proposes the extension of the Stabilisation and Association Process for south-eastern Europe launched in 1999.

11   Commission adopts a communication on the nature of the Charter of Fundamental Rights of the EU.

13–14 The Biarritz Informal European Council debates Austria, the IGC, foreign affairs, the progress of internal reform and QMV, and endorses the EU Charter of Fundamental Rights against the background of British concerns. The summit welcomes the newly-elected Yugoslav President Vojislav Kostunica (IP/00/1148).

20–21 The Third Asia–Europe Meeting (ASEM 3) in Seoul issues a Seoul Declaration for Peace on the Korean Peninsula, updates the Asia–Europe Co-operation Framework (AECF), extends the Asian Trust Fund to a second phase and endorses a number of priority initiatives, on, for instance, educational exchanges, health, migration and global trade «http://asem3.org».

23   Third annual EU–China summit, Beijing (1st summit: 2.4.98, London; 2nd summit: 21.12.99, Beijing).

25   Summit on south-east Europe in the Macedonian capital Skopje decides on closer EU co-operation with the region.

27   EU–China Agreement on insurance licences builds on the landmark May 2000 EU–China accord on Chinese accession to the WTO (IP/00/1227).

30 EU–Russia summit focuses on security in Europe and issues two joint declarations.

30 Commission communication on Latin America and the Caribbean, following the first EU–Latin America summit in June 1999.

November
3 50th Anniversary of the signing of the European Convention on Human Rights.

8 Commission paper on enlargement targets 2002 for first accessions (IP/00/1264).

15–16 Euro–Mediterranean Conference in Marseilles.

20 During a conference in Brussels, Member States pledge their contributions to the 60,000-strong Rapid Reaction Force, planned to be ready for deployment by 2003. A day later (21 November) the candidate countries, Norway and Iceland agreed to contribute.

22 Commission publishes two communications on asylum and immigration policy (IP/00/1340; WiE, 23.11.00).

23–4 The EU's Zagreb summit on the western Balkans.

27–8 Council agrees the 5-year Social Policy Agenda to be approved at Nice (see 28 June 2000).

30 French Prime Minister Jacques Chirac and British PM Tony Blair have a pre-Nice summit meeting.

December
7–9 Nice European Council demonstrates power struggles between larger and smaller Member States and the continued prevalence of national over European interests amongst EU Member States. It nevertheless reaffirms priority of the enlargement process, and 'proclaims' the Charter of Fundamental Rights of the European Union. The Treaty of Nice deals with the 'Amsterdam Leftovers'.

8 Council adopts EURODAC Regulation concerning asylum-seekers and other third-country nationals.

Sources
European Access, 2000.
European Voice, Vol. 6, 2000: *'For the Record'*.
General Report of Activities of the European Union, 2000.
The Week in Europe (WiE), weekly newssheet, paper and internet versions.

Journal of Common Market Studies

Volume 39, Annual Review
September 2001

Documentation of the European Union in 2000

PATRICK OVERY
Exeter University
and
IAN MAYFIELD
University of Portsmouth

A: RECENT TRENDS IN EU DOCUMENTATION

Looking back at the past year, the most striking aspect in the world of EU documentation is the extent to which the themes we identified last year have continued to dominate. These themes include the replacement of print with electronic sources; concern over long-term availability of such sources; tensions between political and economic imperatives in the information market and growing concern about rights of access to documentation. Such concerns have persisted within an institutional context characterized by uncertainty and disorder as Commission reform pursues its labyrinthine path. This confusion has made it difficult to seek answers or to make representation on documentation issues as on others, and it is similarly difficult to feel confident about the satisfactory resolution of the problems outlined here.

We reported last year on the apparent contradiction between the growing provision of free legislative information on the Eur-Lex database and the continued availability, at a price of around £1,000 per annum, of the official legislative database Celex. Reports that these two databases, together with the document delivery service, EUDOR, would be integrated within a single portal during the year 2000 proved to be premature. This move is now planned for some time during 2001. During the past year, however EUR-OP, provider of these databases, has attempted to explain the contradiction by elaborating its policy on legislative databases. Eur-Lex is seen as a means of making EU legislation easily available to as many people as possible – 'the people's Celex', as its early subtitle had it – but is tailored accordingly. That is to say, it is a relatively low-cost resource, with documentation provided within a defined framework and searchable via a fairly crude search engine. It is true to say that Eur-Lex is developing and improving all the time – for example, there will shortly (in Eur-Lex Plus) be access to the pdf archives of the *Official Journal (OJ)* from 1 January 1998 – but it will not be a comprehensive service. Celex, on the other hand, will continue to be the Rolls Royce of EU legislative databases, with powerful search facilities intended for the professional expert. Unfortunately, the qualities of the most sophisticated manifestation of this, the Celex expert search facility, have so far remained opaque to all but a few. To access expert search, users must have a browser which supports Java applets, and with Internet Explorer 4.01 or higher and Netscape 4.5 or higher recommended. Whether or not these are realistic expectations, the fact seems to be that take-up of the service has been much less than anticipated by EUR-OP. The third source, EUDOR, is seen as the official archive, to which users will turn – at a price – for documents not available via the other two. Doubts remain, however, as to how the planned single portal will work and in particular how the interface between free and costed information will be structured. How many users will be aware that many of the documents for sale via EUDOR are available free of charge on other web sites including Europarl (Parliament reports), the Competition DG's web site (merger decisions) and Eur-Lex (*COM* documents)?

Information professionals lobbied hard against the abrupt cessation at the beginning of March 2000 of the free distribution to official information 'Relays' of the printed *Official Journal*. The case was well made, pointing as it did to the greater convenience for users of the printed version, the archiving question – for how long will internet versions of documents remain available? – and questions regarding reliability of networks and the technical and legal difficulties of offering network access to a wide readership. The arguments were to no avail and the trend towards replacement of printed with electronic has continued with, for example, the cessation of the printed debates annex of the *OJ* (to be replaced by CD-Rom). European Documentation Centres recently received a circular in which they were invited to cease taking *COM* documents in print since these were now on the web. Experience suggests that such invitations are shortly followed by compulsion – a worrying prospect given that the availability of *COM* documents on the web is by no means comprehensive. A good example of the archiving problem and also of lack of co-ordination was provided by a recent discussion on the Eurodoc discussion list about access to back issues of *Eurobarometer* reports. In response to an enquiry as to how to get hold of a *Eurobarometer* survey on Europeans and the environment, a knowledgeable correspondent wrote:

> There has never been a systematic distribution system for the special surveys listed on the Eurobarometer website and at the back of each print version of the Eurobarometer survey. A few are available electronically on the Eurobarometer website. Others have been scattered over the websites of the various DGs funding the surveys, with the links unfortunately disappearing over time. So in most cases, a special request has to be made to get a copy. Those with time and energy to pursue such matters might well ask questions about

the appropriateness of such arrangements for gaining access to the results of publicly funded surveys.

The issue of access to documentation came fully to the fore. A year ago, we expressed concern that the apparently worthy intentions of the proposed regulation on access to documents might be subverted in practice given the wide scope of the exceptions provided for by the legislation. In fact, debate on this issue has become enmeshed with an event relating to a separate piece of legislation, an amendment to Council Decision 731 of 1993 on public access to Council documents. In the holiday season of August 2000, the Council unilaterally decided to restrict access to documents on the grounds of security and defence. According to Michael Cashman, rapporteur of the European Parliament's Committee on Citizens' Freedom and Rights, the so-called 'Solana Decision' (after Council Secretary-General Javier Solana), 'threw into confusion the process of defining new rules under the proposed Regulation' (Cashman, 2001). Leaving aside the constitutional issues arising from the fact that this action was taken without consulting Parliament – even though the legislation in question was subject to the co-decision procedure – this decision has been greeted with widespread consternation. The scope of the potential restriction is wide, extending beyond those denominated top secret, secret or confidential to a range of other documents linked to these. Furthermore, according to the pressure group Statewatch, the scope of the restriction has also been extended to other fields, since a later draft of the Council's common position 'deletes the words "in the field of security and defence" thus applying the concept of "sensitive" (changed from "special") documents to all areas of EU activity including justice and home affairs (policing, immigration and asylum, customs and legal co-operation), trade and aid and so on' (Statewatch, 2000). There is also the danger that other institutions will adopt similar restrictions, fear of which is heightened by the fact that the Commission has announced its intention to review its rules on public access. By early 2001, 'Trialogue' discussions aimed at harmonizing the approach of Council, Commission and Parliament on access to documents had failed to make progress:

> After three meetings of the three institutions to resolve the differences between their draft proposals there was little, or no agreement, on a 'compromise'. The process will now – after a three month delay – return to the formal 'co-decision' procedure whereby all three institutions have to agree on the new code of access. This process could take up to eight months to complete. The deadline set by the Amsterdam Treaty agreed in June 1997 was that the new code had to be in place by 1 May 2001. (Statewatch, 2001)

Those wishing to monitor progress on this issue are advised to visit the Statewatch website at «http://www.statewatch.org/».

On a more positive note, there was reason to be optimistic during the year about access to Eurostat data. In February 2000 the new Eurostat website was launched «http://europa.eu.int/comm/eurostat». In addition to a news service and links to information about publications, the site now contains a much increased amount of actual data, with more than 300 statistical indicators available free of charge. Later in the year news began to emerge of a deal to be offered by Eurostat which would offer some 1400 Eurostat publications in pdf format on CD-Rom, with privileged access to the website for subscribers. This deal will cost around €1000, but is expected to be available free of charge to European Documentation Centres (EDCs). If so, this will represent a substantial move towards restoration of the level of statistical provision available in EDCs in the early 1980s, before cutbacks in Eurostat provision began to take hold.

There were other bright spots as new and useful sources of information, particularly websites, continued to appear at a rapid rate. Although there were mixed reviews for some developments, such as the upgrade of the current awareness database, RAPID «http://europa.eu.int/rapid/start/welcome.htm», others were given a more enthusiastic welcome: for example, The European Union in the World «http://europa.eu.int/comm/world/», the new site for EU financial information from the Commission Secretariat-General «http://europa.eu.int/comm/secretariat_general/sgc/info_subv/index_en.htm» and the Treaty of Nice portal «http://europa.eu.int/comm/nice_treaty/index_en.htm». The Council website «http://ue.eu.int/en/summ.htm» now has quite substantial sections on Justice and Home Affairs and the Common Foreign and Security Policy, neither of which is really covered elsewhere in such depth. For further information, see the list of sources which follows or refer to the regular column on EU information developments in the journal *European Access*. It is hard, though, to escape the feeling that such examples of good work are produced despite, rather than because of, the information policies of the Commission and other institutions. The Commission's President, Romano Prodi, and the Education and Culture Commissioner, Viviane Reding, were to have produced a document on information policy by the end of 2000; this had not appeared by the end of the year. A new deadline of 'the middle of the year' was indicated by Prodi in a speech on 29 January setting out the Commission's priorities; this statement hinted at some appreciation of the need for better co-ordination: 'we need to review and renew the European Union's communication and information policy. I believe we need a clear and coherent inter-institutional strategy, and we must implement it in partnership with civil society' (Prodi, 2001).

We must hope that the 'partnership with civil society' will involve full and genuine consultation with the key players in the field. Many of these are uncertain and anxious at present, not least in the EDCs, responsibility for which was moved abruptly around of the end of the year from DG Education and Culture to join other 'information relays' in Press and Communications. This move raises doubts about the continued role of Reding in the formulation of information policy as well as generating concern in higher education circles about the future status of EDCs.

It is very much to be hoped that the current paralysis in Brussels, as Eurocrats await their fates within the reform programme, will soon come to an end. What will follow is hard to predict, but what seems clear is that the forthcoming months will be significant ones for the world of EU documentation and may well provide clear indications about the likely longer-term future in a number of significant areas.

References

Cashman, M. (2001) 'Reforming the Institutions: Public Access to EU Documents'. *European Information*, No. 13, pp. 22–3.

Prodi, R. (2001) 'The Commission's Priorities for 2001'. Conference of Presidents Brussels, 24 January «‹http://europa.eu.int/rapid/cgi/rapcgi.ksh?p_action. gettxt=gt&doc=SPEECH/01/31|0|RAPID&lg=EN».

Statewatch (2000) 'Solana Decision' extended to cover justice and home affairs, trade and aid: 'Solana Two Decision'. *Statewatch News Online*, December «‹http:// www.statewatch.org/news/dec00/06solana2.htm»».

Statewatch (2001) 'Trialogue discussions on new code of access to EU documents collapse with no agreement'. *Statewatch News Online*, January«‹http:// www.statewatch.org/news/2001/feb/06trialogue.htm»».

B: KEY DOCUMENTATION
I. Governance and Institutional Developments

Intergovernmental Conference

The IGC continued in 2000 with the main priority being the reform of the institutions to prepare for enlargement. A number of reports and consultation papers were issued on this theme, including:

Adapting the institutions to make a success of enlargement (*COM*(2000) 34)

Communication concerning the development of the external service (*COM*(2000) 456)

Communication to the Intergovernmental Conference on the reform of the institutions (*COM*(2000) 771)

Externalisation of the management of Community programmes ... (*COM*(2000) 788)

Reforming the Commission (consultative document & action plan) (*COM*(2000) 10)

Reforming the Commission: a White Paper (*COM*(2000) 200) 2 vols

Strategic objectives 2000–2005: 'shaping the new Europe' (*COM*(2000) 154), also issued as *Bulletin of the European Union*. Supplement 1/2000. ISBN 9282892018 cat.no.KA-NF-00-001-EN-C

Reform of the Commission continued under the direction of Neil Kinnock. Most of the above documents are available from the Personnel Service website at «http:// europa.eu.int/comm/reform/refdoc/index_en.htm».

Treaty Reform and Treaty of Nice

Proposals were considered from institutions and Member States for the Treaty to be restructured as a European constitution. At the request of the Commission, the Robert Schuman Centre of the European University Institute presented a report on the reorganization of the treaties on 15 May 2000. It proposes a fundamental treaty, which would contain the essential institutional provisions and the objectives of the Union policies, together with provisions on fundamental rights and European citizenship. Text and background information from «http://www.iue.it/RSC/Treaties.html».

A basic treaty for the EU: Commission communication (*COM*(2000) 434).

The Charter of Fundamental Rights

The Charter was finally issued in the *Official Journal* C 364, 18 December 2000. The text of the charter, together with a comprehensive bibliography and collection of links, is available on a special website at «http://europa.eu.int/comm/justice_home/unit/charte/index_en.html».

Commission communication on the Charter of Fundamental Rights of the EU (*COM*(2000) 559)

Communication on the legal nature of the Charter of Fundamental Rights of the EU (*COM*(2000) 644)

both relate to the ongoing discussion as to whether the charter should be incorporated into the Treaty and what its legal status should be.

The European Council and the Presidency

Because of public perceptions of its lack of transparency, the Council published:

Information handbook of the Council of the EU. ISBN 9282417875 cat.no.BX - 26-98-778-EN-C

Basic texts on transparency concerning the activities of the Council of the EU. ISBN 9282418316 cat.no.BX-26-99-611-EN-C

Council's rules of procedure (*Official Journal*, L149, 23 June 2000). ISBN 9282418863 cat.no.QC-30-00-980-EN-C

and inaugurated a public register of Council documents which will contain references to classified documents and the text of documents released to the public «http://register.consilium.eu.int/isoregister/introEN.htm».

Portugal held the Presidency from January to June 2000 «http://www.portugal.ue-2000.pt/». An extraordinary European Council was held in Lisbon on 23–24 March 2000. The Feira European Council was held on 19–20 June 2000. Conclusions, including important statements about the future of the CFSP and EU involvement in the Middle East peace process, were published in the *Bulletin of the European Union*, 6, 2000, pp. 9–40.

France held the Presidency from July to December 2000 «http://www.presidence-europe.fr/pfue/static/acces5.htm». The Nice European Council was held on 7–9 December 2000 and resulted in the Treaty of Nice: a provisional text is available from the Presidency site. Presidency conclusions for all the above are available at «http://europa.eu.int/council/off/conclu/index.htm».

European Parliament

Communication on the application of 93/109/EC to the June 1999 elections to the European Parliament (*COM*(2000) 843).

Financial Control

Follow-up report on measures taken in the light of the observations of the European Parliament in its 1997 discharge resolution (A5-0004/2000) (*COM*(2000) 224) summarizes the actions taken to combat fraud in the Commission.

The European Anti-Fraud Office (OLAF) published its first report on operational activities (1 June 1999–31 May 2000) «http://europa.eu.int/comm/anti_fraud/index_en.htm».

A proposal was made for the criminal protection of the Community's financial interests: a European prosecutor (Additional IGC contribution) (*COM*(2000) 608).

Summary report on the communications by Member States on their inspection activities and findings and questions of principle relating to traditional own resources, 1998 (*COM*(2000) 107).

Court of Justice

Report by the Working Party on the future of the European Communities' court system (Due report) was issued in January. Available from the Legal Service at «http://europa.eu.int/en/comm/sj/homesjen.htm».

Commission documents on legal matters include:

17th annual report on monitoring the application of Community law (1999) (*COM*(2000) 92) [3 vols.] (also in *Official Journal* C30, 30 January 2001)
Better lawmaking 2000 (pursuant to Art. 9 of the Protocol to the EC Treaty on the application of the principles of subsidiarity & proportionality (*COM*(2000) 772)
Legal aid in civil matters: the problems confronting the cross-border litigant; Green Paper (*COM*(2000) 51)
Reform of the Community courts (*COM*(2000) 109)

A new (5th) edition of *The ABC of Community Law*, by K-D. Borchardt was published in the series European documentation. ISBN 9282878031 cat.no. PD-25-99-221-EN-C

Other Institutions

As the ECSC Treaty expires on 23 July 2002, discussions have begun on the future sharing of its responsibilities:

The future of structured dialogue after the expiry of the ESCS Treaty (*COM*(2000) 588)

II. Internal Policy Developments

Agriculture and Fisheries

Economic performance of selected European fishing fleets annual report 1999. ISBN 9282896005 cat.no. KL-29-00—004-EN-C
The future of young farmers in the EU (European Parliament, DG for Research. Working papers; AGRI 134) cat.no. QA-31-00-239-EN-C

Healthy food for Europe's citizens: the EU & food quality (Europe on the move). ISBN 9282882381 cat.no. PH-26-99-231-EN-C
Special report no.14/2000 on 'Greening the CAP' together with the Commission's replies (Court of Auditors) (*Official Journal* C353, 8.12.2000)

Business

Several reports were issued on financial services in the Community:

1st report on the implementation of the own funds directive (*COM*(2000) 4)
The application of conduct of business rules under Art. 11 of the Investment Services Directive (93/22/EEC) (*COM*(2000) 722)
Economic reform: report on the functioning of Community product & capital markets (*COM*(2000) 881)
EU financial reporting strategy: the way forward (*COM*(2000) 359)
Financial services priorities & progress: 3rd report (*COM*(2000) 692)
Progress on financial services: 2nd report (*COM*(2000) 336)
Progress report on the risk capital action plan (*COM*(2000) 658)
Report on the application of the export prohibition clause, Art.4(1) of the directive on deposit-guarantee schemes (94/19/EC) (*COM*(99) 722)
Upgrading the investment services directive (93/22/EEC) (*COM*(2000) 729)
Challenges for enterprise policy in the knowledge-driven economy (*COM*(2000) 256)
Review of specific Community financial instruments for SMEs (*COM*(2000) 653)
Services of general interest in Europe (*COM*(2000) 580)
Business services in European industry: growth, employment and competitiveness, by L. Rubalcaba-Bermejo. ISBN 9282866971 cat.no. CO-20-98-042-EN-C
Competitiveness of the EU publishing industries: final report. ISBN 928288290X cat.no. CO-25-99-722-EN-C
The contribution of business services to industrial performance: a common policy framework. ISBN 928286670x cat.no. CO-20-98-050-EN-C
European competitiveness report 2000. ISBN 9282905233 cat.no. NB-31-00-918-EN-C
Funding of new technology-based firms by commercial banks in Europe (EUR 17025) ISBN 9282897311 cat. no. NB-NA-17-025-EN-C

Liberalisation of network industries: economic implications and main policy issues (*European Economy. Reports & Studies*, No.4/1999). ISBN 9282876535 cat.no. CM-24-99-413-EN-C

Rural trade: best European practices; local distributive trades in less-favoured rural areas. ISBN 9282890465 cat.no. CT-26-99-174-EN-C

Selling to the public sector in Europe: a practical guide for small and medium-sized companies. ISBN 9282864499 cat.no. CT-17-98-613-EN-C

On tourism, a progress report on the follow-up to the conclusions of the Council on Tourism and Employment (*COM*(2000) 696) was published, also available at «http://europa.eu.int/comm/enterprise/services/tourism/tourism-publications/publications.htm»

Report on the implementation of Directive 95/57/EC on the collection of statistical information in the field of tourism (*COM*(2000) 826)

Towards quality coastal tourism: integrated quality management of coastal tourist destinations. ISBN 9282875652 cat.no. CT-24-99-057-EN-C; also

Towards quality rural tourism. ISBN 9282875547 cat.no. CT-24-99-041-EN-C; and

Towards quality urban tourism. ISBN 9282875431 cat.no. CT-24-99-049-EN-C

Competition

Guidelines on vertical restraints (*Official Journal* C291, 13 October 2000) «http://europa.eu.int/comm/competition/antitrust/legislation/vertical_restraints/guidelines_en.pdf»

8th survey on state aid in the EU (*COM*(2000) 205)

Commission report on…rules for state aid to the steel industry (Steel Aid Code) (*COM*(2000) 83)

Monitoring of Article 95 ECSC steel aid cases, 14th report (*COM*(2000) 685)

Opinion on the White Paper on modernisation of the rules implementing Articles 81 & 82 of the EC Treaty (CES(99)1130)

Report on the application of the agreement between the EC & the US regarding the application of their competition laws…1999 (*COM*(2000) 618)

Report on the application of the Community rules for state aid to the coal industry in 1998 & 1999 (*COM*(2000) 380)

Report on the application of the Merger Regulation thresholds (*COM*(2000) 399)

Report on the Community's anti-dumping & anti-subsidy activities (*COM*(2000) 440)

Report on the evaluation of Reg.1475/95 on…motor vehicle distribution and servicing agreements (*COM*(2000) 743)

Most of these reports are also online at «http://europa.eu.int/comm/competition/index_en.html».

Consumers

Commission report on the experience acquired in the application of Directive 92/59/EEC on general product safety (*COM*(2000) 140)

Report on consumer complaints in respect of distance selling & comparative advertising (*COM*(2000) 127)

Report on the application of Dir.85/374 on liability for defective products (*COM*(2000) 893)

Report on the implementation of Directive 93/13/EEC on unfair terms in consumer contracts (*COM*(2000) 248)

Report on harmonization of consumer price indices in the EU (*COM*(2000) 742)

A White Paper on food safety (*COM*(2000) 719) proposed the establishment of a European Food Authority. «http://europa.eu.int/comm/dgs/health_consumer/library/pub/index_en.html»

The 'Unfair Terms' Directive, Five Years On: Evaluation and Future Perspectives (Brussels Conference, 1–3.7.1999). ISBN 9282883167 cat.no. GT-26-99-530-2A-C

Culture

Report…on the return of cultural objects unlawfully removed from the territory of a member state (*COM*(2000) 325)

Economic and Monetary Issues

Commission recommendation for the 2000 broad economic guidelines (*COM*(2000) 214)

Community support for economic reform programmes & structural adjustment: review & prospects (*COM*(2000) 58)

The contribution of public finances to growth & employment: improving quality & sustainability (*COM*(2000) 846)

Convergence report 2000 (*COM*(2000) 277)

Economic reform: report on the functioning of Community product & capital markets (*COM*(2000) 26 & 881)

Spring 2000 forecasts for 2000–2001 (*European Economy*. Supplement A, 1-2, 2000)

2000 broad economic policy guidelines, Convergence Report 2000, Proposal for the adoption by Greece of the single currency; are reprinted with a statistical annex in *European Economy*, No.70. ISBN 9282896757 cat.no. QC-30-00-067-EN-C

Council recommendation of 19 June 2000 on the broad guidelines of the economic policies of the member states and of the Community. ISBN 9282896757 cat.no. QC-30-00-067-EN-C

Strategies for the EU economy (European Parliament, DG for Research. Working papers; ECON 122) cat.no. QA-31-00-675-EN-C

Documents relating to the practical aspects of the introduction of the euro include:

Changing to the euro: what would happen to a company on 1 January 2002 that had not converted to the euro?: advice to managers (*Euro Papers*, No. 39)

Communications strategy in the last phases of the completion of EMU (*COM*(2000) 57) also (*Euro Papers*, No. 38)

Euro coins: from design to circulation (*Euro Papers*, No.37)

Improving cross-border payments in the euro area (European Parliament, DG for Research. Working papers). ISBN 9282314723 cat.no. QA-33-00-073-EN-C

Practical aspects of the euro: state of play & tasks ahead (*COM*(2000) 443) (also *Euro Papers*, No.41)

Euro papers are available online from the DG for Economic Affairs website at «http://europa.eu.int/comm/economy_finance/document/europap/eupidxen.htm».

Education and Training

Designing tomorrow's education: promoting innovation with new technologies (*COM*(2000) 23)

*e*Learning – designing tomorrow's education (*COM*(2000) 318)

Final report on the implementation of the first phase of the community action programme Leonardo da Vinci (1995–1999) (*COM*(2000) 863)

Implementation of the White Paper 'Teaching & learning – towards the learning society' (*COM*(2000) 750)

Survey into the socio-economic background of Erasmus students (*COM*(2000) 4)

Integrating all young people into society through education & training [2 vols]. ISBN 9282876306 v.1&2 cat.no. C2-98-98-001/2-EN-C

Key data on education in Europe. (The 4th edition of this useful statistical collection now includes data on the applicant countries.) ISBN 9282885372 cat.no. C2-23-99-596-EN-C

Key topics in education in Europe. Vol.2: financing & management of resources in compulsory education; trends in national policies. ISBN 9282885402 cat.no. C2-23-99-605-EN-C

Lifelong learning: the contribution of education systems in the member states of the EU (Eurydice Survey, 2). ISBN 2871162948

Socrates: Community action programme in the field of education (2000–2006): guidelines for applicants. ISBN 9282888851 cat.no. C2-26-99-465-EN-C

Young people's training: key data on vocational training in the EU. ISBN 9282862151 cat.no. C2-19-98-108-EN-C

The European Centre for the Development of Vocational Training (CEDEFOP) published a range of documents, some of which continue earlier series:

An age of learning: vocational training policy at European level. ISBN 9282880516 cat.no. HX-25-99-075-EN-C

The financing of vocational education & training in Germany: financing portrait. ISBN 9282869296 cat.no. HX-22-99-046-EN-C. Also Ireland ISBN 9289600144; Spain ISBN 9282889521 cat.no. TI-27-00-960-EN-C; Sweden ISBN 9282756734 cat.no. TI-28-00-802-EN-C

Identification, assessment & recognition of non-formal learning in Spain. ISBN

9282890058 cat.no. TI-28-00-155-EN-C. Also Greece, ISBN 9282847667 cat.no. TI-28-00-357-EN-C

Internationalising vocational education and training in Europe: prelude to an overdue debate; a discussion paper. ISBN 9282894487 cat.no. TI-29-00-666-EN-C

Making learning visible: identification, assessment & recognition of non-formal education in Europe; by J. Bjørnavold. ISBN 9289600063 cat.no. TI-32-00-871-EN-C

The need for competences due to the increasing use of information and communication technologies. ISBN 9282896560 cat.no. TI-30-00-479-EN-C cat.no. TI-30-00-479-EN-C

Supporting quality in vocational training through networking. ISBN 928288368x cat.no. HX-26-99-271-EN-C

Towards the learning region: education & regional innovation in the EU and US. ISBN 9282885976 cat.no. HX-26-99-441-EN-C

Trends in the development of training & the role of innovation as a transferable practice (TTNet dossier No.1) ISBN 9282893863 cat.no. TI-29-00-513-EN-C

Vocational education & training in France. 2nd edn. ISBN 9282824330 cat.no. HX-10-97-453-EN-C; also Iceland ISBN 9282824799 cat.no. HX-09-97-850-EN-C; the United Kingdom, ISBN 9282827208 cat.no. HX-12-98-271-EN-C

Energy

Action plan to improve energy efficiency in the EC (*COM*(2000) 247)

Recent progress with building the internal electricity market (*COM*(2000) 297)

The EU's oil supply: communication from the Commission (*COM*(2000) 631)

Towards a European strategy for the security of energy supply: Green Paper (*COM*(2000) 769)

Blue book on geothermal resources. ISBN 9282858030

Energising Europe. ISBN 9282893979 cat.no.KO-NA-19619-EN-C

Environment

The Commission published a number of documents relating to climate change in the lead-up to the world conference held at The Hague in November:

Communication on EU policies & measures to reduce greenhouse gas emissions: towards a European Climate Change Programme (ECCP) (*COM*(2000) 88)

Green Paper on greenhouse gas emissions trading within the European Union (*COM* (2000)87)

Implementing the Community strategy to reduce CO_2 emissions from cars: first annual report on the effectiveness of the strategy (*COM*(2000) 615)

Opinion of the Commission…on substances that deplete the ozone layer (*COM*(2000) 96)

Report ... for a monitoring mechanism of Community greenhouse gas emissions (*COM*(2000) 749)

Bringing our needs & responsibilities together: integrating environmental issues with economic policy (*COM*(2000) 576)

Communication on integrated coastal zone management: a strategy for Europe (*COM*(2000) 547)

Communication on the precautionary principle (*COM*(2000) 1)

Developing a new bathing water policy (*COM*(2000) 860)

Environmental issues of PVC: Green Paper (*COM*(2000) 469)

Indicators for the integration of environmental concerns into the Common Agricultural Policy (*COM*(2000) 20)

Promoting sustainable development in the EU non-energy extractive industry (*COM*(2000) 265)

Report on the experience gained in the application of Council Directive 90/313/ EEC of 7 June 1990, on freedom of access to information on the environment (*COM*(2000) 400)

White Paper on environmental liability (*COM*(2000) 66)

Safe operations of mining activities: a follow-up to recent mining accidents (*COM*(2000) 664)

All *COM* documents issued by DG Environment are available at «http://europa. eu.int/ comm/environment/docum/»

The application of the 'polluter pays' principle in Cohesion Fund countries. ISBN 9282868338 cat.no. CX-18-98-396-EN-C

Assessment of indirect & cumulative impacts as well as impact interactions [3 vols]. ISBN 9282880451 cat.no. CR-34-99-001/3-EN-C

The EU eco-industry's export potential. ISBN 9282887200 cat.no. CR-27-99-184-EN-C

The law of sustainable development: general principles. ISBN 9282892875 cat.no.KH-28-00-834-EN-C

Managing Natura 2000 sites: the provisions of Art. 6 of the Habitats Directive. ISBN 9282890481 cat.no.KH-28-00-187-EN-C

Second annual survey on the implementation & enforcement of Community environmental law (January 1998–December 1999). ISBN 9282893243 cat.no.KH-28-00-470-EN-C

Study on environmental reporting by companies. ISBN 9282883116 cat.no. CR-26-99-093-EN-C

Success stories on composting and separate collection. ISBN 9282892956 cat.no. KH-27-00-726-EN-C

Publications of the European Environment Agency include:

Are we moving in the right direction? Indicators on transport & environmental integration in the EU TERM 2000 (Environmental issues series, No.12). ISBN 9291672068 cat.no. TH-28-00-115-EN-C

Emissions of atmospheric pollutants in Europe, 1980–1996 (Topic Report 9/ 2000). ISBN 9291672602 cat.no. TH-32-00-944-EN-C

Environmental signals 2000 (Environmental Assessment Report, No.6). ISBN 929167205x cat.no. TH-28-00-365-EN-C

Guide pour la gestion des déchêts en montagne. ISBN 9282891542 cat.no. KH-28-00-317-FR-C

Household & municipal waste: comparability of data in EEA member countries. ISBN 9291672319 cat.no. TH-29-00-674-EN-C

State & pressures of the marine and coastal Mediterranean environment. ISBN 9291671649 cat.no. GH-24-99-873-EN-C

Sustainable use of Europe's water?: state, prospects and issues. ISBN 9291672513 cat.no. TH-28-00-810-EN-C

Health

Accelerated action targeted at major communicable diseases within the context of poverty reduction (*COM*(2000) 585)

Communication on guidelines...for the safety or health of pregnant workers ... (*COM*(2000) 466)

Communication on the health strategy of the EU (*COM*(2000) 285)

Progress report on the network for the epidemiological surveillance & control of communicable diseases in the Community (*COM*(2000) 471)

Report on the state of young people's health in the European Union «http://europa. eu.int/comm/health/ph/key_doc/index_en.html»

European codification system of the causes & circumstances of accidents at work (Employment & Social Affairs). ISBN 9282847721 cat.no. CE-25-99-843-EN-C

Vade-mecum of civil protection in the EU. ISBN 9282878791 cat.no.CR-25-99-431-EN-C

Publications of the European Agency for Safety & Health at Work include:

Future occupational safety & health research needs and priorities in the member states of the EU. ISBN 9282892549 cat.no. TE-27-00-952-EN-C

Repetitive strain injuries in the member states of the EU: the results of an information request (Systems & Programmes). ISBN 9282888045 cat.no. AS-24-99-704-EN-C

Monitoring the state of occupational safety & health in the EU – pilot study. ISBN 929500700x cat.no TE-29-00-125-EN-C

Occupational safety & health in marketing & procurement. ISBN 9295007018 cat.no TE-30-00-811-EN-C

Research on work-related stress. ISBN 9282892557 cat.no TE-28-00-882-EN-C

Research on work-related low back disorders. ISBN 9295007026 cat.no TE-32-00-273-EN-C

Publications of the European Monitoring Centre for Drugs & Drug Addiction include: Annual report on the state of the drugs problem in the EU. ISBN 9291680974 Evaluation: a key tool for improving drug prevention (EMCDDA Scientific Monograph Series, No.5). ISBN 9291681059 cat.no.TD-28-00-656-EN-C

Information Society

The European Council meetings at Feira and Lisbon both concentrated on the problems and opportunities presented for employment and education by the rise of the 'knowledge-based economy'.

The creation of the .eu internet top level domain (*COM*(2000) 153)

*e*Europe: an information society for all; progress report for the Special European Council, Lisbon 23–24 March 2000 (*COM*(2000) 130). Also: Draft action plan, European Council in Feira, 19–20 June 2000

The *e*Europe updated prepared for the European Council in Nice (*COM*(2000) 783)

EU infrastructures & the year 2000 computer problem (*COM*(99) 651)

Innovation in a knowledge-based economy (*COM*(2000) 567)

Internet domain name system – creating the .eu top level domain (*COM*(2000) 421)

The organisation & management of the internet: international and European policy issues, 1998–2000 (*COM*(2000) 202)

Report to the European Council, Feira, 19–20 June 2000 on the Year 2000 (Y2K) computer problem experience (*COM*(2000) 375)

Strategies for jobs in the information society (*COM*(2000) 48). Also issued as ISBN 928283008x cat.no. CE-25-99-673-EN-C

In the area of telecommunications documents include:

4th communication on the application of Articles 4 & 5 of Dir.89/552/EEC 'Television without frontiers' for the period 1997–98 (*COM*(2000) 442)

6th report on the implementation of the telecommunications regulatory package (*COM*(2000) 814)

Communication … on the development of the Euro-ISDN (integrated services digital network) as a trans-European network (TEN) (*COM*(2000) 267)

The results of the public consultation on the 1999 Communications review & orientations for the new regulatory framework (*COM*(2000) 239)

Unbundled access to the local loop: enabling the competitive provision of a full range of electronic communication services including broadband multimedia & high-speed internet (*COM*(2000) 237)

The European positions for the World Radiocommunications Conference 2000 (WRC-2000) (*COM*(2000) 86)

Results of the WRC-2000 in the context of radio spectrum policy in the EC (*COM*(2000) 811

Texts also available from the Information Society website at «http://europa.eu.int/ comm/information_society/publications/docs/index_en.htm»; «http://europa.eu.int/ comm/information_society/eeurope/documentation/index_en.htm»

The Court of Auditors issued Special Report No.9/2000 concerning trans-European networks (TENs) – telecommunications (*Official Journal* C166, 15 June 2000)

Executive summaries of major reports concerning the growth of electronic publishing were published by the Directorate-General for the Information Society:

Access to capital for the content industries. ISBN 9282905357 cat.no. KK-31-00-562-EN-C

Commercial exploitation of Europe's public sector information. ISBN 9282899349 cat.no. KK-31-00-570-EN-C

Final evaluation of the INFO 2000 programme. ISBN 9282899497 cat.no. KK-31-00-594-EN-C

Impact assessment of the Community activities under INFO 2000. ISBN 9282899446 cat.no. KK-31-00-588-EN-C

IST 2000: Realising an information society for all. ISBN 9289400420 cat.no. KK-30-00-996-EN-C

Internal Market

2000 review of the internal market strategy (*COM*(2000) 257)

Follow-up to the Green Paper on combating counterfeiting & piracy in the single market (*COM*(2000) 789)

An internal market strategy for services (*COM*(2000) 888)

Report on the implementation & effects of Dir.91/250/EEC on the legal protection of computer programs (*COM*(2000) 199)

Results of the 4th phase of SLIM [simplified legislation for the internal market] (*COM*(2000) 56)

Retail payments in the internal market (*COM*(2000) 36)

Electrical & mechanical engineering directory. 2000 edn. ISBN 9282756718 cat.no.CO-24-99-275-EN-C

Guide to the implementation of directives based on the new approach and the global approach. ISBN 9282875008 cat.no.CO-22-99-014-EN-C

Inventory of taxes levied in the member states of the EU. 17th edn. ISBN 9282856631 cat.no. CO-24-99-235-EN-C

Legal aspects of standardisation in the member states of the EC & EFTA; by H. Schepel and J. Falke) 3 vols. Comparative report; Country reports; Deutschland (in German) ISBN 9282889076 cat.no.CO-37-99-001-EN-C

Patinnova '99: patents as an innovation tool; proceedings of the 5th European congress on patents (EUR 17034) . ISBN 9289401168

The rules governing cosmetic products in the European Union: CosmetLex (Vols 1–3: Cosmetics legislation, cosmetics products). ISBN 9282885461 cat.no. NB-26-99-974-EN-C

Justice and Home Affairs

The Commission published the first regular reports on new developments:

Scoreboard to review progress on the creation of an area of 'Freedom, security & justice' in the EU (*COM*(2000) 167)

Biennial update of the scoreboard to review progress on the creation of an area of 'freedom, security & justice' in the EU (*COM*(2000) 782)

Other Commission documents include the following:

Communication on a Community immigration policy (*COM*(2000) 757)

Communication on the establishment of Eurojust (*COM*(2000) 746)

The implementation of Dir. 91/477/EEC on control of the acquisitions & possession of weapons (*COM*(2000) 837)

Mutual recognition of final decisions in criminal matters (*COM*(2000) 495)

The prevention of crime in the EU: reflection on common guidelines and proposals for Community financial support (*COM*(2000) 786)

Report on the activities of the European Monitoring Centre on Racism & Xenophobia (*COM*(2000) 625)

Towards a common asylum procedure & a uniform status, valid throughout the Union, for persons granted asylum (*COM*(2000) 755)

Annual report for 1999 (European ombudsman). ISBN 9282313905 cat.no. QK-28-00-171-EN-C. Also published in *Official Journal*, C260, 11 September 2000

Good practice in mutual legal assistance in criminal matters: statements by the member states of the EU (European Judicial Network) (Council of the EU). ISBN 928241809x cat.no. QC-28-00-179-EN-C

EU action plan on common action for the Russian Federation on combating organised crime (*Official Journal*, C106, 13 April 2000)

The prevention and control of organised crime: EU strategy for the beginning of the new millennium (*Official Journal*, C124, 3 May 2000)

The European Parliament's Directorate-General for Research working papers published working papers on:

Asylum in the EU member states (Civil liberties series) cat.no. PE 168.631

The impact of the Amsterdam Treaty on justice & home affairs issues (Civil liberties series LIBE 110) cat.no. PE 228.145

Trafficking in women (Civil liberties series)

Report on the application of Dir. 92/51/EC ...(*COM*(2000) 17)

Thirty years of free movement of workers in Europe: proceedings of the conference, Brussels, 17–19 December 1998. ISBN 9282897990

The Schengen *acquis* as referred to in Article 1(2) of Council Decision 1999/435/EC was published in the *Official Journal* L239, 22 September 2000

The Schengen Joint Supervisory Authority published the 4th annual report of its activities March 1999–February 2000 at «http://www.cnpdpi.pt/schengen/».

Research

Europe & space: turning to a new chapter (*COM*(2000) 597)

Making a reality of the European Research Area: guidelines for EU research activities (2002–2006) (*COM*(2000) 612)

Programmes 5-year assessment (*COM*(2000) 659)

Research and technological development activities of the EU: 2000 annual report (*COM*(2000) 842)

Towards a European research area (*COM*(2000) 6). Also published as ISBN 9282887219 cat.no. CG-27-99-055-EN-C

Getting more innovation from public research: good practice in technology transfer from large public research institutions. ISBN 9282895807 cat.no. NB-NA-17-026-EN-C

Sequencing the human genome: scientific progress, economic, ethical and social aspects; working document for the STOA Panel (European Parliament, Directorate General for Research) cat.no. PE 167.197

Other STOA Group papers are available from «http://www.europarl.eu.int/stoa/publi/default_en.htm»

Social Policy and the Labour Market

Building an inclusive Europe (*COM*(2000) 79)

The future evolution of social protection from a long-term point of view: safe & sustainable pensions (*COM*(2000) 622)

Social policy agenda: communication from the Commission (*COM*(2000) 379). Also issued in series Employment & Social Affairs. ISBN 9289400498, cat.no. KE-31-00-320-EN-C

Social protection in Europe 1999 (*COM*(2000) 163) also issued in series Employment & Social Affairs. ISBN 9282893464

Social trends: prospects & challenges (*COM*(2000) 82)

EU assistance for employment & human resources: a brief guide to the ESF for future member states (Employment & Social Affairs). ISBN 9282897192

Employment guidelines and policy were a major concern of the Lisbon summit. The following policy documents were issued by the Commission:

Acting locally for employment: a local dimension for the European employment strategy (*COM*(2000) 196)

Community policies in support of employment (*COM*(2000) 78)

Guidelines for member states' employment policies for the year 2000 and Council recommendations (*COM*(2000) 5161 and 6433)

Industrial relations in Europe 2000 (*COM*(2000) 113)

Joint employment report 2000 [with statistical annex] (*COM*(2000) 551)

Several of these were also issued in the series Employment & Social Affairs. The series also included:

Employment in Europe 2000. ISBN 9289401834 cat.no. KE-32-00-217-EN-C
Equal opportunities for women & men in the EU: annual report 1999. ISBN 9282895483
Family issues between gender & generations: seminar report. ISBN 9282895734 cat.no. KE-29-00-981-EN-C
Gender equality in the EU: examples of good practices (1996–2000). ISBN 9282896277 cat.no. KE-30-00-552-EN-C
Report on member states' legal provisions to combat discrimination. ISBN 9282895483 cat.no. KE-27-00-572-EN-C

Reports were issued on the implementation of three important employment law directives:

Report on the application of the directive on the establishment of a European works council ... (*COM*(2000) 188)
Report on ... the protection of young people at work (UK transitional period) (*COM*(2000) 457)
State of implementation of the ... working time directive 93/104/EC (*COM*(2000) 787)

A number of proposals and reports were issued in the area of equal opportunities:
Report ... on the balanced participation of women & men in the decision-making process (*COM*(2000) 120)
Towards a barrier free Europe for people with disabilities (*COM*(2000) 284)
Towards a Community framework strategy on gender equality (2001–2005) (*COM*(2000) 335)

Structural Policy

11th annual report on the Structural Funds 1999 (*COM*(2000) 698 «http://www.inforegio.org/wbdoc/docoffic/official/repor_en.htm»
Annual report of the Cohesion Fund (*COM*(2000) 822)
Commission report on the measures to implement Article 299(2): the outermost regions of the EU (*COM*(2000) 147)
The European Economic Area financial mechanism: 5th annual report (*COM*(2000) 343)
Special report (Court of Auditors) No. 6/99 concerning the principle of additionality; No.7/99 concerning the development of industrial sites (*Official Journal* C68, 9 March 2000)

The EU compendium of spatial planning systems & policies (Regional development studies, 28). New volumes were published on:

Austria. ISBN 9282826864 cat.no. CX-10-97-809-EN-C

Belgium. ISBN 9282830217 cat.no. CX-10-97-542-EN-C

Greece. ISBN 9282826929 cat.no. CX-10-97-558-EN-C

Portugal. ISBN 9282826821 cat.no. CX-10-97-817-EN-C

Sweden. ISBN 9282826848 cat.no. CX-10-97-833-EN-C

UK. ISBN 9282830217 cat.no. CX-10-97-841-EN-C

Evaluating quality of life in European regions and cities (Committee of the Regions)

The impact of economic & monetary union on cohesion (Regional Development Studies, 35). ISBN 9282882918 cat.no. CX-24-99-922-EN-C

Local enterprising localities: area based employment initiatives in the UK (Regional Development Studies, 34). ISBN 9282830217 cat.no. CX-24-99-566-EN-C

Mainstreaming equal opportunities in the Structural Funds (Regional Development Studies, 33). ISBN 9282883183 cat.no. CX-24-99-590-EN-C

Structural actions 2000–2006: commentary and regulations; the Structural Funds, the Cohesion Fund, the instrument for structural policies for pre-accession. ISBN 9282830217 cat.no. CX-24-99-388-EN-C

Structural policies & European territory: the mountains. ISBN 9282889769 cat.no. KN-28-00-204-EN-C

Terra: an experimental laboratory in spatial planning. ISBN 9282830217 cat.no. CX-26-99-506-EN-C

Europe on the right track: transport projects supported by the European Regional Development Fund & the Cohesion Fund. ISBN 928288080x cat.no. CX-25-99-344-EN-C

The urban audit: the yearbook [2 vols]. ISBN 9282892417 (1) 9282892433 (2) cat.no. KN-47-00-001/2-EN-C

Transport

2nd report on ... national road haulage services within a member state (cabotage) (*COM*(2000) 105)

3rd report on ... maritime cabotage (1997–1998) (*COM*(2000) 99)

19th report on ... social legislation relating to road transport (*COM*(2000) 84)

Commission working document ... on the creation of the European Aviation Safety Authority in the Community framework (*COM*(2000) 144)

Communication on ... measures on maritime safety following the sinking of the oil tanker *Erika* (*COM*(2000) 802)

Communication on the safety of the seaborne oil trade (*COM*(2000) 142)

Priorities in EU road safety: progress report & ranking of actions (*COM*(2000) 125)

Protection of air passengers in the EU (*COM*(2000) 365)

Report from the Commission for the Biarritz European Council on the Community's strategy for safety at sea (*COM*(2000) 603)

Towards a safer & more competitive high-quality road transport system in the Community (*COM*(2000) 364)

EU transport in figures: statistical pocketbook 2000. ISBN 9282895718 cat.no. KO-28-00-745-EN-C

III. External Policies and Relations

A new website, The European Union and the World, was launched to provide a joint portal for the six services of the European Commission concerned with external relations. It is an invaluable source of current information and documentation about all aspects of EU involvement in the world and has particularly useful summaries of activities in individual countries or regions «http://europa.eu.int/comm/world/».

Asia

2nd annual report by the European Commission on the Special Administrative Region of Hong Kong (*COM*(2000) 294)

Developing closer relations between Indonesia & the EU (*COM*(2000) 50)

Report on the implementation of the communication 'Building a comprehensive partnership with China' (*COM*(2000) 552)

Common Foreign and Security Policy (CFSP)

Communication concerning the revision of the financial perspective (2001–06); financing of the programme of assistance for the western Balkans; reclassification of aid to Cyprus and Malta (*COM*(2000) 262)

Communication on EU election assistance & observation (*COM*(2000) 191)

Communication on operational conclusions: EU Stabilisation and Association process for countries of SE Europe … (*COM*(2000) 49)

Report … on the feasibility of negotiating a Stabilisation & Association Agreement with the Republic of Croatia (*COM*(2000) 311)

The Tacis Programme annual report 1999 (*COM*(2000) 835)

External Trade

Report … on actions to improve access of EU goods & cross-border services to Japan (*COM*(2000) 638)

2nd & 3rd reports on the situation in world shipbuilding (*COM*(2000) 263 & 730)

A series of books was issued on the Agreement on Trade-Related Aspects of Intellectual Property Rights (TRIPS Agreement)

Copyright & related rights. ISBN 9282838986 CN-16-98-784-EN-C

Enforcement of intellectual property rights. ISBN 928287432x CN-16-98-562-EN-C
Geographical indications. ISBN 9282852083 CN-16-98-855-EN-C
Patent protection. ISBN 9282852083 CN-16-98-546-EN-C

Enlargement

2000 regular report from the Commission on Bulgaria's progress towards accession (*COM*(2000) 701). Also Cyprus (702); Czech Republic (703); Estonia (704); Hungary (705); Latvia (706); Lithuania (707); Malta (708); Poland (709); Romania (710); Slovakia (711); Slovenia (712); Turkey (713)
Also available from DG Enlargement website at «http://europa.eu.int/comm/enlargement/index.htm»
Adapting the institutions to make a success of enlargement: Commission opinion (*COM*(2000) 34). Also published as *Bulletin of the EU*. Supplement 2/2000. ISBN 9282888975 cat.no.KA-NF-00-002-EN-C
Communication on Romania's medium-term economic strategy (*COM*(2000) 463)
Enlargement strategy paper: report on progress towards accession by each of the candidate countries (*COM*(2000) 7000)

The DG for Economic and Financial Affairs launched a new series, Enlargement Papers. The first three titles are:
The financial sector study of the Czech Republic (No.3)
Recent fiscal developments in the candidate countries (No.2)
Seminar on Currency Boards in the context of EU accession (No.1)
Also available in full text at: «http://europa.eu.int/comm/economy_finance/document/enlargement/elpidxen.htm»
Glossary: institutions, policies & enlargement of the EU. ISBN 9282882829 cat.no. PD-26-99-263-EN-C
Preparing for enlargement: devolution in the first wave candidate countries (Committee of the Regions: COR-Studies E-4/99). ISBN 9282885240 cat.no.GF-27-99-015-EN-C
Spatial perspectives for the enlargement of the EU. ISBN 9282881792 cat.no. CX-24-99-962-EN-C

Developing Countries

On 23 June, a new Partnership Agreement was signed at Cotonou in Benin to replace the Lomé Convention. The text was issued as a supplement to *The Courier* (cat.no. NH-AA-00-005-EN-C) and is also available, together with internal agreement on the financing and administration of Community Aid (Council document 10688/1/00 REV.1) at «http://europa.eu.int/comm/development/cotonou/index_en.htm»

Partnership Agreement between the ACP states and the European Community (*COM*(2000) 324) [Proposal for a Council Decision: 3 vols]

A number of working documents were issued relating to the new agreement and to development policy in general:

2000–2006 financial programming of Heading 4 (*COM*(2000) 268)

The Commission & non-governmental organisations: building a stronger partnership (*COM*(2000) 11)

Communication on the compendium providing policy guidelines in specific areas or sectors of cooperation to be approved by the Community within the ACP–EC Council of Ministers (*COM*(2000) 424)

Communication on the 'first come, first served' method for the banana regime and the implications of a 'tariff only' system (*COM*(2000) 621)

Communication promoting sustainable transport in development cooperation (*COM*(2000) 422)

The EC's development policy (*COM*(2000) 212)

The EC external cooperation programmes: policies, management and distribution European Programme for Reconstruction and Development in South Africa: annual report 1998 (*COM*(2000) 8)

Integrating environment & sustainable development into economic and development cooperation policy: elements of a comprehensive strategy (*COM*(2000) 264)

Operational coordination between the Community & the member states of the EU in the field of development cooperation (*COM*(2000) 108)

Report on the implementation of measures intended to promote observance of human rights and democratic principles in external relations for 1996–99 (*COM*(2000) 726)

Human Rights

Action against anti-personnel landmines: reinforcing the contribution of the EU (*COM*(2000) 111)

Annual report on humanitarian aid 1999 (*COM*(2000) 784)

Combating trafficking in human beings & combating the sexual exploitation of children and child pornography (*COM*(2000) 854)

East Timor: looking for a peaceful future; ECHO annual review 1999 (Humanitarian Aid Office) ISBN 928289715x cat.no.KR-30-00-528-EN-C «http://europa.eu.int/comm/echo/en/publicat/publications.htm»

European Union annual report on human rights 1998/99 (Council of the EU, General Secretariat) ISBN 9282417654 cat.no. BX-26-99-764-EN-C

Latin America

EU Mexico Free Trade Agreement (OJ L157 30 June 2000) «http://europa.eu.int/comm/trade/bilateral/mexico/fta.htm»

Mediterranean

Annual report of the MEDA Programme 1999 (*COM*(2000) 472)

Common strategy of the European Council on the Mediterranean region (*Official Journal*, L183 22 July 2000)

Re-invigorating the Barcelona process: communication to prepare the 4th meeting of Euro–Mediterranean foreign ministers (*COM*(2000) 497) and at «http://europa.eu.int/comm/external_relations/med_mideast/euro_med_partnership/key_doc_barcelo_ process.htm»

The Barcelona Process, Five Years on 1995–2000 (Euro–Mediterranean Partnership). ISBN 928940146X cat.no. NF-32-00-128-EN-C

The Euro–Mediterranean Agreement between the European Communities and the State of Israel. Text published in *Official Journal* L147, 21 June 2000 and at «http://europa.eu.int/comm/external_relations/med_mideast/euro_med_partnership/israel _asso_agree.htm».

The Euro–Mediterranean Agreement between the European Communities & Morocco, signed on 26 February 1996, entered into force on 1 March 2000. Full text in *Official Journal* L70, 18 March 2000 and at «http://www.euromed.net/key-docs/association_agreements/morocco.htm».

Journal of Common Market Studies

Volume 39, Annual Review
September 2001

Books on European Integration

BRIAN ARDY
South Bank University
and
JACKIE GOWER
University of Kent at Canterbury

The following list includes all books submitted to the *Journal of Common Market Studies* during 2000, whether these were reviewed or not. Each book is entered only once even though, inevitably, some titles are of relevance to more than one section.

General Studies

Cook, C and Paxton, J: *European Political Facts of the Twentieth Century* (Basingstoke/New York: Palgrave, 5th edn, 2001, ISBN 0333792033); ix+481pp., hb £50.00.

Lane, J-E: *New Public Management* (London/New York: Routledge, 2000, ISBN hb 0415231868, pb 0415231876); x+242pp., hb £55.00, pb £18.99.

Lastenouse, J (ed.): *40 ans des Traités de Rome* (Brussels: Bruylant, 1999, ISBN 2802710869); x+341pp., pb BEF1,100.

Lejeune, Y *et al.* (eds): *Annales d'Études Européennes de l'Université Catholique de Louvain* (Brussels: Etablissements Emile Bruylant, 2000, ISBN 2802713957); xi+365pp., pb BEF 3400.

Marsh, I (ed.): *Sociology: Making Sense of Society* (Harlow: Pearson Education, 2nd edn, 2000, ISBN 0582369436); xiv+840pp., pb £19.99.

Navari, C: *Intern ationalism and the State in the Twentieth Century* (London: Routledge, 2000, ISBN hb 0415097479, pb 0415097487); vi+373pp., hb 60.00, pb £19.99.

Plumb, L; Tongue, C and Wijsenbeek, F: *Shaping Europe: Reflections of Three MEPs* (London: Federal Trust, 2000, ISBN 090157399X); 157pp., pb £12.95.

Sakwa, R and Stevens, A (eds): *Contemporary Europe* (Basingstoke: Palgrave, 2000, ISBN 0333772709); xix+283pp., pb £15.99.

Shore, C: *Building Europe: The Cultural Politics of European Integration* (London: Routledge, 2000, ISBN hb 0415180147, pb 0415180155); xii+258pp., hb £50.00, pb £15.99.

Stein, E: *Thoughts from a Bridge* (Michigan: University of Michigan Press, 2000, ISBN 0472110594); xv+497pp., hb £37.00/$59.50.

Weidenfeld, W and Wessels, W (eds): *Europa von A bis Z: Taschenbuch der Europäischen Integration* (Bonn: Europa Union Verlag, 2000, ISBN 3771305853); 464pp., pb np.

Weidenfeld, W and Wessels, W (eds): *Jahrbuch der Europäischen Integration 1999/ 2000* (Bonn: Europa Union Verlag, 2000, ISBN 3771305942); 531pp., pb np.

Government and Institutions

Bergman, T and Damgaard, E (eds): *Delegation and Accountability in European Integration: The Nordic Parliamentary Democracies and the European Union* (London: Frank Cass, 2000, ISBN hb 0714650668, pb 0714681156); 180pp., hb £39.50/$57.50, pb £17.50/$26.50.

Blondel, J and Cotta, M (eds): *The Nature of Party Government: A Comparative European Perspective* (Basingstoke: Palgrave, 2001, ISBN 0333681991); x+241pp., hb £45.00.

Bornschier, V (ed.): *State-building in Europe: The Revitalization of Western European Integration* (Cambridge: Cambridge University Press, 2000, ISBN hb 0521781035, pb 0521786193); xvi+326pp., hb £40.00/$64.95, pb £14.95/$22.95.

Burgess, M: *Federalism and European Union: The Building of Europe, 1950 –2000* (London: Routledge, 2000, ISBN hb 0415226465, pb 0415226473); xiii+290pp., hb £60.00, pb £19.99.

Chandler, J A (ed): *Comparative Public Administration* (London/New York: Routledge, 2000, ISBN hb 0415184576, pb 0415184584); xi+275pp., hb £55.00, pb £18.99.

Corbett, R; Jacobs, F and Shackleton, M: *The European Parliament* (London: John Harper, 4th edn, 2000, ISBN hb 0953627829, pb 0953627810); xv+363pp., hb £37.50, pb £14.95.

Day, A J (ed): *Directory of European Union Political Parties* (London: John Harper, 2000, ISBN pb 0953627853, hb 0953627861); viii+267pp., pb £37.50, pb £14.95.

de Búrca, G and Scott, J (eds): *Constitutional Change in the EU: From Uniformity to Flexibility?* (Portland, Oregon: Hart, 2000, ISBN 1841131032); xxviii+372pp., hb £30.00.

de Schoutheete, P: *The Case for Europe: Unity, Diversity, and Democracy in the European Union* (Boulder, Col./London: Lynne Rienner, 2000, ISBN hb 1555878989, pb 1555879004); xvii+118pp., hb £33.95, pb £9.50.

Eriksen, E O and Fossum, J E (eds): *Democracy in the European Union: Integration Through Deliberation?* (London: Routledge, 2000, ISBN hb 0415225914, pb 0415225922); xiii+310pp., hb £55.00, pb £18.99.

Greven, M T and Pauly, L W (eds): *Democracy Beyond the State? The European Dilemma and the Emerging Global Order* (Lanham, Maryland: Rowman and Littlefield, 2000, ISBN hb 0847699005, pb 0847699013); vii+191pp., hb £51.00/ $65.00, pb £19.95/$24.95.

Ladrech, R: *Social Democracy and the Challenge of European Union* (Boulder, Col./ London: Lynne Rienner, 2000, ISBN 1555879020); xi+165pp., hb £37.50.

Magnette, P: *L'Europe, l'État et la Démocratie* (Brussels: Éditions Complexe, 2000, ISBN hb 2870278144, pb 2800412453); 261pp., hb BEF898/ FF139 , pb BEF850/ FF157.

Magnette, P and Remacle, E (eds): *Le Nouveau Modèle Européen. Volume 2: Les Politiques Internes et Externes* (Brussels: Editions de l'Université de Bruxelles, 2000, ISBN hb 2800412380, pb 2800412372); 242pp., hb BEF1250/FF231, pb BF895/FF165.

Mannners, I: *Substance and Symbolism: An Anatomy of Cooperation in the New Europe* (Aldershot: Ashgate, 2000, ISBN 0754611922); x+289pp., hb £42.50.

Milward, A S: *The European Rescue of the Nation-State* (London: Routledge, 2nd edn, 2000, ISBN hb 0415216281, pb 041521629X); xv+466pp., hb £60.00, pb £23.99.

Moser, P, Schneider, G and Kirchgässner G (eds): *Decision Rules in the European Union: A Rational Choice Perspective* (Basingstoke: Palgrave, 2000, ISBN 0333710797); xii+302pp., hb £47.50.

Neunreither, K and Wiener A (eds): *European Integration After Amsterdam* (Oxford: Oxford University Press, 2000, ISBN hb 019829641X, pb 0198296401); xii+384pp., hb £50.00, pb £18.99.

Notermans, T: *Money, Markets, and the State: Social Democratic Economic Policies Since 1918* (New York: Cambridge University Press, 2000, ISBN 0521633397); xix+302pp., hb £37.50/$59.95.

Nugent, N (ed.): *At the Heart of the Union: Studies of the European Commission* (Basingstoke: Palgrave, 2nd edn, 2000, ISBN hb 0333918304, pb 0333918374); xiii+332pp., hb £50.00, pb £16.99.

Nugent, N: *The European Commission* (Basingstoke/New York: Palgrave, 2001, ISBN hb 0333587421, pb 033358743X); xiii+366pp., hb £49.50, pb £17.50.

Peterson, J and Bomberg, E: *Decision Making in the European Union* (Basingstoke: Palgrave, 2000, ISBN hb 0333604911, pb 033360492X); 352pp., hb £47.50 hb, pb £15.99.

Pierre, J (ed.): *Debating Governance: Authority, Steering and Democracy* (Oxford: Oxford University Press, 2000, ISBN hb 0198295146, pb 0198297726); xi+251pp., hb £35.00, pb £16.99.

Rosamond, B: *Theories of European Integration* (Basingstoke: Palgrave, 2000, ISBN hb 0333647165, pb 0333647173); xiii+232pp., hb £42.50, £13.99.

Schmitter, P C: *How to Democratize the European Union ... and Why Bother?* (Lanham, Maryland: Rowman and Littlefield, 2000, ISBN hb 0847699048, pb 0847699056); viii+150pp., hb £46.00/$59.00, pb £14.95/$17.95.

Wallace, H and Wallace, W (eds): *Policy-Making in the European Union* (New York: Oxford University Press, 4th edn, 2000, ISBN 019878242X); xxxiii+610pp., pb £17.99.

Internal Policies and the Law

Ackrill, R: *The Common Agricultural Policy* (Sheffield: Sheffield Academic Press/ UACES, 2000, ISBN 1841271268); 246pp., pb £10.95/$16.95.

Bogaert, G and Lohmann, U: *Commercial Agency and Distribution Agreements: Law and Practice in the Member States of the European Union* (London: Kluwer Law, 3rd edn, 2000, ISBN 9041197486); xlvii+707pp., hb £140.00.

Drakeford, M: *Privatisation and Social Policy* (Harlow: Pearson Education, 2000, ISBN 0582356407); xi+242pp., pb £17.99.

Geddes, A: *Immigration and European Integration: Towards Fortress Europe?* (Manchester: Manchester University Press, 2000, ISBN hb 0719056888, pb 0719056896); xii+196pp., hb £40.00, pb £14.99.

Hilson, C: *Regulating Pollution: A UK and EC Perspective* (Oxford/Portland, Oregon: Hart, 2000, ISBN 1841130944); xxiii+190pp., hb £25.00.

Jacqué, J. P., Bieber, R., Haag, M *et al.*: *Commentaire J. Megret: Le Droit de la CE et de l'Union Européenne. Volume 9* (Brussels: Editions de l'Université de Bruxelles, 2nd edn, 2000, ISBN 2800412364); 639pp., hb BEF4500/FF832.

Johnson, R W M: *Reforming EU Farm Policy: Lessons from New Zealand* (London: Institute of Economic Affairs, 2000, ISBN 0255364849); 84pp., pb £8.00.

Kempees, P (ed.): *A Systematic Guide to the Case-Law of the European Court of Human Rights 1997–1998 Volume IV* (London: Kluwer Law International, 2000, ISBN 9041112235); xxiii+966pp., hb £184.00.

Kilpatrick, C; Novitz, T and Skidmore, P (eds): *The Future of Remedies in Europe* (Oxford/Portland, Oregon: Hart, 2000, ISBN 1841130826); xlii+303pp., hb £35.00.

Koslowski, R: *Migrants and Citizens: Demographic Change in the European State System* (Ithaca: Cornell University Press, 2000, ISBN 0801437148); xi+232pp., hb £25.95.

Larouche, P: *Competition Law and Regulation in European Telecommunications* (Portland, Oregon: Hart, 2000, ISBN 184113144X); xxxvii+466pp., hb £45.00.

Lehmkuhl, D: *The Importance of Small Differences: European Integration and Road Haulage Associations in Germany and the Netherlands* (Amsterdam: Thela Thesis, 1999, ISBN 9051704860); 234pp., pb Dfl49,50/£16.95/$33.00.

Lenaerts, K and Arts, D: *Procedural Law of the European Union* (London: Sweet and Maxwell, 1999, ISBN 0421651709); cxxviii+539pp., pb £30.00.

Lenaerts, K and Van Nuffel, P: *Constitutional Law of the European Union* (London: Sweet and Maxwell, 1999, ISBN 0421651806); cxliii+717pp., pb £28.00.

Littlewood, P: *Social Exclusion in Europe: Problems and Paradigms* (Aldershot: Ashgate, 1999, ISBN 1840147172); xiii+254pp., hb £39.95.

Lo Faro, A: *Regulating Social Europe: Reality & Myth of Collective Bargaining in the EC Legal Order* (Portland, Oregon: Hart, 2000, ISBN 1901362906); vi+192pp., hb £25.00.

Maher, I and O'Connor, T: *Competition Law: Alignment and Reform* (Dublin: Round Hall Sweet and Maxwell, 1999, ISBN 1899738525); lxvii+514pp., hb £65.00.

Mancini, G F: *Democracy & Constitutionalism in the European Union* (Portland, Oregon: Hart, 2000, ISBN 1841131148); xxvii+268pp., hb £30.00.

O'Keeffe, D and Twomey, P (eds): *Legal Issues of the Amsterdam Treaty* (Oxford: Hart, 1999, ISBN 1841130028); xli+425pp., hb £40.00.

Ordóñez Solís, D: *La Igualdad entre Hombres y Mujeres en el Derecho Europeo* (Madrid: Ministerio de Trabajo y Asuntos Sociales, 1999); 448pp., pb np.

Raffaelli, E A: *Antitrust Between EC Law and National Law* (Brussels/Milan: Bruylant/Guiffré, 2000, ISBN 2802713868); xv+538pp., pb BEF3,800.

Schonberg, S: *Legitimate Expectations in Administrative Law* (Oxford: Oxford University Press, 2000, ISBN 0198299478); lxvii+270pp., hb £40.00.

Senkovic, P: *L'Évolution de la Responsabilité de l'Etat Législateur sous l'Influence du Droit Communautaire* (Brussels: Bruylant, 2000, ISBN 2802713582); xvi+490pp., pb BEF3,300BEF.

Shaw, J: *Law of the European Union* (Basingstoke: Palgrave, 3rd edn, 2000, ISBN 0333924916); lxii+591pp., pb £14.99.

Stefanou, C and Xanthaki, H: *A Legal and Political Interpretation of Article 215(2) [new Article 288(2)] of the Treaty of Rome* (Aldershot: Dartmouth/Ashgate, 2000, ISBN 1840144289); vii+236pp., hb £39.95.

Usher, J. A. : *The Law of Money and Financial Services in the European Community* (New York: Oxford University Press, 2nd edn, 2000, ISBN 0198298773); xliv+255pp., hb £65.00.

van Selm, J (ed): *Kosovo's Refugees in the European Union* (London/New York: Pinter, 2000, ISBN hb 1855676400, pb 1855676419); x+239pp., hb £50.00, pb £15.99.

Vanhove, N: *Regional Policy: A European Approach* (Aldershot/Brookfield, Vermont: Ashgate, 3rd edn, 1999, ISBN 1840149949); xx+639pp., hb £55.00.

Weiler, J H H (ed): *The EU, the WTO and the NAFTA: Towards a Common Law of International Trade* (New York: Oxford University Press, 2000, ISBN 0198298749); xx+238pp., hb £40.00.

Wesseling, R: *The Modernization of EC Antitrust Law* (Oxford/Portland, Oregon: Hart, 2000, ISBN 1841131210); xix+252pp., hb £35.00.

Zimmermann, R and Whittaker, S (eds): *Good Faith in European Contract Law* (Cambridge: Cambridge University Press, 2000, ISBN 0521771900); xxxiii+720pp., hb £75.00/$120.00.

External Relations and Developments

Abe, A: *Japan and the European Union* (London: Athlone Press, 1999, ISBN 0485115565); xii+196pp., £45.00 hb.

Baun, M J: *A Wider Europe: The Process and Politics of European Union Enlargement* (Lanham, Maryland: Rowman and Littlefield, 2000, ISBN hb 0847690369, pb 0847690377); xxi+257pp., £52.00/$69.00 hb, £17.95/$22.95 pb.

Brewin, C: *The European Union and Cyprus* (Huntingdon, Cambridgeshire: Eothen Press, 2000, ISBN hb 0906719313, pb 0906719240); xii+290pp., hb £29.95 hb, pb £19.50.

Cordell, K (ed): *Poland and the European Union* (London/New York: Routledge, 2000, ISBN 0415238854); xvi+208pp., hb £55.00.

Guay, T R: *The United States and the European Union: The Political Economy of a Relationship* (Sheffield: Sheffield Academic Press/UACES, 1999, ISBN 1850759987); 134pp., pb £10.95/$16.95.

Lawton, T C; Rosenau, J N and Verdun, A C (eds): *Strange Power: Shaping the Parameters of International Relations and International Political Economy* (Aldershot: Ashgate, 2000, ISBN hb 0754613240, pb 0754613291); xxii+453pp., £55.00 hb, pb £19.95.

Lippert, B (ed): *Osterweiterung der Europäischen Union: Die Doppelte Reifeprüfung* (Bonn: Europa Union Verlag, 2000, ISBN 377130590X); 378pp., hb np.

Lord, C (ed): *Central Europe: Core or Periphery?* (Copenhagen: Copenhagen Business School Press, 2000, ISBN 8716134478); 255pp., hb £21.00/$34/DKK 236.

Missiroli, A: *CFSP, Defence and Flexibility/PESC, Defense et Flexibilité* (Paris: Institute for Security Studies of WEU, 2000, ISBN 10177566); viii+57pp., pb np.

Palard, J (ed): *Les Relations internationales des régions en Europe* (Québec: Laval University Press, 1999, ISBN 00142123); 654-887pp., pb $20.00.

Rengger, N J : *International Relations, Political Theory and the Problem of Order: Beyond International Relations Theory?* (London: Routledge, 2000, ISBN hb 0415095832, pb 0415095840); xx+232pp., hb £55.00, pb £17.99.

Rotfeld, A D (ed.): *SIPRI Yearbook 2000: Armaments, Disarmament and International Security* (Solna, Sweden: Oxford University Press/SIPRI, 2000, ISBN 0199241627); xlii+758pp., hb £60.00.

Salmon, T C (ed.): *Issues in International Relations* (London: Routledge, 2000, ISBN hb 1857288319, pb 1857288327); xiii+319pp., hb £50.00, pb £15.99.

van Dijck, P and Faber, G (eds): *The External Economic Dimension of the European Union* (The Hague: Kluwer Law International, 2000, ISBN 9041113835); xxvii+387pp., hb £54.50.

Zielonka, J (ed): *Paradoxes of European Foreign Policy* (London: Kluwer Law International, ISBN 9041105719); 171pp., hb £39.00.

Economic Developments in Europe and Beyond

Alho K E O (ed.): *Economics of the Northern Dimension* (Helsinki: ETLA, Research Insitute of the Finnish Economy, 2000, ISBN 9516283195); 226pp., hb np.

Bara, Z and Csaba, L: *Small Economies Adjustment to Global Tendencies* (Budapest: Aula, 2000, ISBN 9639215899); xiv+430pp., pb np.

Braunerhjelm, P; Faini, R; Norman, V; Ruane, F and Seabright, P: *Integration and the Regions of Europe: How the Right Policies Can Prevent Polarization* (London: CEPR, 2000, ISBN 1898128464); xv+115pp., pb £25.00.

Chesnais, F; Ietto-Gillies, G and Simonetti, R (eds): *European Integration and Global Corporate Strategies* (London/New York: Routledge, 2000, ISBN 0415212782); xvii+276pp., hb £65.00.

Crouch, C (ed): *After the Euro: Shaping Institutions for Governance in the Wake of European Monetary Union* (New York: Oxford University Press, 2000, ISBN 0198296398); xii+290pp., hb £40.00.

de Grauwe, P: *Economics of Monetary Union* (Oxford: Oxford University Press, 2000, ISBN 0198776322); vii+243pp., pb £20.99.

Dyson, K: *The Politics of the Euro-Zone: Stability or Breakdown?* (Oxford: Oxford University Press, 2000, ISBN hb 0199241643, pb 0199241651); x+311pp., hb £40.00 hb, pb £14.99.

Eijffinger, SCW and De Haan, J: *European Monetary and Fiscal Policy* (Oxford: Oxford University Press, 2000, ISBN 0198776160); xiv+199pp., pb £20.99.

Favero, C; Freixas, X; Persson, T and Wyplosz, C: *One Money, Many Currencies: Monitoring the European Central Bank 2* (London: CEPR, 2000, ISBN 189812843X); 74pp., pb £30.00/$45.00.

Gros, D, Davanne, O, Emerson, M, Mayer, T, Tabellini, G and Thygesen, N: *Quo Vadis Euro: The Cost of Muddling Through: 2nd Macroeconomic Policy Report from the Macroeconomic Policy Group* (Brussels: CEPS, 2000, ISBN 9290792957); vii+64pp., pb €25.00.

Henning, C. R. and Padoan, P. C. : *Transatlantic Perspectives on the Euro* (Washington: Brookings, 2000, ISBN 0815735596); x+123pp., pb $14.95.

Heston, A and Lipsey R E (eds): *International and Interarea Comparisons of Income, Output, and Prices* (Chicago: University of Chicago Press, 1999, ISBN 0226331105); xii+530pp., hb £56.00/US$80.00.

Hoekman, B and Zarrouk, J (eds): *Catching up with the Competition: Trade Opportunities and Challenges for Arab Countries* (Michigan: University of Michigan Press, 2000, ISBN 047211154X); xiv+340pp., hb £37.00/$59.50.

Hölscher, J (ed.): *Financial Turbulence and Capital Markets in Transition Countries* (Basingstoke/New York: Palgrave, 2000, ISBN 0333800419); xx+197pp., £45.00 hb.

Kaplan, S N (ed.): *Mergers and Productivity* (Chicago/London: Chicago University Press, 2000, ISBN 0226424316); x+337pp., hb £28.00/$40.00.

Levitt, M and Lord, C: *The Political Economy of Monetary Union* (Basingstoke: Palgrave, 2000, ISBN hb 0333717104, pb 0333717112); ix+277pp., hb £47.50, pb £15.99.

McKay, D.: *Federalism and European Union: A Political Economy Perspective* (Oxford: Oxford University Press, 1999, ISBN 0198296770); viii+200pp., pb £15.99.

Millar, C M; Grant, R M and Choi C J (eds): *International Business: Emerging Issues and Emerging Markets* (Basingstoke/New York: Palgrave/St. Martin's Press, 2000, ISBN 0333771001); xv+322pp., hb £45.00.

Morck, R K (ed.): *Concentrated Corporate Ownership* (Chicago: University of Chicago Press, 2000, ISBN 0226536785); xiii+387pp., hb £39.50/$62.00.

Noble, G W and Ravenhill, J (eds): *The Asian Financial Crisis and the Architecture of Global Finance* (Cambridge: Cambridge University Press, 2000, ISBN hb 0521790913, pb 0521794226); xvi+310pp., hb £40.00/$64.95, pb £14.95/$22.95.

Odell, J. S.: *Negotiating the World Economy* (Ithaca: Cornell University Press, 2000, ISBN hb 0801437431, pb 0801486467); xiii+252pp., hb £34.50, pb £14.95.

OECD: *EMU: Facts, Challenges and Policies* (Paris: OECD, 1999, ISBN 9264170278); 216pp., pb £21.00/$39.00.

OECD: *EMU: One Year On* (Paris: OECD, 2000, ISBN 9264173639); 194pp., pb £25.00/$39.00.

Overturf, S F: *Money and European Union* (Basingstoke: Palgrave, 2000, ISBN 0333913833); xi+307pp., pb £13.99.

Scharpf, F W and Schmidt, V A (eds): *Welfare and Work in the Open Economy, Volume One: From Vulnerability to Competitiveness* (New York: Oxford University Press, 2000, ISBN hb 0199240876, pb 0199240884); xiv+403pp., hb £45.00, pb £20.00.

Scharpf, F W and Schmidt, V A (eds): *Welfare and Work in the Open Economy, Volume Two: Diverse Responses to Common Challenges* (New York: Oxford University Press, 2000, ISBN hb 0199240914, pb 0199240922); xxi+656pp., hb £50.00, pb £20.00.

Smith, A: *The Return to Europe: The Reintegration of Eastern Europe into the European Economy* (Basingstoke: Palgrave, 2000, ISBN 0333740459); xiv+215pp., hb £42.50.

Smith, V L : *Bargaining and Market Behaviour: Essays in Experimental Economics* (Cambridge: Cambridge University Press, 2000, ISBN 0521584507); xii+461pp., hb £55.00/$90.00.

Stephen, R: *Vehicle of Influence: Building a European Car Market* (Michigan: University of Michigan Press, 2000, ISBN 0472111213); xiv+220pp., hb £31.00/$49.50.

Walsh, J. I. : *European Monetary Integration and Domestic Politics: Britain, France and Italy* (Boulder, Col./London: Lynne Rienner, 2000, ISBN 1555878237); x+182pp., hb £37.50.

Member States

Arter, D: *Scandinavian Politics Today* (Manchester/New York: Manchester University Press, 1999, ISBN hb 0719051320, pb 0719051339); xiv+366pp., hb £50.80, pb £16.99.

Bieler, A: *Globalisation and Enlargement of the European Union: Austrian and Swedish Social Forces in the Struggle Over Membership* (London: Routledge, 2000, ISBN 0415213126); xii+196pp., hb £55.00.

Dooge, J and Barrington, R (eds): *A Vital National Interest: Ireland in Europe 1973–1998* (Dublin: Institute of Public Administration, 1999, ISBN 1902448227); xx+358pp., pb IR£20.00/€25.39.

Ellison, J: *Threatening Europe: Britain and the Creation of the European Community, 1955–58* (Basingstoke: Palgrave, 2000, ISBN 0333753631); xiii+310pp., hb £45.00.

Gibbons, J: *Spanish Politics Today* (Manchester: Manchester University Press, 1999, ISBN hb 0719049458, pb 0719049466); xvi+174pp., hb £40.00, pb £9.99.

Grant, W: *Pressure Groups and British Politics* (Basingstoke/New York: Palgrave/St. Martin's Press, 2000, ISBN hb 0333744845, pb 0333744853); xii+250pp., hb £42.50, pb £13.99.

Howarth, D J: *The French Road to European Monetary Union* (Basingstoke: Palgrave, 2000, ISBN 0333920961); xi+239pp., hb £42.50.

Hyde-Price, A: *Germany & European Order: Enlarging NATO and EU* (Manchester: Manchester University Press, 2000, ISBN hb 0719054273, pb 0719054281); xvii+270pp., hb £40.00, pb £13.99.

Maclean, M and Trouille, J-M (eds): *France, Germany and Britain: Partners in a Changing World* (Basingstoke/New York: Palgrave, 2001, ISBN 0333921607); xxi+208pp., hb £42.50.

MacLennan, J C: *Spain and the Process of European Integration* (Basingstoke: Palgrave, 2000, ISBN 0333928865); 223pp., hb £45.00.

Mather, J: *The European Union and British Democracy: Towards Convergence* (Basingstoke/New York: Palgrave/St. Martin's Press, 2000, ISBN 0333776488); xvii+230pp., hb £42.50.

Mitchell, M: *Austria* (Oxford: ABC-CLIO, 1999, ISBN 1851092978); xxiii+271pp., hb £50.00.

O'Donnell, R (ed): *Europe: The Irish Experience* (Dublin: Institute of European Affairs, 2000, ISBN 1874109486); x+233pp., pb IR£15.00/€19.00.

Phillips, D G: *Germany and the Transnational Building Blocks for Post-National Community* (Westport, Conn: Praeger, 2000, ISBN 0275964906); x+190pp., hb £52.95.

Young, J W: *Britain and European Unity 1945-1999* (Basingstoke: Palgrve, 2nd edn, 2000, ISBN hb 0333741110, pb 0333741129); xii+237pp., hb £42.50, pb £13.50.

Index